'Krishnamurti is one of the greatest philosophers of the age.'
– The Dalai Lama, Madras, 1995

'If the world lost people who are concerned
with what Krishnamurti is concerned with,
I think it would lose its centre.'
– Iris Murdoch

'Krishnamurti's work is permeated by the
essence of the scientific approach,
in its highest and purest form.'
– David Bohm FRS

'I feel the meaning of Krishnamurti for our time
is that one has to think for oneself
and not be swayed by any outside religions
or spiritual authorities.'
– Van Morrison

Questioning Krishnamurti

J. Krishnamurti in dialogue

Thorsons

An Imprint of HarperCollins*Publishers*

Thorsons
An Imprint of HarperCollins*Publishers*
77–85 Fulham Palace Road,
Hammersmith, London W6 8JB
1160 Battery Street
San Francisco, California 94111–1213

Published by Thorsons 1996

1 3 5 7 9 10 8 6 4 2

A catalogue record for this book
is available from the British Library

ISBN 0 7225 3284 9

Printed in Great Britain by
Caledonian International Book Manufacturer, Glasgow

Audio and video tapes of most of the conversations are available.

For additional information, write to:
Krishnamurti Foundation Trust Ltd
Brockwood Park, Bramdean,
Hampshire SO24 0LQ, England

Krishnamurti Foundation of America
PO Box 1560
Ojai, CA 93023
USA

Contents

I think before we begin it should be made clear what we mean by discussion. To me it is a process of discovery through exposing oneself to the fact. That is, in discussion I discover myself, the habit of my thought, the way I proceed to think, my reactions, the way I reason, not only intellectually but inwardly . . . I feel that if we could be serious for an hour or so and really fathom, delve into, ourselves as much as we can, we should be able to release, not through any action of will, a certain sense of energy that is awake all the time, which is beyond thought.

New Delhi, 8 January 1961

We are human beings, not labels.

Colombo, 13 January 1957

Foreword

Both the life and teaching of Jiddu Krishnamurti (1895–1986) have aroused considerable controversy, ranging from adulation as a 'World Teacher', a twentieth-century Maitreya or Messiah, to the view that he was a fallible, if extraordinary, human being. Many who knew him felt overwhelmed, deeply awed even, by a sense of sacredness and unconditional love flowing from him. Others felt something of this, and a few also felt badly wronged or slighted, and have responded with a pained ambivalence. Even for those close to him for years, his personality has remained in some ways an enigma. But whatever the perhaps inevitable mystery of the person, the books, videos and tapes are there to show how for more than half a century Krishnamurti argued passionately that the problems facing us demand a radical transformation of human consciousness.

Was he asking the impossible? Did Krishnamurti undergo such a transformation himself? And if he did, what relevance does this have for the rest of us?

This book consists of fourteen conversations, in the last two decades of his life, in which these questions were debated. Those taking part include scientists, a Buddhist scholar, philosophers, artists and a Jesuit priest. None of them could be called 'devotees', but were people who came to question, clarify and challenge. This was something that Krishnamurti had in his lifetime always urged his listeners and readers to do – not perhaps always successfully.

A question that throbs like a pulse in this book is: can human beings live without conflict? Throughout these dialogues, Krishnamurti maintains that this can happen only when outer conflict, be it with another person or collectively in war, is seen to arise from inner conflict within the individual. The root of such conflict is a mistaken but powerful focus on 'what should be', rather than on 'what is', whether in ourselves or others. Or, to put it another way, ideals and objectives are insidiously found more attractive than looking at and understanding facts. Usually, if the fact – that which happens – is displeasing, our tendency is to resist, escape from, or suppress it. But this 'running away from the fact', as Krishnamurti calls it, is dangerous. By reacting in this way, he argues, we split off a fictitious but strong sense of self from what we experience, the 'observer' from the 'observed'. This separative self – which is a figment of thought based on inevitably limited experience, a kind of mental marionette – is for him the heart of violence, whether between two people or two nations. This is not, he contends, a problem that just a few unbalanced people have: the whole of humanity is caught in it.

The many implications of this key and difficult notion of 'the observer is the observed', sketched only very briefly here, are discussed in depth with David Bohm, a Fellow of the Royal Society and, like a few outstanding theoretical physicists, also a philosopher.

What then can be done? Instead of a plan of action, Krishnamurti invites the listener to 'remain with what is' in his or her life non-judgmentally, to test whether what is being experienced will then disclose and clarify its significance. In so doing, he argues, we explore not just our own consciousness but human consciousness as a whole. This is not, therefore, 'neurotic, lopsided, selfish' introspection. We are instead 'observing without an observer', in which there is no movement of thought, no labelling, no justification, no condemnation, no desire to change, but a sense of affection and care. Nor is this some kind of mystical, or otherworldly, notion. At the end of the conversation with Asit Chandmal and David Bohm, Krishnamurti cites his own response at the time of his brother Nitya's death: 'there was absolutely no moving from that ... from that sorrow, that shock, that feeling ... K didn't go after comfort ... there is no other path except that.' Then another dimension of mind can come into play. The difficulties we may have in 'staying with' experience in this way are discussed with the American professor of philosophy, Renée Weber.

This is a clear instance of how Krishnamurti's 'teaching' goes to the

heart of the kind of experience that we all share. He puts to us
propositions about such experience, which he invites us not to accept
but to test. In his dialogue with Bernard Levin, he castigates dogma
and belief as blocks to understanding. It is by serious testing and
experimenting – to see whether what is said is false or not – that we
can find out the truth for ourselves. Any other way of evaluating
reality, such as reliance on authority or scripture, he sees as turning us
into 'second-hand people'.

As the reply to the final question in this book makes clear,
Krishnamurti disclaimed any status as some kind of 'role model' for
the rest of us. As he said in a talk in 1983, 'the speaker is speaking for
himself, not for anybody else. He may be deceiving himself, he may
be trying to pretend to be something or other. He may be, you don't
know. So have a great deal of scepticism: doubt, question ...' Not only
did he disclaim such a role, he argued strongly that to seek any kind
of exemplar, whether in himself or in anyone else, is psychologically
crippling. By creating a childlike dependency, conformity, and a
temporary, but ultimately false, sense of security in the authority of
another, it 'atrophies the brain'. It is also religiously, and often
politically, divisive, since the proliferation of such exemplars
inevitably creates barriers for the 'faithful' between 'them' and 'us'.
And like inner conflict, this dull subservience wastes the energy
needed to explore and respond anew to an ever-changing reality – to
the essence of life itself.

In most of these talks, these issues, including the discussion of
death with the playwright and broadcaster Ronald Eyre, are treated
with a passion and humour that the editor has tried but failed to
adequately reproduce.

Is what Krishnamurti says a product of Oriental religious
philosophy and alien to Western ways of thought? The reader may
find an answer to this in the conversations with the Buddhist scholar,
Walpola Rahula, and the Jesuit priest, Eugene Schallert. These may
surprise people who have pigeon-holed Krishnamurti as an 'Eastern
mystic'. In fact there are many significant echoes of Krishnamurti's
concerns in Western thought. As Iris Murdoch points out, being and
becoming have been constantly debated in Western philosophy, and
she enlists Plato to elucidate some of Krishnamurti's arguments.
Thomas Hobbes's remark that 'whosoever looks into himself shall

know the thoughts and passions of all other men' can remind one of Krishnamurti's 'I am the world'. It would not be difficult to cite other examples.

There have also been Western philosophers who have approached the problem of the self in ways akin to Krishnamurti's – though without, it also seems fair to say, the far-ranging and powerful implications he draws for our everyday experience. When Wittgenstein says that 'private sensations and the self are all part of the same picture and they stand and fall together', some readers may feel there is no difference between that and 'the observer is the observed'. The 'elusiveness of the 'I' ' has taxed the minds of philosophers like Hume and Ryle and many others. Yet despite all this activity there is still no philosophical or psychological consensus on personal identity and consciousness. And neuroscientists, for their part, have searched for, and so far failed to find, a 'homunculus' or 'control centre' in the brain.

Whether Krishnamurti cuts through the jumble of conflicting views on the self by pinning down what thought can and cannot do is something the reader can explore. But in any event he makes a radical and liberating appeal to us to 'clear the decks' and to set aside everything that has been affirmed untestably by religious 'authorities', philosophers, psychologists, gurus, and indeed anyone, including himself, in these matters. The world cries out for a new culture in which we cease to be 'second-hand people' and resolve instead to 'find out' for ourselves. What such a culture would imply is explored with Pupul Jayakar, a friend and cultural adviser to Indira Ghandi.

For the first-time reader, the range and vocabulary of these conversations may seem daunting. Is this philosophy, psychology, or religion? Or all three? Krishnamurti himself did not like giving a name to what he talked about. His agenda was very open-ended, always totally free to cover any aspect of the human condition. For Krishnamurti, a religious view of life is inseparable from exploring whether we mistakenly apply the biological model of evolution to the psychological sphere; and whether the computer is an accurate simulation of the human brain. For him, these are not incidental but crucial issues that determine the quality of our lives, not just topics of intellectual interest.

Also, he decided early in his life not to use a specialized vocabulary.

This means that he uses simple words to describe often complex states of mind. There are of course many advantages in this but it can also sometimes call for a kind of decoding by the reader. At times he can be said to redefine words: 'passion', for example, is described as 'sustained energy in which there is no movement of thought'; and depending on the context the word 'knowledge' is often used in a psychological sense to cover our likes and dislikes, beliefs, prejudices, conclusions about ourselves and others. 'Conflict' nearly always refers to inner conflict.

At the same time his vocabulary is fluid, constantly being revised. Although always concerned to define his terms he can caution us about definitions, because they can so easily condition and blinker the way we think. Repeatedly he warns that 'the word is not the thing, the description is not the described'. Words, rightly used, are only hints, clues to truths that must be lived.

While Krishnamurti always stresses that one must 'start very near' – with oneself – in order to 'go very far', it will be apparent from the opening conversation, with Jonas Salk, that he saw the situation of each of us as inseparable from what one might call a 'planetary view' of the human condition. We have grown increasingly aware of our planetary interdependence in trade and monetary matters and have set up bodies such as the World Trade Organization and the International Monetary Fund. We have seen the need for World Conferences on the environment and on population. We have understood that to forecast the weather of one country as accurately as possible a satellite system has to scan the world's weather as a whole. Krishnamurti puts before us something more fundamental, a testable, worldwide account of the way that human minds work, wherever they are, of our psychological common ground. Right action, in whatever sphere, he saw as flowing only from an understanding of that, starting with one's own mind. This also includes, in his view, seeing that religious beliefs and national identities are being clung to neurotically, and that the psychological apartheid this creates seriously threatens human survival.

Krishnamurti has, it seems, stood back and looked at the whole human picture, both personal and planetary. The question then arises: can any kind of *organization*, however well-intended, succeed without our *also* doing this? Are we, all the time, putting the cart before the horse? And are we capable of doing anything else? Will something happen if we put these questions to ourselves seriously?

Some forty books have been published of Krishnamurti's talks and dialogues, nearly all of them translated into the world's major languages. The CD-ROM of his teaching, covering the years 1933 to 1986 – the earlier years he described as 'patchy' – contains the equivalent of some 200 average-sized books. Other material, transcripts, tapes, letters, would amount to the equivalent of perhaps a further hundred. What effect has this massive outpouring had? Has anyone been radically transformed?

Krishnamurti's own answer to the first question, in New York in the eighties, was: 'very little'. On the second one he said, shortly before his death, that nobody had got in touch with that consciousness of which he had spoken. He added, 'perhaps they will somewhat if they live the teachings'.

For some of us this may be the point where, perhaps with a sigh of relief, one puts the book back on the bottom shelf. So it was all just too difficult after all. Yet the questions Krishnamurti puts do not go away so easily. Remarks such as 'intelligence is understanding what love is', or 'be unprepared for the unknown', linger in the mind. And looking around for a heartening sign (what would that be exactly?) that someone else has done it, has changed fundamentally, seems like furtive sidling out of a role of one's own – a touch of the artful dodger.

Only when one has done everything one can to test and apply what he says is one in a position to judge that Krishnamurti is demanding the impossible. That is the quandary he confronts us with.

One could explain what Krishnamurti says as a massive and endless inquiry into the state of the human being. But the value of all explanations, including this one, is bound to fade after a while. As Krishnamurti put it, 'let us be very clear where explanations end and where real perception or experiencing begins. You can go only so far with explanations, and the rest of the journey you must take by yourself.'

This book offers such a journey.

David Skitt

What Is of Most Concern to You?

Jonas Salk, MD, developer of the anti-poliomyelitis vaccine and director of the Salk Institute for Biological Studies in San Diego, California.

Krishnamurti: What shall we talk about?

Jonas Salk: I'd like you to tell me what is your deepest interest, your deepest concern.

K: It is rather difficult to put it into words, isn't it, but seeing what the world is becoming, I think any serious man must be concerned about the future, about what is going to happen to mankind. Especially if one has children, what is their future? Are they going to repeat the same old pattern that human beings have been following for a million years, more or less? Or is there going to be a fundamental change in their psyche, their whole consciousness? That is the real question – not atomic war or conventional war – but whether it has to be man against man.

JS: Yes, I am sure you must have an opinion about that.

K: I don't know if I have an opinion. I have observed a great deal, talked to a great many people in my life, and there are very few who are really concerned, committed to discovering if there is a different way of living, a global relationship, global intercomm-unication, not merely stumbling over language, not the religious and political divisions and all that nonsense, but really finding out if we can live on this Earth peacefully, without killing each other endlessly. I think that is the real issue we are now facing. And we think the crisis is outside us, but it is in us, in our consciousness.

JS: So what you are saying is that we have now come face to face with ourselves.

K: Yes, with ourselves and with our relationship to the world, both externally and inwardly.

JS: So the fundamental issue confronting us is relationship:

1

relationship to ourselves and relationship to each other, and I might
even go so far as to say to the world and the cosmos. We are really
confronted with that eternal question of the meaning of our lives.

K: Yes, that's right. Either we give a meaning to our life intellectually,
fix a goal and work towards that, which becomes so artificial,
unnatural, or we understand the whole structure of ourselves.
We have now advanced so extraordinarily technologically – it's
fantastic what they are doing, as you know – but in the other, the
psychological field, we have hardly moved at all. We are what we
have been for the last umpteen years.

JS: Even to the point of having developed what we call artificial
intelligence without recognizing that we need to learn how to
use our own natural intelligence.

K: Sir, have we natural intelligence or have we destroyed it?

JS: It's innate, and we destroy it in each individual as they come
along. I think we are born with natural intelligence.

K: I really would like to question that, whether we are born with
natural intelligence.

JS: We are born with the capacity, the potential for that, in the
same way that we are born with the capacity for language. But it
must then be exercised, activated, brought out in the course of
life's experiences. And that is why we really need to understand
what I like to think of as the conditions and circumstances for
evoking that potential.

K: As long as we are conditioned...

JS: We are always conditionable, that's in our nature.

K: But is it possible to uncondition ourselves, or must it go on?

JS: Are you asking if it is possible to uncondition the individual
who has become conditioned?

K: Can the individual conditioned by society, language, the climate,
literature, newspapers, by everything that has shaped, impressed
and influenced him ever step out of this conditioning?

JS: With great difficulty, because it does have a tendency to become
fixed, and this is why we must give attention to the young, to
each new generation that is brought into and shaped by the
social context, shaped by those circumstances. We have an
opportunity with new and as yet unshaped, unformed minds to
influence them in a healthier fashion.

K: One has come into contact, if I may speak about it, with lots of young people, thousands of them. From the age of five to twelve they seem intelligent, curious, awake, full of energy, vitality and beauty. After that age the parents, society, newspapers, their own friends, the family, are responsible for the whole thing seeming to drown them, to make them so ugly, vicious. You know the whole human race has become like that. So is it possible to educate them differently?

JS: I think so. I have said in something I wrote not long ago that we are in need of an immunizing education. The analogy I am using is of immunizing against a crippling disease. In this instance I am thinking of the crippling of the mind, not merely the crippling of the body.

K: Could we go into that a little bit? What is it that basically, not superficially, cripples the mind? Basically, if I may ask, is it knowledge?

JS: Wrong knowledge.

K: I am using the word 'knowledge', whether it be right or wrong, in the sense of psychological knowledge. Apart from academic knowledge, scientific knowledge, the technology of the computer and so on, apart from all that, has Man been helped inwardly by knowledge?

JS: Are you referring to the kind of knowledge that comes from experience?

K: Yes, such knowledge is after all the gathering of experience.

JS: I see two kinds of knowledge: I see the organized body of knowledge that comes, let us say, through science; and I see the kind of knowledge that comes through human experience.

K: Human experience – just take human experience. We have had wars for probably ten thousand years or so. And in the old days you killed by arrows or club, two or three or a hundred people at the most. Now you kill by the million.

JS: Much more efficiently.

K: Yes, you are up in the air and you don't know whom you are killing. It might be your own family, your own friends. So has that experience of thousands of years of war taught Man anything about not killing?

JS: Well, it has taught me something. I see no sense in it, and there are growing numbers of people who are becoming conscious of the absurdity of that kind of behaviour.

K: After ten thousand years! You follow me?

JS: I follow you.

K: We must question whether there is any learning at all or just blind wandering. After ten thousand years or so, human beings haven't learnt a very simple thing: don't kill somebody, that for God's sake, you are killing yourself, you are killing your future. And that hasn't been learnt.

JS: It has been learnt by some but not all of us.

K: Of course there are exceptions. Let's leave the exceptions, they will always be there, fortunately.

JS: Fortunately, that's a very important point.

K: But the majority, who vote for war, for presidents, for prime ministers, and all the rest of it, haven't learnt a thing, they will destroy humanity.

JS: The ultimate destruction has not happened yet. You are quite right, but we need to become aware of that new danger, and something must arise within us now.

K: Sir, I would like to go into this because I am questioning whether experience has taught Man anything, except to be more brutal, more selfish, more self-centred, more concerned with himself and his little group, his little family, or whatever. Tribal consciousness, which has become glorified as national consciousness, is destroying us. So if ten thousand years, more or less, has not taught Man to stop killing, there is something wrong.

JS: I'd like to offer a suggestion, a way of looking at this question. I'd like to look at it from an evolutionary point of view, and speculate that we are evolving through a period of time, in which the exception to which you referred earlier may some day become the rule. Now how might this happen? It has to happen or else there will be nothing to speak about after the event.

K: Of course.

JS: We are confronting a crisis now. That crisis is imminent, it gets closer and closer.

K: Yes, sir, that's what we said.

JS: So that we may very well have to enter the arena ourselves in a conscious way. As we are fully conscious, aware of the risk and danger, some effort must be made, some way must be invented to raise the consciousness of the world as a whole, however difficult that may be.

K: I understand all this, sir. I have talked to a great many politicians and their argument is that you and people like you must enter the arena. Now, wait a minute. We always deal with a crisis, not with what has brought about the crisis. When the crisis arises our response is: deal with the crisis, don't bother about the past, don't bother about anything else, just deal with the crisis.

JS: That's wrong.

K: That's what they are all doing.

JS: I understand that. And that's why they need the wisdom of those like yourself, who see the future, can see the 'handwriting on the wall', and will act before the wall begins to crumble.

K: So what I am saying is: shouldn't we inquire into the cause of all this? Not just say, well, here is a crisis, deal with it.

JS: Yes, I agree with you.

K: That's what the politicians are saying. I mean the cause of all this is obviously the desire to live safely, protected, be secure inwardly. I divide myself as a family, then as a small group of people, and so on and so on.

JS: We are going to discover that we are all one family.

K: Ah!

JS: And our greatest security will come from being concerned about others in our family. It will be of no great advantage to us to have others suffer and be a threat to us as well as to themselves, which is the state of affairs now.

K: But I am pointing out that we haven't learnt through suffering, we haven't learnt from the agony of wars. So what makes us learn, change? What are the factors and the depth of it? Why are human beings, who have lived on it for so long, destroying this poor unfortunate Earth, and destroying each other? What is the cause of all this? Not speculations about the cause, but the actual, deep human cause? Unless we find that we will go on with this for the rest of our days.

JS: That's quite right. So you are asking about the cause.

K: Or causation that has brought Man to this present crisis.

JS: As I see it, war is something that men engage in to satisfy the need

for survival under circumstances of threat, when there is
something to be gained by war. Now when the time comes when
nothing is to be gained, and everything is to be lost, we may give a
second thought to this.

K: But we have lost, sir. You understand? Every war is a lost war.
Why haven't we learnt that? The historians, all the great
scholars, have written about it and Man has remained tribal,
petty, self-centred. So what will make him change? The
immediacy of change, not gradually in the future, because time
may be the enemy of Man. Evolution may be the enemy.

JS: The enemy? Evolution may be the only solution.

K: If Man hasn't learnt after all this suffering and is simply
perpetuating this thing...

JS: He hasn't evolved sufficiently as yet. The conditions have not, as
yet, been propitious for solving the problems that precipitate war.

K: Sir, if we have children, what is their future? War? And how am
I, if one is a parent, how is one to see all this? How is one to
awaken, to be aware of all that is going on, and of the
relationship of our children to what is going on? And if they
don't change this thing will go on endlessly.

JS: Therefore a change is imperative. How are we going to bring it
about?

K: That's what I am asking. Change is imperative. But if the change
depends on evolution, which means time and all the rest of it,
we are going to destroy ourselves.

JS: But I think we have to deliberately and consciously accelerate the
evolutionary process. Until now we have been evolving
unconsciously, which has led to the condition that you have just
described. A new, a different kind of change must occur, a change
in our consciousness, in which we are using our intelligence.

K: Agreed, sir. So I am asking what are the causes of this? If I can
find the cause, every cause has an end. If I can find the cause or
many causes that have brought human beings to the present
state, then I can go after them.

JS: Let me suggest another way of looking at it. Let us assume, for the
sake of argument, that the causes that have led to this will persist
unless some outside intervention is brought to bear to change the
direction. Let me suggest the possibility of looking at the positive

elements in human beings, the possibility of strengthening those.

K: That means time.

JS: Everything in the human realm occurs in time. I am suggesting that we accelerate or foreshorten the time, that we not leave it only to time and to chance, that we begin to intervene in our own evolution to that extent, and become the co-authors of our evolution.

K: I understand that. Now I am asking a question that perhaps may not have an answer – I think myself it does – which is, can time end? This way of thinking that means give me a few more days before you slaughter me. During those few days I must change.

JS: I think time ends in the following sense: the past ends and the future begins.

K: Which means what? For the past to end, which is one of the most complex things, memory, knowledge, desire, hope, all that has to end.

JS: Let me give you an illustration of the ending of something and the beginning of something new. When it was observed that the Earth was round and not flat there was a change in perception. The same thing happened when it became apparent that it was the Earth that revolved around the Sun.

K: Sir, my question is this: is time an enemy or a help? The human brain has infinite capacity technologically, but we don't seem to apply that extraordinary capacity inwardly.

JS: Let's focus on that. That's the central issue. I agree.

K: Yes, that's what I am saying. If we could focus that tremendous energy on this, we would change instantly.

JS: Instantly, there you have it.

K: Now what will make Man focus that capacity, that energy, that drive, on this one point, the content of his consciousness? Sorrow hasn't helped him; better communication hasn't helped him; the fact is nothing has helped – God, church, religions, better statesmen, the latest gurus, none of that.

JS: That's right.

K: So can I put all that aside and not depend on anybody, scientists, doctors, psychologists, anybody?

JS: What you are saying is that the means has not yet been invented for accomplishing what you have in mind.

K: I don't think it is a question of means, the means is the end.

JS: I accept that.

K: Therefore don't look for a means. See that these people have not helped you in the least; on the contrary, they have led you up the wrong path. So leave them.

JS: They are not the means. Because they do not serve the ends of which we are speaking.

K: The authority outside is not the means, so look inside. That requires, sir, tremendous – I don't like to use the word – 'courage'; but it means to stand alone, not depend on or be attached to anything. And who is going to do this? Just one or two?

JS: That's the challenge.

K: So I say, for God's sake wake up to that, not to the means, not to the end.

JS: I share your view as to where the solution lies and that it is perhaps the most difficult of all the things that human beings have been confronted with. That is why it's left to the last. We have done all the easy things, like manipulating artificial intelligence, but without developing our own intelligence. It is understandable because we are in a sense both the cause and the effect.

K: The cause becomes the effect, and the effect becomes the cause, and so on, we keep in that chain.

JS: Yes, now since we are at a point at which the human race can become extinct, it seems to me that the only invention, if I may use that term, we are awaiting is to find the means for exercising self-restraint upon all the factors and conditions and circumstances that have led to war.

K: I wonder, this may be irrelevant, but you know the world is bent on pleasure. You see it in America more than anywhere else, a tremendous drive for pleasure, for sport, to be entertained all the time. In school here the children want to be entertained, not to learn. You go to the East, and there they want to learn.

JS: That can be pleasurable too.

K: Yes, of course, but Man is driven to find and continue in pleasure. Apparently that has been the historical process: pleasure whether in the church, the mass, all the circus that goes on in the name of religion, or on the football field, all that has existed from antiquity. Being entertained by specialists may be one of our difficulties, you know, that whole world of entertainers. Every magazine is a form of entertainment, with a few good articles here and there. So Man's drive is not only to escape fear, but the drive for pleasure. They go together, like two sides of the same coin. But we forget the other side, fear, and pursue pleasure. That may be one of the reasons why this crisis is coming.

JS: It will not be the first time that a species will have become extinct. I think we must ask whether there are some cultures or societies that are more likely to endure than others, that have the characteristics and attributes necessary to overcome the problems and weaknesses to which you have been drawing attention. It seems to me that you are prophesying a time of great difficulty and great danger. And you are pointing out the differences that exist amongst peoples and cultures and individuals, some of whom might be the exceptional ones who will survive and endure after the holocaust.

K: That means one or two, or half a dozen people, survive out of all the mess. No, I can't agree to that.

JS: I am not recommending that. I am simply giving a picture, a number, a quality and a quantity to it so as to make people aware of their responsibility in respect to that future.

K: Sir, responsibility implies not only to your little family, but you are responsible as a human being for the rest of humanity.

JS: I think I showed you the title of an address I gave in India, which was 'Are We Being Good Ancestors?' We have a responsibility as ancestors for the future. I share your view completely. And the sooner we become aware of this and begin to address ourselves to this consciously as an imminent threat the better.

K: Again, I would like to point out that there are exceptions, but the vast majority who are not in the way of looking at things elect the governors, presidents, prime ministers or the totalitarians who are suppressing everything. So as the majority elect those, or the few gather power to themselves and dictate to others, we are at their mercy, we are in their hands, even the most exceptional people. So far they haven't done it, but they may say, 'you can't speak here any more, or write any more, don't come here.' At the same time there is the urge to find security, to find some kind of peace somewhere.

JS: Would you be willing to say that those who are now ruling, leading, are somehow lacking in wisdom?

K: Oh, obviously, sir.

JS: Would you say that there are some who have the wisdom with which to lead and to guide?

K: Not when the mass of people want to be guided by somebody they elect, or by tyrannies they don't elect. What I am really asking is: how is a man, a human being, who is no longer an 'individual' – for me, individuality doesn't exist, we are human beings, we are humanity...

JS: Right, we are members of the species, we are cells of humankind.

K: We are humanity, our consciousness is not mine, it is human mind, human heart, human love. All that is human. And by emphasizing, as they are doing now, the individual, fulfilling yourself, do whatever you want to do, you know the whole thing, that is destroying human relationship.

JS: Yes, that is fundamental.

K: There is no love, there is no compassion in all this. Just a vast mass moving in a hopeless direction, and electing these extraordinary people to lead them. And they lead them to destruction. My point is that this has happened time after time, century after century. And unless you are serious you give up, turn your back on it. I know several people who have said to me, 'don't be a fool, you can't change Man, go away, retire. Go to the Himalayas and beg and live and die.' I don't feel like that.

JS: Nor do I.

K: Of course not. They have seen all this as hopeless. For me, I don't see it as either hopeful or hopeless. I have said this is the state of things, they have got to change.

JS: This is the reality.

K: And change instantly.

JS: Exactly. All right, having agreed upon that, where do we go from here?

K: I can't go very far if I don't start very near. The 'very near' is this.

JS: All right, let's start right here, right here. What do we do?

K: If I don't start *right here* but start *over there* I can't do anything. So I start here. Now I ask: who is the 'me' who is struggling for all this? Who is 'I', who is the self? What makes me behave this way, why do I react like this? You follow, sir?

JS: Oh yes, I follow.

K: So that I begin to see myself, not theoretically but in a mirror of relationship with my wife, with my friends, how I behave, how I think, and in that relationship I begin to see what I am.

JS: Yes, you can see yourself only through reflection in another.

K: Through relationship. In that there may be affection, there may be anger, there may be jealousy. I discover in all that the monstrous creature hidden in me, including the idea that there is something extraordinarily spiritual in me, all that I begin to discover. The illusions and the lies that Man has lived with. And in that relationship I see that if I want to change I break the mirror. Which means I break the content of my whole consciousness. And perhaps out of that, breaking down the content, there is love, there is compassion, there is intelligence. There is no intelligence except the intelligence of compassion.

JS: Well, having agreed on what the ultimate resolution can be, and having agreed that one has to begin here and now...

K: Yes, sir, change now, not wait for evolution to throttle you.

JS: Evolution can begin now.

K: If you like to put it that way. Evolution in the sense of moving from this, breaking this down to something that thought cannot project.

JS: When I use the phrase 'evolution can begin now', I am speaking of a mutation event.

K: A mutation, I agree. Mutation is not evolution.

JS: But I am going to add one other factor that I think is important. I believe that some individuals see the world as you and I do, there are others besides ourselves who see the problems and the solution that you speak of. Now let us refer to such individuals as exceptional, extraordinary. We might even think of them as unusual, as mutations, if you like.

K: Biological freaks! (laughs)

JS: If you like. Curious in some way, different from the rest. Can they be gathered together, can they be selected? Will they select each other and come together?

K: Yes, they will come together, not select each other.

JS: I am using the term in the sense of coming together because there is some sense of recognition, something that draws them together,

11

some self-selecting mechanism. Now can you imagine that making a difference?

K: Perhaps a little.

JS: Can you imagine anything else making a difference?

K: Not imagine, sir. Could we put it this way? Death has been one of the most extraordinary factors in life. We have avoided looking at it, because we are afraid of what it is. We cling to all the things we have known, and we don't want to let that go when we die. We can't take it with us but, etc, etc. Now to die to all the things I am attached to. To die, not say, 'what will happen if I die, is there another reward?' Because unless dying and living go together...

JS: Yes, death is part of life.

K: Death is part of life. But very few move in that direction.

JS: I agree. We are talking now about the same exceptional individuals.

K: And those exceptional individuals – I am not pessimistic or optimistic, I am just looking at the facts – have they affected mankind?

JS: Not sufficiently, not yet. My contention is that if we do something about it consciously and deliberately we can make it happen sooner.

K: But consciously and deliberately may be another continuation of the self-centredness.

JS: That is part of the conditioning we must not include. That must be excluded. It must be species-centredness, if you like, humankind-centredness, humanity-centredness. It cannot be the same *self*-centredness to which you have been referring up to now. That will be the mutation event.

K: Yes, sir, the end of self-centredness. You know the monks, the nuns or the sannyasis of India have tried to do this through meditation, by joining orders, by renouncing the world. Once when I was in Kashmir I was walking behind a group of monks, about a dozen of them. It was beautiful country, a river on one side, flowers, birds and an extraordinary blue sky. Everything was really laughing, the Earth was smiling. And these monks never, never looked at anything. They kept their heads down, repeating some words in Sanskrit – I couldn't gather what they were – and that was all. They put on blinkers and said, '*there* is safety.' That's what we have done, religiously, politically. One can deceive oneself enormously. Deception is one of our factors.

JS: Deception, and denial, negation.

K: Sir, we never start, as in Buddhism and Hinduism, with doubt. Doubt is an extraordinary factor. But we don't use it, we don't doubt all that is going on around us.

JS: That is very unhealthy. Healthy doubt is necessary, we must question rather than accept the answers that have been given us.

K: Scepticism, of course. So nobody else can answer *my* problems. I have to resolve them myself. So don't create problems. I won't enter into that. The mind that is *trained* to resolve problems is always *finding* problems. But if the brain is not trained and educated to solve problems, it is free from problems. It can face problems but it is essentially free.

JS: There are some brains, if you like, some minds that create problems and some that solve problems. What you are posing now is the question: can we solve the ultimate problem with which we are confronted, which is, 'can we go on as a species?' Or will we destroy ourselves?

K: Yes, that's why I brought in death earlier, death to things that I have gathered psychologically.

JS: We have to accept the death of those things of the past that are no longer valuable and allow the birth of those new things that are necessary for a new future. I quite agree that the past must come to an end. War must come to an end.

K: The brain must of course record, but the brain is recording constantly. It is recording and then it plays the tape.

JS: It is recording constantly and it is recognizing. It is re-cognizing. It is re-examining what it already knows. Now we must at this point in time recognize what has happened in the past, and become aware that there must be a new way.

K: Which means, don't record. Why should I record? Language and so on, let's leave those out, but why should I record anything psychologically? You hurt me, suppose. You say some brutal thing to me, why should I record it?

JS: I would relegate it to what I call the 'forgettery'.

K: No, why should I record it? Or somebody flatters me, why should I record it? What a bore it is to react in the same old pattern!

JS: It records itself, but it must be relegated.

K: No, watch it, sir, whether it is possible not to record at all. Psychologically, I mean, not the recording of driving a car or this or that, but psychologically not to record anything.

JS: Are you able to do that?

K: Oh, yes.

JS: You must be able to discriminate between what you record and what you don't record.

K: The memory is selective.

JS: Yes, and that was why I used that humorous way of putting it: you select by putting some things in the memory and some in the 'forgettery'. We are selecting that which we choose.

K: I have to record how to drive a car or how to speak a language. If I have to learn a skill I have to record it. In the physical world I have to record how to go from here to my house or to Paris, I have to do various things, I have to record all that. But I am asking, why should there be recording of any psychological event which then emphasizes the self, the 'me', self-centred activity and all the rest of it?

JS: Well, let's deal with that for a moment because it seems to be very central to what you are saying, and to what I implied earlier when I used the word 'self-restraint'. I think we are talking about the same category of phenomena, the need perhaps to liberate ourselves from those experiences in life that make us vindictive, that make it difficult for us to join together to relate to those who may have injured us in the past. And we see this amongst nations now, between religious groups and others, who are incapable of forgiving the present generation who have nothing to do with the events perpetrated at some previous time in history.

K: Yes, sir.

JS: So we are now beginning to approach the question that I posed earlier: what is it that we must do, what might we do now, to deal with the cause of the effects that we want to avoid? You have identified these as psychological, as being within the human mind.

K: The first thing I would say is, don't identify yourself with anything – with a group, with a country, with a God, with ideologies. Don't identify. Because that which you identify with must be protected – your country, your God, your conclusions, your experience, your biases. This identification is a form of self-centred activity.

JS: Let us assume for the sake of argument that there is a need to relate to things or to each other. This is the basis for religion – the meaning of the word 'religio' is to tie together – and there is a need that human beings have for relationship. Yet they may very well enter into relationships that are harmful, that are in fact self-destructive. Now is it possible to address ourselves to the kinds of relationship which, if developed, would allow us to relinquish those that are now harmful? For example, the most fundamental relationship is to ourselves, not in the self-centred sense, but to ourselves as members of the human species, and to each other.

K: That is, my relationship as a human being with the rest of humanity. Now, just a minute. Relationship implies two: my relationship with you, with another. But I *am* humanity, I am not separate from my brother across the ocean.

JS: You are not.

K: I am humanity. Therefore if I have this quality of love I have established a relationship, there is relationship.

JS: I think that it exists. I think you have it and your brothers across the sea have it, in all of the countries of the world this exists, but we are also taught to hate. We are taught to hate each other. We are taught to separate ourselves from the other.

K: Not only, sir, taught, but isn't there this feeling of possessiveness in which there is security and pleasure? I possess my property, I possess my wife, I possess my children, I possess my God. I am trying to say that this sense of isolating process is so strong in us that we can't *train* ourselves to be out of it. I say, see the *fact* that you are the rest of mankind, for God's sake see it!

JS: Well, what you are saying is that we are both individual and also related to the rest of humankind.

K: No, I say you are not an individual. Your thinking is not yours. Your consciousness is not yours because every human being suffers, every human being goes through hell, turmoil, anxiety, agony, every human being, whether west or east, north, south, goes through this. So we are human beings, not, 'I am a separate human who is related to other human beings': I am the rest of humanity. And if I see that fact I will not kill another.

JS: Now contrast that with what exists today.

K: What exists today? I am an individual, I must fulfil my own desires, my own urges, my own instincts, my own whatever it is and that is creating havoc.

JS: Now we want to transform one state to another.

K: You can't transform.

JS: All right, what can you do?

K: Change, mutate. You can't change one form into another form. See the truth that you actually are the rest of mankind. Sir, when you see that, when you feel it in – if I may use the word – your guts, your blood, then your whole activity, whole attitude, whole way of living changes. Then you have a relationship that is not two images fighting each other. A relationship that is living, alive, full of something, beauty. But again we come back to the exception.

JS: They exist. Now let's focus on that.

K: Suppose, sir, you are one of the exceptions – just suppose, as it were. What's your relationship with me who is just an ordinary person? Have you any relationship with me?

JS: We are the same species.

K: Yes, but you have stepped out of that, you are an exception. That's what we are talking about. You are an exception and I am not, right? What is your relationship with me? Have you any? Or you are outside trying to help me.

JS: No, I have a relationship with you and a responsibility because your well-being will influence my well-being. Our well-being is one and the same.

K: But you are an exception, you are not psychologically accumulating things. You are out of that category and I am all the time gathering, you know, all the rest of it. There is a vast division between freedom and the man who is in prison. I am in a prison of my own making and of the making of politicians, books and all the rest of it. I am in prison, you are not, you are free. And I would like to be like you.

JS: I would like to help liberate you.

K: Therefore what's your relationship? A helper? Or you have real compassion, not *for* me, but the *flame* of it, the perfume, the depth, the beauty, the vitality and intelligence of compassion, love. That's all. That will have much more effect than your decision to help me.

JS: We are in complete agreement here. That's how I see the exceptional. I see that the exceptional individuals possess the quality of compassion.

K: And compassion cannot be put together by thought.

JS: It exists.

K: But how can it exist when I have hate in my heart, when I want to kill somebody, when I am crying for myself? There must be freedom from all that before the other is.

JS: I am focusing my attention now on the exceptional. And do the exceptional ones have hatred in their hearts?

K: Sir, it is like the sun, the sunshine isn't yours or mine. We share it. But the moment it is *my* sunshine it becomes childish. So all that you can be is like the sun, give me compassion, love, intelligence, nothing else – don't say, do this, don't do that – then I fall into the trap that all the churches, the religions have made. Freedom means, sir, to be out of the prison – the prison that Man has built for himself. And you who are free, *be there*. That's all. You can't do anything.

JS: I hear you say something very positive, very important, very significant. I hear you say that there are people, a group of individuals, who possess these qualities for emanating something that could help the rest of humankind.

K: But you see there is this whole concept – I don't want to go into it, it's too irrelevant – that there are people who help, not guide, who *tell* you what to do, then it all becomes so silly. Rather it is simply like the sun, the sun giving light. If you want to sit in the sun, you sit in it, if you don't, you sit in the shade.

JS: So it's that kind of enlightenment. That *is* enlightenment.

Are You Not Saying What the Buddha Said?

Walpola Rahula, *international authority on Buddhism and author of the* Encyclopaedia Britannica *entry on the Buddha.*
David Bohm, *in his lifetime a Fellow of the Royal Society and professor of theoretical physics at Birkbeck College, University of London.*
TK Parchure, *MD, physician to Krishnamurti.*
G Narayan, *formerly director of Krishnamurti Foundation India's Rishi Valley School.*
Irmgaard Schloegel, *Buddhist scholar.*

Walpola Rahula: I have been following your teaching – if I may use that word – from my younger days. I have read most of your books with great interest, and I have wanted to have this discussion with you for a long time.

To someone who knows Buddha's teaching fairly well, your teaching is quite familiar, not something new to him. What the Buddha taught 2,500 years ago you teach today in a new idiom, a new style, a new garb. When I read your books I often write in the margin, comparing what you say with the Buddha, sometimes I even quote chapter and verse, or the text – not only Buddha's original teaching, but also the ideas of the later Buddhist philosophers – those too you put in practically the same way. I was surprised how well and beautifully you expressed them.

So to begin with I want to mention briefly a few points that are common to Buddha's teaching and yours. For instance, Buddha did not accept the notion of a creator-God who rules this world and rewards and punishes people for their actions. Nor do you, I believe. Buddha did not accept the old Vedic, Brahmanic idea of an eternal, permanent everlasting, unchanging soul or *atman* – Buddha denied this. Nor do you, I think, accept that notion.

Buddha begins his teaching from the premise that human life is a predicament, suffering, conflict, sorrow. And your books always emphasize that. Also, Buddha says that what causes this conflict, suffering, is the selfishness created by the wrong idea of my self, my *atman*. I think you say that too.

Buddha says that when one is free from desire, attachment, from the self, one is free from suffering and conflict. And you said somewhere, I remember, that freedom means freedom from all attachment. That is exactly what Buddha taught, from *all* attachment – there is no discrimination between attachment that is good and attachment that is bad – of course there is in ordinary practical life, but ultimately there is no such division.

Then there is the seeing of truth, the realization of truth, that is, to see things as they are; when you do that, you see reality, you see truth and are free from conflict. I think you have said this very often – in, for example, the book *Truth and Actuality*. This is quite well known in Buddhist thought as *samvrti-satya* and *paramartha-satya*: *samvrti-satya* is the conventional truth, and *paramartha-satya* is the absolute or ultimate truth. And you can't see the ultimate or absolute truth without seeing the conventional or relative truth. That is the Buddhist attitude. I think you say the same thing.

On the more popular level, but very importantly, you always say that you must not depend on authority – anybody's authority, anybody's teaching. You must realize it yourself, see it for yourself. This is a very well known teaching in Buddhism. Buddha said, don't accept anything just because it is said by religion or scripture, or by a teacher or guru, only accept it if you see for yourself that it is right, if you see it is wrong or bad then reject it.

In a very interesting discussion that you had with Swami Venkatesananda, he asked about the importance of gurus, and your answer was always: what can a guru do? It is up to you to do it, a guru can't save you. This is exactly the Buddhist attitude – that you should not accept authority. After reading the whole of this discussion in your book *The Awakening of Intelligence*, I wrote that Buddha has said these things too, and summarized them in two lines in the *Dhammapada*: you must make the effort, the Buddhas only teach. This is in the *Dhammapada* that you read long ago when you were young.

Another very important thing is your emphasis on awareness

or mindfulness. This is something that is extremely important in Buddha's teaching, to be mindful. I myself was surprised when I read in the *Mahaparinibbanasutra*, a discourse about the last month of his life, that wherever he stopped and talked to his disciples he always said: be aware, cultivate awareness, mindfulness. It is called the presence of mindfulness. This is also a very strong point in your teaching, which I very much appreciate and follow.

Then another interesting thing is your constant emphasis on impermanence. This is one of the fundamental things in Buddha's teaching, everything is impermanent, there is nothing permanent. And in the book *Freedom from the Known* you have said that to discern nothing is permanent is of tremendous importance – for only then is the mind free. That is in complete accordance with the Four Noble Truths of the Buddha.

There is another point showing how your teaching and the Buddha's go together. I think in *Freedom from the Known*, you say that control and outward discipline are not the way, nor has an undisciplined life any value. When I read this I wrote in the margin: a Brahmin asked the Buddha, how did you attain these spiritual heights, by what precepts, what discipline, what knowledge? Buddha said, not by knowledge, not by discipline, not by precepts, nor without them. That is the important thing – not with these things, but not without them either. It is exactly what you say: you condemn slavery to discipline but without discipline life has no value. That is exactly how it is in Zen Buddhism – there is no Zen Buddhism, Zen is Buddhism. In Zen, slavery to discipline is seen as attachment, and that is very much condemned, but there is no Buddhist sect in the world where discipline is so much emphasized.

We have many other things to talk about but to begin with I want to say that there is fundamental agreement on these things, and there is no conflict between you and the Buddha. Of course you are not a Buddhist, as you say.

K: No, sir.

WR: And I myself don't know what I am, it does not matter. But there is hardly any difference between your teaching and the Buddha's, it is just that you say the same thing in a way that is fascinating for Man today, and for tomorrow's Man. And now I would like to know what you think about all this.

K: May I ask, sir, with due respect, why you compare?

WR: This is because when I read your books as a Buddhist scholar, as one who has studied Buddhist texts, I always see that it is the same thing.

K: Yes, sir, but if I may ask, what is the necessity of comparing?

WR: There is no necessity.

K: If you were not a scholar of Buddhism and all the sutras and sayings of the Buddha, if you had not gone very deeply into Buddhism, how would it strike you on reading these books, without the background of all that?

WR: That I can't tell you because I was never without that background. One is conditioned, it is a conditioning. We are all conditioned. Therefore I cannot answer that question because I don't know what the position would be.

K: So if I may point out, I hope you don't mind...

WR: No, not at all.

K: ...does knowledge condition human beings – knowledge of scriptures, knowledge of what the saints have said and so on, the whole gamut of so-called sacred books, does that help mankind at all?

WR: Scriptures and all our knowledge condition Man, there is no doubt about that. But I should say that knowledge is not absolutely unnecessary. Buddha has pointed out very clearly that if you want to cross the river and there is no bridge, you build a boat and cross with its help. But if, on the other shore, you think, oh, this boat has been very useful, very helpful to me, I can't leave it here, I will carry it on my shoulders, that is a wrong action. What you should say is: of course this boat was very helpful to me but I have crossed the river, it is no more use to me, so I'll leave it here for somebody else. That is the attitude towards knowledge and learning. Buddha says that even the teachings, not only those, even the virtues, the so-called moral virtues, are also like the boat and have a relative and conditioned value.

K: I would like to question that. I am not doubting what you are saying, sir. But I would like to question whether knowledge has the quality of liberating the mind.

WR: I don't think *knowledge* can liberate.

K: Knowledge can't, but the quality, the strength, the sense of capacity, the sense of value that you derive from knowledge, the feeling that you know, the weight of knowledge – doesn't that strengthen you, the self?

WR: Certainly.

K: Does knowledge actually condition Man? Let's put it that way. The word 'knowledge' all of us surely take to mean accumulation of information, accumulation of experience, accumulation of various facts, theories and principles, the past and present, all that bundle we call knowledge. Does, then, the past help? Because knowledge *is* the past.

WR: All that past, all that knowledge, disappears the moment you see the truth.

K: But can a mind that is burdened with knowledge see truth?

WR: Of course if the mind is burdened, crowded and covered with knowledge...

K: It is, generally it is. Most minds are filled and crippled with knowledge. I am using the word 'crippled' in the sense of weighed down. Can such a mind perceive what is truth? Or must it be free from knowledge?

WR: To see the truth the mind must be free from all knowledge.

K: Yes, so why should one accumulate knowledge and then abandon it, and then seek truth? You follow what I am saying?

WR: Well, I think that in our ordinary life, most of the things that happen are useful at the beginning. For instance, as schoolchildren we can't write without ruled paper but today I can write without it.

K: Wait a minute, sir, I agree. When you are at school or university, we need lines to write on and all the rest of it, but does not the beginning, which might condition the future as we grow up, matter enormously? You understand what I am saying? I don't know if I am making myself clear. Does freedom lie at the end or at the beginning?

WR: Freedom has no beginning, no end.

K: Would you say that freedom is limited by knowledge?

WR: Freedom is not limited by knowledge, perhaps knowledge that is acquired and wrongly applied may obstruct freedom.

K: No, there is no wrong or right accumulation of knowledge. I may do certain ugly things and repent, or carry on with those ugly things, which is again part of my knowledge. But I am asking if knowledge leads to freedom? As you say, discipline is necessary at the beginning. And as you grow older, mature, acquire capacities and so on, does that discipline not condition the mind so that it can never abandon discipline in the usual sense of that word?

WR: Yes, I understand. You agree that discipline at the beginning, at a certain level is necessary.

K: I am questioning that, sir. When I say questioning it, I don't mean I doubt it or am saying it is not necessary, but I am questioning it in order to inquire.

WR: I should say at a certain level it is necessary, but if you can never abandon it... I am talking from the Buddhist point of view. There are two stages in Buddhism with regard to the Way: for people who are on the Way but have not yet arrived, there are disciplines, precepts and all those things that are good and bad, right and wrong. And an *arhat* who has realized the truth has no discipline because he is beyond that.

K: Yes, I understand this.

WR: But that is a fact in life.

K: I am questioning that, sir.

WR: I have no doubt about it in my mind.

K: Then we have stopped inquiring.

WR: No, it is not so.

K: I mean we are talking about knowledge: knowledge being useful or necessary, as a boat to cross the river. I want to inquire into that fact or that simile to see whether it is the truth – whether it has the quality of truth – let's put it that way for the moment.

WR: You mean the simile or the teaching?

K: The whole of that. Which means, sir... which means accepting evolution.

WR: Yes, accepting it.

K: Evolution, so gradually, step by step, advancing, and ultimately reaching. First I discipline, control, use effort, and as I get more capacity, more energy, more strength, I abandon that and move on.

WR: There is no plan like that, there is no plan.

K: No, I am not saying there is a plan. I am asking, or inquiring, whether there is such a movement, such progress at all.

WR: What do you think?

K: What do I think? No.

Irmgaard Schloegel: I very much agree with you, I can't believe that there is.

WR: Yes, all right, there is no progress like that.

K: We must go into this very carefully, because the whole religious tradition, Buddhist, Hindu and Christian, all the religious and non-religious attitudes are caught up in time, in evolution – I will be better, I will be good, I will eventually blossom in goodness. Right? I am saying that there is a root of untruth in this. Sorry to put it that way.

IS: I entirely agree with that for the very good reason that, as far as we know, ever since human beings have existed, we have always known that we *should* be good. If it were possible to progress by something like this we would not be the human beings that we are today. We would all have progressed sufficiently.

K: Have we progressed at all?

IS: Precisely, we have not progressed – very little, if at all.

K: We may have progressed technologically, scientifically, hygienically and all the rest of it but psychologically, inwardly, we have not – we are what we were ten thousand or more years ago.

IS: So the fact that we know we should do good, and have evolved so many systems of how to do it, has not managed to help us to become good. As I see it there is a specific obstacle in all of us, and it is working through this obstacle – because most of us want in our hearts to be good but most of us do not bring it about – that seems to me at stake.

K: We have accepted evolution. Biologically there is evolution. We have transferred that biological fact into psychological existence, thinking that we will evolve psychologically.

WR: No, I don't think that is the attitude.

K: But that is what it means when you say 'gradually'.

WR: No, I don't say 'gradually'. I don't say that. The realization of truth, attainment of truth, or seeing the truth, is without a plan, is without a scheme.

K: Is out of time.

WR: Out of time, exactly.

K: Which is quite different from saying that my mind, which has evolved through centuries, for millennia, which is conditioned by time, which is evolution, which is the acquiring of more and more knowledge, will reveal the extraordinary truth.

WR: It is not that knowledge that will reveal truth.

K: Therefore why should I accumulate knowledge?

WR: How can you avoid it?

K: Psychologically avoid it, not technologically.

WR: Even psychologically, how can you do that?

K: Ah, that's a different matter.

WR: Yes, how can you do that? Because you are conditioned.

K: Wait a minute, sir. Let's go into it a little more. Biologically, physically, from childhood up to a certain age, adolescence, maturity and so on, we evolve, that is a fact. A little oak tree grows into a gigantic oak tree, that is a fact. Now, is it a fact, or have we simply assumed it is, that we must *grow psychologically*? Which means, psychologically, that *eventually* I will achieve truth, or truth will take place if I *prepare* the ground.

WR: No, that is a wrong conclusion, that is a wrong point of view, the realization of truth is revolution not evolution.

K: Therefore, can the mind be *free psychologically* of the idea of progress?

WR: It can be.

K: No, not 'can be', it must be.

WR: That is what I have said – revolution is not evolution, a gradual process.

K: So psychologically can there be a revolution?

WR: Yes, certainly.

K: Which means what? No time.

WR: There is no time in it.

K: But all the religions, all the scriptures, whether it is Islam or whatever, have maintained you must go through certain systems.

WR: But not Buddhism.

K: Wait a minute. I wouldn't even say Buddhism, I don't know. I haven't read about it, except when I was a boy, but that has gone out of my mind. When you say, you must discipline first and then eventually let go of that discipline...

WR: No, I don't say that. I don't perceive it like that, and neither did Buddha.

K: Then, please, I may be mistaken.

WR: The question I have to ask you is: how does the realization of truth come about?

K: Ah, that's quite a different matter.

WR: What I am saying is that we are conditioned. Nobody can *tell* us that, however much they try. The revolution is to *see* that you are conditioned. The moment you see that, it has no time, it is an entire revolution, and that is the truth.

K: Suppose one is conditioned in the pattern of evolution – I have been, I am, I shall be. That is evolution. No?

WR: Yes.

K: My action was ugly yesterday, but today I am learning about that ugliness and freeing myself and tomorrow I will be free of it. That is our whole attitude, the psychological structure of our being. This is an everyday fact.

WR: Do we see that? Understanding may be intellectual, merely verbal.

K: No, I am not talking either intellectually or verbally, I mean that structure is a fact. I will *try* to be good.

WR: There is no question of *trying* to be good.

K: No, sir, not according to the Buddha, not according to scripture, but the average human being in everyday life says 'I am not as good as I should be, but – give me a couple of weeks or years – and eventually I will be awfully good.'

WR: Certainly that is the attitude that practically everybody has.

K: Practically everybody. Now wait a minute. That is our conditioning – the Christian, the Buddhist, the whole world is conditioned by this idea, which may have come from biological progress and moved into the psychological field.

WR: Yes, that's a good way of putting it.

K: Now how is a man or woman, a human being, to break this pattern without bringing in time? You understand my question?

WR: Yes. It is only by seeing.

K: No, I can't see if I am caught in this blasted ugliness of progress. You say it is only by seeing, and I say I can't see.

WR: Then you can't.

K: No, but I want to inquire into it, sir. That is, why have we given 'progress' such importance, psychologically?

IS: I am not a scholar but a practitioner. For me personally as a Westerner, as a one-time scientist, I have found the most satisfactory answer in the Buddhist teaching that I blind myself, I am my own obstacle. As long as I, with all my bundle of conditioning am here, I cannot see and act.

K: That doesn't help me. You are saying that you have learnt that.

IS: I have learnt it but I have done so in the same way as one learns to play a piano, rather than in the way of studying a subject.

K: Again, playing the piano, which means practice. So what are we talking about at the end of this?

G Narayan: There seems to be a difficulty here. Knowledge has a certain fascination, a certain power, one accumulates knowledge, whether it is Buddhist or scientific, and it gives you a peculiar sense of freedom – though it is not freedom – in the realm of conventional reality. And after years of study one finds it very difficult to get out of this because for twenty or so years you arrive at this point and value it, but it hasn't got the quality of what you might call truth. The difficulty with all practice seems to be that when you practise you achieve something; and the achievement is of the conventional-reality type, it has got a certain power, a certain fascination, a certain capacity, maybe a certain clarity.

WR: Because of that you get attached to it.

GN: Yes, and to break away from it is much more difficult than for a beginner; a beginner who has not got these things may see something more directly than a man who has a great deal of acquired wisdom.

WR: That depends on the individual, you can't generalize.

K: If I may point out, one can generalize as a principle. But let's come back to where we were. We are all caught in this idea of progress, right?

WR: We had just come to an agreement on that point, that humanity accepts the fact that progress is a gradual evolution. As you said, they accept it as true biologically, and can prove it there, so they apply the same theory to the psychological area. We agreed that that is the human position.

K: Is that position the truth? I have accepted that there is progress in

27

the sense of biological evolution and have then gradually transferred that to psychological existence. Now is that the truth?

WR: Now I see what you are questioning. I don't think it is the truth.

K: Therefore I abandon the whole idea of discipline.

WR: I should have said there is no question of abandoning it. If you abandon it consciously...

K: No, sir, just a minute. I see what human beings have done, which is to move from the biological to the psychological, and there they have invented this idea that eventually you will come to the godhead or enlightenment, reach Brahman or whatever, Nirvana, paradise or hell. If you see the truth of that, actually not theoretically, then it is finished.

WR: Absolutely, that is what I have been saying all the time.

K: Why should I then acquire knowledge of scriptures, of this or that, psychologically?

WR: There is no reason.

K: Then why do I read the Buddha?

WR: As I have said, we are all conditioned.

David Bohm: Could I ask a question: do you accept that you are conditioned?

K: Dr Bohm asks: do we all accept that we *are* conditioned?

WR: I don't know whether you accept it or not, I accept it. To be in time is to be conditioned.

DB: Well, what I mean to say is this: I think that Krishnaji has said, at least in some of our discussions, that he was not deeply conditioned in the beginning and therefore had a certain insight that would not be common. Is that fair?

K: Please, don't refer to me – I may be a biological freak, so leave me out of it. What we are trying to discuss, sir, is this: can we admit the truth that psychologically there is no movement forward – the truth of it, not the idea of it. You understand?

WR: I understand.

K: The truth of it, not 'I accept the idea of it', the idea is not the truth. So do we as human beings see the truth or falseness of what we have done?

WR: You mean, human beings generally?

K: The whole world.

WR: No, they don't see it.

K: Therefore when you tell them, get more knowledge, read this, read that, scriptures, what the Buddha said, what Christ said, if he existed at all, and so on, they are full of this accumulative instinct that will help them to jump or propel themselves into heaven.

DB: When we say we are all conditioned, how do we know that we are all conditioned? That is really what I wanted to say.

K: Yes, his point is, sir, are all human beings conditioned?

DB: What I wanted to emphasize is that if we say we are all conditioned there could be two ways of responding to that. One way could be to accumulate knowledge about our conditioning, to say we observe the common human experience, we can look at people and see that they are generally conditioned. The other way would be to say, do we see in a more direct way that we are all conditioned? That's what I was trying to get at.

K: But does that help in this matter? I mean there may or there may not be.

DB: The point I am trying to make is that if we say that we are all conditioned then I think there is nothing else to do but some kind of disciplined or gradual approach. That is, you begin with your conditioning.

K: Not necessarily, I don't see that.

DB: Well, let's try to pursue this. That's the way I take the implication of his question that if we all begin conditioned...

K: ...which we are.

DB: ...then what can we do for the next step?

WR: There is nothing called 'the next step'.

DB: How can we be free of the conditioning as we do whatever we do?

WR: The freedom from conditioning is to see.

DB: Well, the same question, how do we see?

WR: Of course many people have tried various ways.

K: No, there are not various ways. The moment you say a 'way', you have already a conditioned person on the 'way'.

WR: That is what I say. And you are also conditioning by your talks, they are also conditioning. Trying to uncondition the mind is also conditioning it.

K: No, I question that statement, whether what K is talking about conditions the mind – the mind being the brain, thoughts, feelings, the whole human psychological existence. I doubt it, I question it. If I may suggest, we are going off from the central issue.

WR: The question is how to see it – is that it?

K: No, sir, no. Not 'how', there is no how. First let us see this simple fact: do I, as a human being, see that I am representative of all humanity – I am a human being, and therefore I represent all humanity. Right?

IS: In an individual way.

K: No, as a human being, I represent you, the whole world, because I suffer, I go through agony etc, so does every human being. So do I, as a human being, see the falseness of the step human beings have taken by moving from the biological to the psychological with the same mentality? There, biologically, there is progress, from the little to the big and so on, from the wheel to the jet. As a human being, do I see the mischief that human beings have created by moving from there to this? Do I see it, as I see this table? Or do I say, 'yes, I accept the theory of it, the idea of it' and then we are lost. And the theory, the idea are therefore knowledge.

IS: If I see it as I see this table then it is no longer a theory.

K: It is then a fact. But the moment you move away from the fact it becomes idea, knowledge, and the pursuit of that. You move further away from the fact. I don't know if I am making myself clear.

WR: Yes, I guess that is so.

K: What is so? Human beings moving away?

WR: Human beings are caught in this.

K: Yes, it is a fact, isn't it, that there is biological progress, from a little tree to a gigantic tree, from baby to boyhood, to adolescence. Now we have moved with that mentality, with that fact, into the psychological field, and have assumed as a fact that we progress there, which is a false movement. I wonder if I am making myself clear?

DB: Are you saying that this is part of the conditioning?

K: No, leave the conditioning aside for the moment. I don't want to enter into that. But why have we applied the fact of biological growth to the psychological field, why? It is a fact that we have, but why have we done this?

IS: I want to *become* something.

K: Which is, you want satisfaction, safety, certainty, a sense of achievement.

IS: And it is in the wanting.

K: So why doesn't a human being see what he has done – actually, not theoretically?

IS: An ordinary human being.

K: You, I, X, Y.

IS: I do not like to see it, I fear it.

K: Therefore you are living in an illusion.

IS: Naturally.

K: Why?

IS: I want to be something that I fear at the same time not to see. This is where the divide is.

K: No, Madam, when you see what you have done there is no fear.

IS: But the fact is that I usually do not see it.

K: Why don't you see it?

IS: I suspect because of fear. I don't know why.

K: You are entering into quite a different field, when you talk of fear. I would just like to inquire, why human beings have done this, played this game for millennia. Why this living in this false structure, and then people come along and say, be unselfish, be this and all the rest of it – why?

IS: All of us have a very strong irrational side.

K: I am questioning all this. It is because we are living not with facts but with ideas and knowledge.

WR: Certainly.

K: The fact is that biologically there is evolution, psychologically there isn't. And so we give importance to knowledge, ideas, theories, philosophy and all the rest of it.

WR: You don't see at all that there can be a certain development, an evolution, even psychologically?

K: No.

WR: But take a man with a bad criminal record who lies, steals and so on – you can explain to him certain very fundamental, elementary things, and he changes, in the conventional sense, into a better man, no longer stealing, no longer telling lies or wanting to kill others.

K: A terrorist, for example.

WR: A man like that can change.

K: Are you saying, sir, a man who is evil, 'evil' in quotes, like the terrorists around the world, what is their future? Are you asking that?

WR: Don't you agree that you can explain to a criminal like that the wrongness of his behaviour? Because he understands what you have said, either because of his own thinking or because of your personal influence or whatever, he transforms himself, he changes.

K: I am not sure, sir, whether you can talk to a criminal, in the orthodox sense of that word, at all.

WR: That I don't know.

K: You can pacify him, you know, give him a reward and this and that, but an actual criminally-minded man, will he ever listen to any sanity? The terrorist – will he listen to you, to your sanity? Of course not.

WR: That you can't say, I don't know. I am not at all positive about it. But until I have more proof I can't say that.

K: I have no proof either, but you can see what is happening.

WR: What is happening is that there are terrorists and we don't know whether any of them have transformed themselves into good men. We have no proof.

K: You see that is my whole point – the bad man evolving into the good man.

WR: In the popular and the conventional sense, that certainly happens, one can't deny that.

K: Yes, we know that, we have dozens of examples.

WR: Don't we accept that at all?

K: No, wait a minute, sir. A bad man who tells lies, is cruel and so on, probably one day he realizes it is an ugly business and says, 'I'll change and become good', but that is not goodness. Goodness is not born out of badness.

WR: Certainly not.

K: Therefore the 'bad man', in quotes, can never *become* the good man, non-quotes. Goodness is not the opposite of the bad.

WR: At that level it is.

K: At any level.

WR: I don't agree.

GN: We might put it this way. At the *conventional* level the bad man becomes the good man. I think we would call that 'psychological progress'. That's something we do, the human mind does.

K: Of course, you are wearing yellow and I am wearing brown, we have the opposites of night and day, man and woman, and so on. But is there an opposite of fear? Is there an opposite of goodness? Is love the opposite of hate? The opposite, which means duality.

WR: I would say that we are talking in dualistic terms.

K: All language is dualistic.

WR: You can't talk, I can't talk, without a dualistic approach.

K: Yes, for comparing. But I am not talking of that.

WR: At the present moment you are speaking about the absolute, the ultimate ... when we talk of good and bad we are talking dualistically.

K: That's why I want to move away. Goodness is never the opposite of bad. So what are we talking about when we say 'I will move, change, from my conditioning, which is bad, to freedom from my conditioning, which is good'? Therefore freedom is the opposite of my conditioning. Therefore it is not freedom at all. That freedom is born out of my conditioning because I am caught in this prison and I want to be free. Freedom is not a *reaction* to the prison.

WR: I don't quite follow.

K: Sir, could we consider for a minute: is love the opposite of hate?

WR: The only thing you can say is: where there is love there is no hate.

K: No, I am asking a different question. I am asking: is hate the opposite of affection, love? If it is, then in that affection, in that love, there is hate, because it is born out of hate, out of the opposite. All opposites are born out of their own opposites. No?

WR: I don't know. That is what you say.

K: But it is a fact, sir. Look, I am afraid, and I cultivate courage, you know, to put away fear. I take a drink, or whatever, all the rest of it, to get rid of fear. And at the end of it I say that I am very courageous. All the war heroes and the rest of them are given medals for this. Because they are frightened, they say, 'we must go and kill', or do something or other, and they become very courageous, heroes.

WR: That is not courage.

K: I am saying anything born out of its opposite contains its own opposite.

WR: How?

K: Sir, if someone hates you and then says, 'I must love', that love is born out of hate. Because he knows what hate is and he says, 'I must not be this, but I must be that.' So that is the opposite of this. Therefore that opposite contains this.

WR: I don't know whether it is the opposite.

K: That is how we live, sir. This is what we do. I am sexual, I must not be sexual. I take a vow of celibacy – not I – people take a vow of celibacy, which is the opposite. So they are always caught in this corridor of opposites. And I question the whole corridor. I don't think it exists; we have invented it, but actually it doesn't exist. I mean, please this is just an explanation, don't accept anything, sir.

IS: Personally, I regard, as a working hypothesis, this channel of opposites as a humanizing factor, and we are caught in it.

K: Oh no, that is not a humanizing factor. That is like saying, 'I have been a tribal entity, now I have become a nation, and then ultimately I will become international': it is still tribalism going on.

DB: I think both of you are saying that we do in some sense make progress, in that we are not as barbaric as we were before.

IS: That is what I mean by the humanizing factor.

K: I question whether it is humanizing.

DB: Are you saying that this is not genuine progress? You see in the past people were far more barbaric generally than they are today, and therefore would you say that that really doesn't mean very much?

K: We are still barbarous.

DB: Yes, we are, but some people say we are not as barbaric as we were.

K: Not 'as'.

DB: Let's see if we can get this straight. Now, would you say that that is not important, that that is not significant?

K: No, when I say I am better than I was – it has no meaning.

DB: I think we should clarify that.

WR: In the relative, dualistic sense I don't accept that, I can't see that. But in the absolute, ultimate sense there is nothing like that.

K: No, not ultimately – I won't even accept that word 'ultimately'. I see how the opposite is born in everyday life, not ultimately. I am greedy, that's a fact. I try to become non-greedy, which is non-fact, but if I remain with the fact that I am greedy, then I can do something about it actually, now. Therefore there is no opposite. Sir, take violence and non-violence. Non-violence is the opposite of violence, an ideal. So non-violence is non-fact. Violence is the only fact. So I can then deal with facts, not with non-facts.

WR: So what is your point?

K: My point is that there is no duality even in daily life. It is the invention of all the philosophers, intellectuals, Utopians, idealists who say there is the opposite, work for that. The fact is I am violent, that's all, let me deal with that. And to deal with it, don't invent non-violence.

IS: The question now is: how am I going to deal with it, having accepted the fact that I am violent ...

K: Not accepted, it's a fact.

IS: ... having seen it.

K: Then we can proceed, I'll show you. I must see what I am doing now. I am avoiding the fact and running away to non-fact. That is what is happening in the world. So don't run, but *remain with the fact*. Can you do it?

IS: Well, the question is: *can* one do it? One can, but one often does not like doing it.

K: Of course you can do it. When you see something dangerous you say, 'it's dangerous so I won't go near it.' *Running away from the fact is dangerous.* So that's finished, you don't run away. That doesn't mean you train, that you practise not to run, *you don't run.* I think the gurus, the philosophers, have invented the running. Sorry.

WR: There is no running away, that is entirely different, it is a wrong way of putting it.

K: No, sir.

WR: You can't run away.

K: No, I am saying, don't run, then you see. Don't run, then you see. But we say, 'I can't see because I am caught in that.'

WR: I quite see that, what you are saying I see very well.

K: So there is no duality.

WR: Where?

K: Now, in daily life, not ultimately.

WR: What is duality?

K: Duality is the opposite. Violence and non-violence. You know, the whole of India has been practising non-violence, which is nonsense. There is only violence, let me deal with that. Let human beings deal with violence, not with the ideal of non-violence.

WR: I agree that if you see the fact, we must handle that.

K: Therefore there is no progress.

WR: That is just a word you can use anyway.

K: No, not anyway. When I have an ideal, to achieve that ideal I need time. Right? Therefore I will evolve to that. So no ideals – only facts.

WR: What is the difference, what is the argument between us? We agree that there are only facts.

K: Which means, sir, that to look at facts time is not necessary.

WR: Absolutely not.

K: Therefore if time is not necessary I can see it now.

WR: Yes, agreed.

K: You can see it now. Why don't you?

WR: Why don't you? That is another question.

K: No, not another question.

DB: If you take it seriously that time is not necessary one could perhaps clear up the whole thing right now.

WR: Yes, that does not mean all human beings can do it, there are people who can do it.

K: No, if I can see it, you can see it.

WR: I don't think so, I don't agree with you.

K: It is not a question of agreement or disagreement. When we have ideals away from facts time is necessary to get there, progress is necessary. I must have knowledge to progress. All that comes in. Right? So can you abandon ideals?

WR: It is possible.

K: Ah, no, the moment you use the word 'possible' time is there.

WR: I mean seeing the facts is possible.

K: Do it now, sir – forgive me, I am not being authoritarian – when you say it is possible you have already moved away.

WR: I mean to say, I must say, that not everybody can do it.

K: How do you know?

WR: That is a fact.

K: No, I won't accept that.

IS: Perhaps I can come in with a concrete example. If I stand on a high springboard over a swimming pool and I cannot swim, and I am told, 'Just jump in and relax completely and the water will carry you', this is perfectly true, I can swim. There is nothing that prevents me except that I am frightened of doing it. That is I think the issue. Of course we can do it, there is no difficulty but there is this basic fear, which does not stand to reason, that makes us shy away.

K: Please forgive me, I am not talking of that, we are not saying that. But if one realizes that one is greedy, why do we invent non-greed?

IS: I wouldn't know because it seems to me so obvious that if I am greedy then I am greedy.

K: So why do we have the opposite – why? All the religions say we must not be greedy, all the philosophers, if they are worth their salt, say don't be greedy, or something else. Or they say if you are greedy you will not reach heaven. So they have always cultivated through tradition, through saints, the whole gamut, this idea of the opposite. So I don't accept that. I say *that* is an escape from *this*.

IS: Which it is. It is at best a half-way stage.

K: It is an escape from this, right? And it won't solve this problem. So to deal with the problem, to remove it, I can't have one foot *there* and one foot *here*. I must have both my feet *here*.

IS: And if both my feet are here?

K: Wait, that is a simile, a simile. So I have no opposite which implies time, progress, practising, trying, becoming, the whole gamut of that.

IS: So I see I am greedy or I am violent.

K: Now we have to go into something entirely different. Can a human being be free of greed *now*? That's the question. Not eventually. You see I am not interested in not being greedy next life, who cares, or the day after tomorrow, I want to be free of sorrow, pain, now. So I have no ideals at all. Right, sir? Then I have only this fact: I am greedy. What is greed? The very word is condemnatory. The word 'greed' has been in my mind for centuries and the word immediately condemns the fact. By saying, 'I am greedy' I have already condemned it. Now can I look at that fact without the word with all its intimations, its content, its tradition? Look at it. You cannot understand the depth and feeling of greed or be free of it if you are caught in words. So as my whole being is concerned with greed it says, 'all right I won't be caught in it, I won't use the word greed.' Right? Now is that feeling of greed devoid of the word, divorced from the word 'greed'?

IS: No, it isn't, please go on.

K: So as my mind is full of words and caught in words, can it look at greed without the word?

WR: That is really seeing the fact.

K: Then only do I see the fact, then only do I see the fact.

WR: Yes, without the word.

K: This is where the difficulty lies. I want to be free of greed because everything in my blood, my tradition, my upbringing, my education, says be free of that ugly thing. So all the time I am making an *effort* to be free of it. Right? I was not educated, thank God, on those lines. So I say, all right, I have only the fact, the fact that I am greedy. I want to understand the nature and structure of that word, that feeling. What is it, what is the nature of that feeling? Is it a remembrance? If it is a remembrance I am looking at it, the present greed, with past remembrances. The past remembrances have said condemn it. Can I look at it without past remembrances?

I'll go into this a little more because the past remembrance condemns greed and therefore strengthens it. If it is something new, I won't condemn it. But because it is new but made old by remembrances, memories, experience, I condemn it. So can I look at it without the word, without the association of words? That doesn't need discipline or practice, that doesn't need a guide. Just this – can I look at it without the word? Can I look at that tree, woman, man, sky, heaven, without the word and find out? But if someone comes along and says, 'I'll show you how to do it', then I am lost. And 'how to do it' is the whole business of the sacred books. Sorry. All the gurus, the bishops, the popes, the whole of that.

How Do We See That Which Is Most Real?

Father Eugene Schallert, in his lifetime of the Society of Jesus, and a professor of sociology at the University of San Francisco.

Eugene Schallert: Perhaps we should start by exploring with each other the discovering of that which is most real in the world in which we live, and how we learn to see that which is most real.

Krishnamurti: Sir, would you say that to see the whole complex human problem very clearly, not only politically, religiously, socially, but also including morality, and a sense of 'otherness' – if we can use that word – mustn't one have total freedom?

ES: Yes, I don't see how one can explore anything of relevance to the world in which we live without an awareness of one's own inner freedom. If we feel we are somehow limited or constricted in our approach to social, economic or political, and moral problems – in particular religious problems – then we explore them from some base other than the real one, which is the base of being free.

K: Yes, sir, but most religions and most cultures, whether of Asia, India, Europe or America, condition the mind a great deal. As you travel you notice how in each country and each culture they have taken tremendous pains to shape the mind.

ES: I suppose the function of culture is to shape the mind – I don't think it is a very effective function – but it is a function of culture to provide in a sense a buffer between the person and the overwhelming dimensions of human existence. I think that cultures do in a sense soften or attempt to make things manageable or 'doable' in some way.

K: Yes, but I was thinking really of how the world is divided politically, socially, morally and especially in the religious field, which should be the unifying factor of all cultures. There one sees how religions have separated Man.

ES: Yes, indeed.

K: The Catholic, the Protestant, the Hindu, the Muslim, and they're all saying we're seeking one thing.

ES: Yes, even within the framework of any given religion there is a great tendency for people to divide, one sub-group against another sub-group . . .

K: Of course.

ES: . . . and this seems to be indigenous.

K: Therefore freedom is the negation of conditioning by any culture, by any religious division or political division.

ES: I think that in some sense ultimate freedom is the negation of such conditioning. The struggle for freedom is precisely the attempt to break through, undercut, or get at that which underlies these various conditioning processes. The conditioning processes themselves go on in each human being, in each flower, in each animal, and the task in the pursuit of freedom is precisely to break through somehow or other to that which is ultimately real.

K: I'm just wondering what we mean by conditioning?

ES: Conditioning in cultures throughout history and across space is quite varied, as you know. Conditioning for example in the Western world of today has been achieved primarily through the process of the enlightenment, of rational-logical processes, which I suppose are productive in the sense that without them you wouldn't have television cameras to talk to. At the same time with television cameras we may not see anything. I suspect that the primary conditioning agency in our world is the totality of the kinds of thoughts, categories, concepts or constructs – I call them fantasies – that people deal with and which somehow they think are real.

K: Yes, sir, but don't these conditionings separate Man?

ES: Unquestionably, yes. They separate Man both within himself and outwardly.

K: So if we are concerned with peace, with ending war, with living in a world in which this terrible violence, separation, brutality and all the rest of it is to end, and it seems to me that is the function of any serious religious man – because I feel religion is the only factor that unifies Man . . .

ES: Yes.

K: . . . not politics, economics and so on. But instead of bringing

Man together religions have separated Man.

ES: I'm not sure that that's quite right. I think religion has been *defined* by cultures as a unifying force between men. There's not an awful lot of historical evidence that it has ever *achieved* this.

K: No.

ES: This may also be a function of the limiting dimensions of any given religion, or the inability of religious people to in some way or other transcend their own religious concepts or legends or myths or dogmas – whatever you want to call them. And I think that there is in fact a deeper base for unity.

K: One can't get to the deeper unless one is free from the outer. I mean, my mind won't go very, very deeply unless there is a freedom from belief and from dogma.

ES: I think that's true in a sense. I think that there must be within Man a sense, a consciousness, experience, something, a sense of his own inner freedom before he can be appropriately religious – before he can allow religious categories as analytical categories to have any meaning for him. Somehow or other he must be human and free before he can ever think of being religious. What has happened is just the opposite.

K: Yes, we are saying, seeing what the world is now actually, not conceptually, but the actual fact of separation, wars, the terrible all-pervasive violence, I feel it is the religious mind that can bring real unity to human beings.

ES: I would rather say it is the 'human' or the 'seeing' mind that may be susceptible to some exhilaration, if you will, not in the sense of stimulus but some exhilaration relative to the phenomenon of being itself that can bring people together or achieve an end to the conflicts that we are experiencing.

K: Could we approach this by asking: what separates Man, what divides human beings?

ES: I think that ultimately it is 'Man-ness'.

K: What do you mean by 'Man-ness'?

ES: What I mean is that our tendency to think about ourselves as Man or human, rather than as being, separates us from the world in which we live – from the tree, the flower, the sunset, the sea, the lake, the river, the animal, the bird, the fish – and ultimately from each other.

K: From each other.

ES: Yes, ultimately it is from each other.

K: And that is given strength by or through these separative religions. I want to get at something. Is reality or truth to be approached through any particular religion? Or is it approachable or perceivable only when the organized religious belief and propaganda, dogma and all the conceptual way of living, completely go?

ES: I am not sure if it is appropriate to say that it should go completely, for a lot of other reasons posterior to the phenomenon of being human or simply of being in the first place. If we're going to get at the question of truth, which I think is the question of understanding or seeing, we have to somehow get at the question of being, and the whole inner dynamics and evolutionary character of being. If we can't get at that level in the beginning, somehow we really won't get at whatever value the teachings of the various religions offer men. If those teachings are not relevant to existence, to being, to seeing, to understanding, to loving, or to an end of conflict in a negative sense, then somehow or other those teachings are really not relevant for Man. They're unimportant.

K: I agree, but the fact remains – just look at it – if one is born a Hindu or a Muslim and is conditioned by that, in that culture, in that behavioural pattern, and conditioned by a series of beliefs imposed, carefully cultivated by various religious orders and sanctions, books and all the rest of it: and another is conditioned by Christianity – there is no meeting point, except conceptually.

ES: Krishnaji, do you mean that in order for a man to simply be free, he will somehow have to rid himself not only of political, cultural and social but also of the religious – particularly religious – doctrines, dogmas or myths that are associated with him as a religious person?

K: That's right. Because you see, after all, what is important in living is unity, harmony between human beings. That can only come about if there is harmony in each one; and that harmony is not possible if there is any form of division inside or outside, externally or internally. Externally, if there is political division, geographical division, national division, there must obviously be conflict; and if there is inward division, that must obviously breed great conflict, which expresses itself in violence, brutality, aggressiveness and all the rest of it. So human beings are brought up in this way. And a Hindu and a Muslim are at each other all the time, or the Arab and the Jew, or the American, the Russian, you follow?

ES: What we are dealing with here is not so much the imposition of harmony on the human being from without . . .

K: Oh, no!

ES: . . . or the imposition of disharmony on the human being from without. My hands are perfectly harmonious with each other, my fingers move together and my eyes move with my hands. But there may be conflict in my mind, or between my mind and my feelings insofar as I have internalized certain concepts or ideas which are then in conflict.

K: That's right.

ES: What I must discover if I am to be free is that there is in fact harmony within me, and if I am to be one with you I must somehow or other discover from my hand what it's like to be a part of something. Because my hand is already harmoniously existing with my arm and with my body – and with you. But then my mind sets up these strange dualities.

K: That's the problem, sir. Are these dualities created artificially? First of all because you are a Protestant, I am a Catholic, or I am a Communist and you are a Capitalist? Are they created artificially because each society has its own vested interest, each group has its own particular form of security? Or is the division created in oneself by the 'me' and the 'not me'? You understand what I mean?

ES: I understand what you mean.

K: The 'me' is my ego, my selfishness, my ambitions, greed, envy and that separates, excludes you from entering that field.

ES: Really the more one is conscious of his selfishness, his greed, his ambition, or on the other side of the fence, his security or even his peace in a superficial sense, the more unconscious is he of the inner self who is in fact already one with you, however much he may be unaware of that.

K: Wait, just a minute, sir. That becomes a dangerous thing. Because the Hindus have maintained, as most religions have, that in you there is harmony, there is God, there is reality, and all that you have to do is peel off the layers of corruption, hypocrisy, stupidity and gradually come to that point where you are established in harmony, because you've already got it.

ES: I think the Hindus don't have a monopoly on that particular way of thinking . . .

K: No, of course not!

ES: . . . we Catholics have the same problem. (laughs)

K: The same problem, of course!

ES: I think what we're confronted with is a discovery. With a discovery of seeing, of understanding, of living, of trusting – all these primary sorts of words, we're confronted with the discovering of these things. And peeling back layers is not, I think, the way to discover them. Whether it be layers of corruption, of goodness or evil, whatever, that is not the way to discover them. One does not abstract from or pretend away his sense of evil within himself in order to find himself. What is required it seems to me is a penetrating, empathetic, open, free mind.

K: Yes, sir, but how does one come to it? With all the mischief one is brought up in or lives in, is it possible to put all that aside and do so effortlessly? For the moment there is effort there is distortion.

ES: I am sure that is true. Without effort – that is without activity, behaviour, too much conversation – but certainly not without the expenditure of enormous amounts of energy.

K: That energy can come only if there is no effort.

ES: Precisely, it can come only in the absence of effort.

K: If there is no friction then you have an abundance of energy!

ES: Precisely, friction destroys, dissipates energy.

K: Friction exists when there is separation . . .

ES: Right.

K: . . . between what is right and what is wrong. Between what is called evil and what is called good. If I am trying to be good then I create friction. So really the problem is how to have this abundance of energy that will come when there is no conflict. And one needs that tremendous energy to discover what truth is.

ES: Or what goodness is. I think if we deal with goodness in the sense that you use it there – 'one tries to be good' – we're dealing with codes, with law, with moral goodness in some sense.

K: No, I don't mean that. Goodness flowers only in freedom, it

were all at your

fingertips

ws, any religious sanctions, or any

nstraints.

s. So if we're going to discover the

goodness, and of being, we have to

e reasons why we have not

have within ourselves this strange

face of things and never to leave that.

ted.

uppose you and I know nothing,

ve no belief, no dogma, nothing.

live rightly, to be good – not find

o be good.

Now, to do that I have to inquire, I have to observe. Observation is only possible when there is no division.

ES: Observation is that which eliminates the divisions.

K: Yes, when the mind is capable of observing without division then I perceive, then there is perception.

ES: In any seeing that is more than conceptual or categorical seeing or observing mental constructs, a truth is encountered, and being and truth and goodness are all the same thing.

K: Of course.

ES: So the question then is why do I have to think about truth as though it were associated with the logical consistency of categories . . .

K: Of course.

ES: . . . rather than think about truth as though it were associated with my being itself. If I have to somehow or other always partialize my world – we spoke of the dualities – to think of, as we frequently do or did in the Catholic religion, of the duality of body and soul . . .

K: . . . and of good and evil.

ES: . . . and good and evil incarnate in one form or another – if we have to always think that way, then we shall never find what it means to be good, or to be truthful, or to be at all.

K: Yes, that's right.

ES: I think this is the problem, and as you suggested there are so many centuries of cultural conditioning from all perspectives that it's difficult.

K: And human beings are brought up in this dualistic way of living.

ES: Yes, and maybe we could do this better if we did not consider the obvious dualities of good and evil, of the sacred and profane, of right and wrong, of truth and falsehood.

K: Right, right.

ES: We wouldn't take any of these dualities, but somehow or other come to grips with the duality that bedevils us most, the duality of you and me, of man and woman.

K: Yes, the duality of me and you. Now what is the root of that? What is the source of this division as me and you? We and they. Politically, religiously – you follow?

ES: There cannot be any source of this in us because we are one – like the fingers on my hand.

K: Sir, when you say we are one that is an assumption. I don't know I am one. Only when the division actually ceases can I say – then I don't have to say I am one. There is a unity. I want to go into this a little bit because, as human beings live, there is only me and you, my God and your God, my country and your country, my doctrine – (laughs) you follow? This me and you, me and you. Now, the 'me' is the conditioned entity.

ES: Yes, the 'me' is the conditioned entity.

K: Let's go step by step. The 'me' is the conditioned entity brought about, nurtured, through culture, society, religion, through conceptual, ideological living. The 'me' that is selfish, the 'me' that gets angry, violent, the 'me' that says I love you, I don't love you, all that is 'me'. That 'me' is the root of separation.

ES: Unquestionably. In fact the very terminology you use portrays the substance of your idea. The word 'me' is an objective pronoun. Once I have made of myself something out there to look at I shall never see anything that is real because I am not out there to be looked at! Once I make freedom something out there to pursue then I shall never achieve freedom. Once I make freedom something out there that someone will *give* me then I shall never achieve freedom.

K: All authority, all that can be pushed aside. There is me and you. As long as this division exists there must be conflict between you and me.

ES: Unquestionably.

K: And there is not only conflict between you and me but there is conflict within me.

ES: Once you have objectified yourself there must be conflict within you.

K: So I want to find out whether this 'me' can end, so that – not so that – merely end.

ES: Yes, because there is obviously no 'so that' if the 'me' ends.

K: Now, is it possible to completely empty the mind of the 'me'? Not only at the conscious level, but at the deep unconscious roots of one's being.

ES: I think it's not only possible but it's the price that we must pay for being, for being good or being true or being at all, living. To live, the price we must pay is to rid ourselves of 'me-ness'.

K: Is there a process, a system, a method, to end the 'me'?

ES: No, I don't think there is any process or method.

K: Therefore there are no choices. It must be done instantly! Now on this we must be very clear. All the religions have maintained processes. The whole evolutionary system psychologically is a process. If you say, and to me that is a reality, that it cannot possibly be a process – which means a matter of time, degree, gradualness – then there is only one problem: which is to end it instantly.

ES: That is to destroy the monster at one step.

K: Instantly!

ES: Yes, that is unquestionably what must be done. We must destroy 'me-ness'.

K: No, I wouldn't say destroy, but the ending of the 'me' with all the accumulation, all the experiences, dogma, everything it has accumulated consciously and unconsciously. Can that whole content be thrown out? Not by effort, by me. If I say thrown out by me it is still the 'me'. Or if I throw it out by exertion of will it is still the 'me'. The 'me' remains.

ES: Yes, clearly it is not an act or an activity of the mind, nor an activity of the will, nor an activity of feeling, nor an activity of the body which will help me to see.

K: To see, yes.

ES: And since we in this world are so wrapped up with doing, having and acting, we don't really understand reflectively and profoundly what takes place before we act or before we possess. It seems incumbent upon us to reflect backwards and see that there is seeing before seeing takes place – in the two senses of the word seeing – just as there is loving before one becomes aware of loving and certainly just as there is being before one becomes aware of being. Is the question reflecting backwards inwardly, deeply enough?

K: Now, just a minute, sir. That's the difficulty, because the 'me' is both at a conscious level and at the deeper levels of consciousness. Can the conscious mind examine the unconscious 'me' and expose it? Or the content of consciousness *is* the 'me'.

ES: No, the self transcends the content of consciousness. The 'me' may well be the content of consciousness, but the 'me' is not the I, the 'me' is not the self.

K: Wait, I include in the 'me', the self, the ego, the whole conceptual ideation about myself: the higher self, the lower self, the soul – all of that is the content of my consciousness, which makes the I, which makes the ego, which is the 'me'.

ES: It certainly makes the 'me', yes. I agree that it makes that objective self that I can examine and analyse and look at, compare, that I can be violent with others about. The summation of the whole thing that you put in the word 'me' is explanatory of a history, of a whole multiplicity of present relationships, but it's still not getting at the reality.

K: No, the reality cannot be got at, or it cannot flower, if the 'me' is there.

ES: Whenever, as I said before, I insist upon 'me' viewing 'you' then the reality cannot flower and freedom will not be.

K: So the content of my consciousness is the 'me', my ego, my self, my ideation, my thoughts, my ambitions, my greed, all that is the 'me'. My nation, my desire for security, for pleasure, for sex, my desire to do this or that. All that is the content of my consciousness. As long as that content remains, there must be separation between you and me, between good and bad, and the whole division takes place. Now, we are saying that the emptying of that content is not a process of time.

ES: Nor is it subject to methodology.

K: Or to methodology. So then what is one to do? Let's look at it. Let's take a little time over this because it is quite important. Most people say you must practise, you must strive, you must make a tremendous effort, live in a disciplined way, control, suppress, you know?

ES: I am very familiar with all that. (laughs)

K: That's all out.

ES: That has not been helpful.

K: So how is the content to be emptied with one stroke, as it were?

ES: I would say – and maybe we could pursue this together – the content cannot be emptied by a negative action of repudiation of the content.

K: No, obviously.

ES: So that is a blind alley.

K: Obviously. By denying it you are putting it under the carpet. I mean it is like locking it up, it is still there.

ES: It's a pretence.

K: That's just it, sir. One has to see this. One has to be tremendously honest in this otherwise one plays tricks with oneself, one deceives oneself.

ES: Yes.

K: I see clearly and logically that the 'me' is the mischief in the world.

ES: Well, I don't see that so logically as simply intuitively.

K: All right.

ES: It's not the result of a discursive act, it's not a dialectical . . .

K: No, of course not, it's not analytical, dialectical. You see it. A selfish human being, whether he's politically high or low, you see the selfishness of human beings and how destructive they are. Now the question is: can this content be emptied, so that the mind is really empty and active and therefore capable of perception?

ES: Probably the content cannot be simply emptied. I think that the content can be put in a perspective or can be seen for its inadequacy or inappropriateness by a very energetic act of simply seeing. That's why I said in the beginning that so long as I look at the truths of any given religion I am not finding truth itself. The way I discover the relative value of the truths of any given religion is precisely by seeing truth itself. Truth itself, not as an object.

K: No, the mind cannot perceive the truth if there is division. That I must stick to.

ES: Once you have division of any kind . . .

K: It's finished.

ES: . . . then you're at the categorical level and you will not see.

K: Therefore my question is whether the mind can empty its content. Wait sir, this is really – you follow?

ES: I follow what you are saying and I think you are devising a new methodology.

K: Ah, no, I am not devising a new methodology. I don't believe in methods! I think they are the most mechanical and destructive things.

ES: But having said that, you come back and say, but if the mind is really to see it must empty itself of content. Isn't this a method?

K: No!

ES: But why, sir, is it not a method?

K: I'll show you. It is not a method because we said as long as there is division there must be conflict. That is so politically, religiously. We are saying that division exists because of the 'me', which is the content of my consciousness, and that the emptying of the mind brings unity. I see this not logically but as fact. Not conceptually. I see what is taking place in the world – I see how absurd, how cruel all this is, and the perception of that empties the mind. The very perceiving is the act of emptying.

ES: What you're suggesting is that the perception of the inappropriateness of the content of consciousness or of the 'me', the perception of the inadequacy of this content or truthlessness of the 'me', is in itself the discovery of being.

K: That's right.

ES: I think we should pursue that because I wonder if the perception is in fact that negative or might in fact be very positive. It is rather in the simple seeing of the being of things – and it wouldn't have to be me or you in the objective sense. It could be through this table or my hand or whatever that I discover the inadequacy of such things as the content of consciousness or through me or you in the objective sense. So it may be through a rather profound display of intellectual or rather personal energy that being simply makes itself visible to me by reason of the display. It's dissipating and at the same time it's easy to deal with concepts, we've agreed on that. It's easy to create concepts. It's easier, I maintain, to see simply prior to concepts.

K: Of course. Seeing!

ES: Just simple seeing.

K: But, sir, there is no perception if that perception is through an image.

ES: There is no perception if it is through an image. I think that is very true.

K: Now, the mind has images.

ES: The mind is bedevilled with images!

K: (laughs) That's just it, it has images. I have an image of you and you have an image of me. These images are built through contact, through relationship, through you saying this, you hurting me, and I – you know. It's built, it is there. Which is memory. The brain cells themselves are the residue of memory that forms the image. Now the question then is: memory, which is knowledge, is necessary to function technically; and to walk home or drive home, I need memory. Therefore memory has a place as knowledge but knowledge as image has no place in relationship between human beings.

ES: I still think we are avoiding the issue at hand. Because I think what you have said about memory is, as you suggested, terribly important, but I don't think that memory or the repudiation of memory . . .

K: Ah no, I don't . . .

ES: . . . or consciousness or the repudiation of the content of consciousness is the solution of the problem. I think what we have to ask is: how is it, Krishnaji, that you – and I'm not talking methodology now – saw? Or that you see? I know that you have seen. And don't tell me what you eliminated in order to describe to me how you see!

K: I'll tell you how I saw. You simply see!

ES: Yes, now suppose you say to someone who has had no such

experience, 'you simply see', because I say the same thing myself
all the time: 'well, you simply see' and people say – how? If we
are to be teachers we must somehow or other deal with this. 'Let
me take you by the hand and I will show you how to see.'

K: I'll show you. I think that is fairly simple. First of all one has to see
what the world is, see what is around you, see! Don't take sides.

ES: Yes, I think our terminology may get in the way here. Suppose,
rather than saying one must start by seeing what the world is,
we said: one must see the world. Not be concerned with
natures or categories.

K: That's it. See the world. See the world as it is. Don't translate it
in terms of your concepts.

ES: Now again could I say see the world as it is '. . .ising'?

K: Yes, put it that way. (laughs)

ES: Does that help? I mean we are trying to . . .

K: See the world as it is! You cannot see the world as it is if you
interpret it through your terminology, your categories, your
temperament, your prejudices. See it as it is, violent, brutal,
whatever it is.

ES: Or good or beautiful.

K: Whatever it is. Can you look at it that way? Which means: can
you look at a tree without the image of the tree, the botanical
description and all the naming? Just look at the tree.

ES: Once you have discovered – and it's not easy in our world to
discover this – the simple experience of seeing the tree without
thinking 'treeness' or its nature, or as you say, its botany and
things of that kind, then what would you suggest is the next
step in the pursuit of seeing?

K: Then seeing myself as I am.

ES: Underneath the content of your consciousness.

K: See it all – not underneath. I haven't begun yet! I see what I am,
therefore self-knowing. There must be observation of myself as
I am without saying how terrible, how ugly, how beautiful, how
sentimental. Just to be aware – all the movement of myself,
conscious as well as unconscious. I begin with the tree, not as a
methodical process. I see that. And I also must see, in this way,
myself, the hypocrisy, the tricks I play – you follow? The whole
of that. Watchfulness. Without any choice – just watch. Know

myself. Knowing myself all the time.

ES: But in a non-analytical fashion.

 K: Of course. But the mind is trained to be analytical. So I have to pursue that – why am I analytical? Watch it, seeing the futility of it! It takes time, analysis, and you can never really be analysed whether by a professional or yourself, so see the futility, the absurdity, the danger of it! So what are you doing then? You are seeing things as they are, actually what is taking place.

ES: My tendency would be to say that when we discuss this we may use these words, like seeing the self in its fullness, with all its negative and positive polarities, and realize the futility of looking analytically at certain dimensions of the self, yet find ourselves saying – but I still have to see.

 K: Yes, of course.

ES: Because at this point I have not yet seen. All I have seen are the analytical categories I've used to take myself apart somehow in little pieces.

 K: That's why I ask, sir, can you look at the tree without the knowledge?

ES: Without the prior conditioning.

 K: Without the prior conditioning. Can you look at a flower without any word?

ES: I can see how one must somehow or other be able to look at the self. I must be able to look at you, Krishnamurti, and not use the word Krishnamurti. Otherwise I will not see you.

 K: That's right.

ES: This is true. Now after I have learned, through thinking, to say somehow or other I must see you and not even use the word . . .

 K: The word, the form, the image, the content of that image and all the rest of it.

ES: Whatever the word denotes I must not use.

 K: So that requires tremendous watchfulness. Watchfulness in the sense of not involving correction, not saying I must, I must not. Watching.

ES: When you use the word watching – and I think again because we are teaching we must be careful of our words . . .

 K: Being aware, whatever, it doesn't matter what word you use.

ES: Observation has the connotation of putting something out there to look at under a microscope as a scientist would do, and I think that is what we don't want to teach.

K: No, of course.

ES: So if you could use again, Krishnaji, the word watching.

K: It is watching, being aware, choicelessly aware.

ES: Choicelessly aware, fine.

K: Choicelessly aware of this dualistic, analytical, conceptual way of living. Be aware of it. Don't correct it, don't say this is right, be aware of it. And we are aware of this intensely when there is a crisis.

ES: I think we have another problem that precedes this one by an inch: what kinds of question can I ask myself in order to be aware of you and not use the categories or to be aware of the fact that in being aware of you I am using the categories and the stereotypes and all these other funny images that I use all the time? Is there some way in which I can address myself to you, using certain kinds of words – not ideas – words that don't relate to ideas at all – that somehow or other will teach me or you or whoever that there is something more important or significant in you than your name or nature or content or consciousness or your good or your evil. What words would you use if you were to teach a young person – or an old person, because we all have the problem – in order to make it understandable in a non-rational or, better, in a pre-rational way, that you are more than your name connotes?

K: I wouldn't, I think, use that word. Be choicelessly aware. Because to choose, as we do, is one of our great conflicts.

ES: And for some strange reason we associate choice with freedom, which is the antithesis of freedom, which is absurd!

K: Of course!

ES: But now, to be freely aware . . .

K: Freely, choicelessly.

ES: . . . freely aware, yes. Now suppose that someone says: but, sir, I don't understand completely what you mean by choicelessly aware, can you show me?

K: I'll show you, yes. First of all, choice implies duality; and there is choice at a certain level. I choose that carpet as better than the other one. At that level choice must exist. But when there is choice in awareness of yourself, it implies duality, it implies effort.

ES: Choice implies a highly developed consciousness of limitation.

K: Yes, choice also implies conformity.

ES: And choice implies conformity, yes, to cultural conditionings.

K: Conformity means imitation, which means more conflict. Trying to live up to something. So there must be an understanding of that word not only verbally but inwardly, the meaning of it, the significance of it. That is, I understand the full significance of choice, the entirety of choice.

ES: May I attempt to translate this now? Would you say that choiceless awareness means that I am somehow or other conscious of your presence to the within of me and I don't need the choice. The choice is irrelevant, the choice is abstract, the choice has to do with the categories. When I don't feel, having seen you, that I must choose you or choose to like you or choose to love you – that any choice is involved, then would you say I have choiceless awareness of you?

K: Yes, but you see, sir, is there in love, choice? I love. Is there choice?

ES: There is no choice in love.

K: No, that's just it. Choice is a process of the intellect. I'll explain this as much as we can discuss, go into, it. But see the significance of it. Now, to be aware, what does that mean, to be aware? To be aware of things about you outwardly and also to be aware inwardly, of what is happening, of your motives, your anxiety. To be aware, again, choicelessly.

Watch, look, listen. So that you are watching without any movement of thought. Thought is the image, thought is the word. To watch without thought coming and pushing you in any direction. Just to watch.

ES: I think you used a better word before when you said to be aware. Because it is an act of existence rather than an act of the mind or feeling.

K: Of course.

ES: So then we have to – I have to somehow or other become eventually, and therefore be aware, in a pre-cognitive sense, of your presence.

K: Be aware, that's right.

ES: And this antecedes choice and makes choice unnecessary.

K: Yes. There is no choice. Be aware.

ES: Be aware. Choiceless awareness, yes.

K: Now, from that there is an awareness of the 'me', an awareness of how hypocritical the whole movement of the 'me' and the 'you' is.

ES: Sir, you're moving backwards now, we've already . . .

K: Purposely, I know. I moved back so that we relate it to that. So there is this quality of mind that is free from the 'me' and therefore there is no separation. I don't say 'we are one' but we discover unity as a living thing, not as a conceptual thing, when there is this sense of choiceless attention.

ES: Yes.

The conversation continued later the same day.

ES: You have said that in order to achieve this seeing that we have been discussing one must arrive at a state in which one is attentive and freely, or choicelessly, attentive to the other. Perhaps if we could say, can give his undivided attention to the other?

K: Yes.

ES: And before we take the next step, could I say that we are really not looking for an answer to the question: what is seeing? Are we not looking for seeing itself?

K: Is there an answer, sir, when there is real perception – actually of what is?

ES: No, perception is not an answer.

K: But when there is perception of what is – what is in the world, what is in me – that perception, not a conceptual perception but actual perception that the world is me and I am the world, there is no division between the world and me, I am the world. Then there is perception. What takes place in that perception? That's what you're asking, is it, sir?

ES: Yes, the word itself is difficult to use because, in a sense, we have for so long taken each other, our dualities, our world, for granted – and because of this, I think we have in some way made it impossible or difficult for us to simply perceive.

K: Right sir, yes sir.

ES: But once we can handle this and say what we are really interested in is the simple perception that precedes all rational, logical knowledge of any kind, or all of our biases, and all of our prejudices, and from which these biases do not come . . .

K: . . . or rather, putting it this way, there is no perception if there is a bias.

ES: A bias is precisely that which makes perception impossible, when I do not *want* to perceive you.

K: Of course, I build a barrier, whether of religion, politics or whatever it is.

ES: Now, if it is true that in the seeing, the perception of you, what is needed within me is not me . . .

K: Yes, that's right.

ES: . . . and what is needed within you is not you, then when we speak of perception, are we not, in some way or other, speaking of such things as oneness or truth?

K: I would not come to that yet. To me, it is seeing that I am the world, or seeing – whether I'm a Hindu, Buddhist or Christian – that we are the same, psychologically; inwardly we are all in a state of confusion, battle, misery, sorrow, with an appalling sense of loneliness, of despair. That is the common ground of all humanity. There is perception of that. Now what takes place when there is that perception?

ES: That is what we're trying to pursue and to explain – without explaining it!

K: That is what we're going to share together. There is perception of sorrow, let's take that. My son, my brother, my father dies. What takes place, generally, is that I escape from it. Because I can't face this sense of tremendous danger, loneliness and despair, I escape from it, into ideology, concepts, in a dozen ways. Now, to perceive the escape – just to perceive it, not check it or control it, not say I mustn't – just to be aware, choicelessly again, that you are escaping – then the escape stops. The momentum of escape is a wastage of energy. You've stopped that energy – not you have stopped – perception has ended the wastage. Therefore, you have more energy. Then, when there is no escape, you are faced with the fact of what is. That is, you have lost somebody, there is death, loneliness, despair. That is exactly what is. There, again, a perception of what is.

ES: I think I see the direction you are taking. What you are saying is

that when I perceive that you are sorrowful – because I don't
perceive sorrow, it doesn't exist by itself – what I perceive is that
you have been separated and this is a source of sorrow because
now your father is dead and you are separated. And in
perceiving that sorrow is associated with separation . . .

K: Not quite, sir, not yet. The fact is I've lost somebody. That's a
fact: burned, gone; and it is something gone finally, and I feel
tremendously lonely. That's a fact: lonely, without any sense of
relationship, without a sense of any security. I'm completely at
the end.

ES: Many people speak of this, saying 'I am empty now'.

K: Yes, there is an awareness of emptiness, loneliness, despair. I
am saying, when you don't escape, there is this conservation of
energy when I'm facing the fear of my loneliness. I meet it, I'm
aware of it. There is an awareness of this fear of loneliness.

ES: But how can you give your undivided attention to someone
whom you have lost, simply and finally?

K: I have lost him finally. But now we're examining the state of the
mind that has lost. The mind that is saying, 'I've lost everything,
I'm really in desperate sorrow'. And there is fear. See that fear.
Don't run away, don't escape, don't try to smother it by courage
and all the rest of it. See that fear. Be choicelessly aware of that
fear. Then, in that awareness, fear disappears. It does disappear.
Now you have greater energy.

ES: Yes, and we have all experienced that, seeing how fear disarms
fear.

K: Now, why is there sorrow? What is sorrow, self-pity?

ES: Well, when it's associated with anxiety or fear then we will have
to call it self-pity.

K: Self-pity, yes. What does that mean, self-pity? You see, that
means the 'me' is more important than the person who is dead.

ES: So you didn't give your undivided attention.

K: I never loved that man.

ES: Precisely, yes.

K: My child, I never loved that child. I never loved my wife or
husband, sister. In this state of awareness there is the discovery
that love never existed.

ES: In the discovery of a sorrow associated with grief or separation

or fear, there is the discovery that love has been horribly
limited, if it existed at all.

K: Not limited, I didn't have it! I couldn't have it! Love means
something entirely different. So now there is tremendous
energy. You follow, sir? No escape, no fear, no sense of self-pity,
concern about myself, my anxiety. So out of this sense of sorrow
there is this bubbling energy which is really love.

ES: Which is really love, yes. So now we have discovered that when
one gives this undivided attention to another . . .

K: Ah, no! I am not giving my attention to the person who is dead:
my father, my son, my brother. There has been attention to the
state of my mind, the mind that says 'I suffer'.

ES: Yes, but we have been trying to examine what 'I suffer' means in
the context of what choiceless attention means.

K: Yes, so I find love is a total attention . . .

ES: Love is a total attention.

K: . . . without any division. This is really important because, you
see, sir, for us love is pleasure, sexual, and love is fear, love is
jealousy, love is possessiveness, domination, aggressiveness –
you follow? We use that word to cover up all this: love of God,
love of Man, love of country, love of – and so on. All that is *love
of my concern about myself.*

ES: All that is self-love.

K: Obviously.

ES: But it's the 'me' that is being loved, not the self that is being . . .

K: Yes, that's it – no love. That's a tremendous discovery. That
requires great honesty, to say: 'I've never really loved anybody,
I've pretended, I've exploited, I've adjusted myself to somebody,
but the fact is that I have never known what it means to love'.
That is tremendous honesty, sir, to say that I thought I loved and
have never found it. Now I have come upon something that is
real, which is, I have watched what is and moved from there.
There is an awareness of what is and that awareness moves. It is
a living thing – not something that comes to a conclusion.

ES: Now, why is it that in our attempt to pursue the question of
undivided or choiceless attention, or simple seeing, that we, very
naturally – not really logically but very naturally – slipped into
the question of simple loving as opposed to fictitious, fraudulent

or conditioned loving? There must be something about the loving and the seeing process which is so similar that we can slip from seeing to loving and really be discussing the same thing. And as we move – well, move is not a good word . . .

K: No.

ES: . . . as we become aware, as we develop this undivided attention, this choiceless awareness . . .

K: If I may suggest, don't use the word 'develop', that means time. Be aware, be aware of the carpet in your room, the colour, the shape, the form – be aware of that. Don't say 'I like it, don't like it, this is good, this is bad'. Just be aware of it. Then from that grows the flame of awareness, if one can so call it.

ES: But, you see, haven't you said the same thing in different words by saying, 'Be aware of the other, of the carpet, of the tree, of the universe within which you live'. And then you translate into another level of perception and you say, 'Love the carpet, love the tree, love the universe', and you don't feel there's any difference between being aware or seeing undividedly and loving undividedly or unconditionally.

K: When you are so aware, there is that quality of love. You don't have to say be or not be – it is there! It is like a perfume in a flower, it is there!

ES: They're not different sides of the same coin, they're the same coin.

K: The same coin.

ES: With no sides at all. So that to see in this undivided, choiceless way and to love in this choiceless way must be one and the same thing.

K: It is, sir. But, you see, the difficulty is: we are so eager to get this thing that we lose the real thread, the beauty of it.

ES: Now suppose that we were to move our discussion another step and say that as far as we can perceive, to be aware and to love are one and the same thing. Could we move one step further and say: to be is the same as to see and to love?

K: Now what do you mean by the words, to be? Everybody says 'I am'. The whole younger generation at present says 'I want to be'. What does that mean?

ES: I'm sure it means very little. I think it means be active.

K: That's all.

ES: Or be possessive.

K: Yes, be possessive, be angry, be violent: I am. That is what I am.

ES: So then the word 'to be' has a connotation about it that is associated with activity, which can only follow from this inner energy which is what 'to be' means.

K: Yes, sir. All this brings us to the question whether Man can change at all. That seems to me one of the major questions in the present world. The structure and nature of human beings have to change.

ES: Well, when you use words like 'structure' and 'nature', those mean categories to me.

K: No, structure in the sense of the way he lives.

ES: Can his life-style change?

K: Yes, the way he lives, the appalling pettiness, the ugliness, the violence, you know, what is going on.

ES: I would say that there should be nothing but despair about the question of change, if what we're dealing with is the creation of new categories to replace old categories.

K: No, I don't mean that.

ES: If, on the other hand, it is a question of changing from the without to the within, and can men do this, from the 'to do' to the 'to be', from the pretence of love to love, from the perception of categories to seeing, can men change in that direction, I would ask – 'do men?' And they do. You have done it, I have done it. Men do it.

K: Because, as he has lived, Man has lived with such appalling brutality, such deception, such lies, hypocrisy and all the rest of it. If I have a son, a brother, that's my concern, my responsibility. Not to change him but to see what my responsibility is. I don't want him to imitate me or conform to my pattern, which is absurd, or to my belief, I have none of that. So I say, look, how is it possible for a human being to change – not into a particular pattern – to bring about a total psychological revolution?

ES: If I were to start someplace, Krishnaji, I believe I would start with you. Not because I think you need changing – because I don't, not because I think you would want to change, but because I think you want to teach. You want to share. You have received so much joy from understanding and from loving . . .

K: Yes, sir.

ES: . . . that this radiates from within you. Now, if you wanted to teach someone that there's more to be seen than is seen and the more is not quantitative but in depth, maybe I would want to change you in this direction: that when you speak of the world and its conflict, tensions, violence and hypocrisy, that you address yourself also – which I'm sure you have done but don't speak of – to the question not only of the endurance of inner or exterior conflict, but also of the endurance of inner joy.

K: Sir, now, wait a minute.

ES: This is always there when you talk, but it is not expressed.

K: When does joy come? When I don't seek it, it happens. I don't have to cultivate it, the mind hasn't to pursue it.

ES: Yes, the mind cannot pursue joy.

K: Therefore an understanding must take place of what is pleasure and what is joy. That's where we mix our . . .

ES: We mix our levels, yes.

K: To understand pleasure is far more important than to understand joy. Because we want pleasure, we pursue pleasure. Everything is our pleasure. The whole moral, social structure is based on this enormous pleasure. And pleasure breeds fear, insecurity and all the rest of it. Now, in the understanding of pleasure, the other thing comes. You don't have to talk about it, the other thing flows like a fountain. You don't even call it joy or ecstasy or whatever.

ES: Are you saying, then, that in the understanding of fear or of pleasure, or in both, we find death? A death to the dissipation of energy that keeps us from being joyous?

K: That's right.

ES: . . . and from seeing, and being loving or simply being. They're all the same thing.

K: You see, through negation, the positive is. To assert the positive is to negate the real.

ES: But as we have said before, to negate the categories is really not what we're dealing with. Nor are we dealing with the negation of seeing simply. We're dealing with the negation of all the obstacles, like pleasure, because unless you negate pleasure you will never be joyous and when you're joyous, you're also quite pleasurable.

K: Oh, you don't talk about it. The moment you're conscious that you're joyous, it goes. It is like being happy and saying 'how happy I am', it becomes nonsense when you say that.

ES: Yes, because you've rationalized it, put it in a category, and it now becomes something to speculate about rather than to be. At the same time, since we are pursuing as deeply as we can – pursuing seeing and understanding and loving, or this undivided attention – since we're pursuing that, and we have found that one cannot pursue it except by negating fear or negating pleasure . . .

K: Understanding pleasure, the whole nature of it.

ES: . . . then we must ask ourselves: well, if these are not the avenues to seeing or loving or being, then I suppose we will ultimately get to the question of being or being one. Because we want to discover that you are one with the world and the world is one with you and you are one with myself and I am one with you. We want to discover that. So we've seen that seeing and loving and an awareness of being must take place, and seeing what to do to get rid of these things that get in the way of the most exhilarating of all experiences or realities, the reality of just being: *I am*, enough, I don't need these things to be, *here I am*. Then what would you think would be the next step? – and we're not talking about process and method.

K: From what?

ES: From this undivided attention, that we discussed earlier, and from this loving, which we found to be the same as choiceless attention, and from this being that we found to be the same as loving and seeing or understanding, and now we're trying to pursue your experience of – I don't like to use the word 'oneness' because that gets us to the end before the middle. But what does one do next? After one has seen and loved and been, then what . . .

K: What happens next? One *lives*!

ES: One lives, so that to live is the same as to love in any real sense?

K: Then it also means, sir, doesn't it, the understanding of death. Because to love one must die.

ES: Unquestionably, yes.

K: So there must be the investigation, understanding, awareness of what it means to die. Without that there is no love.

ES: But could this not be a fiction, because who is to tell us what it's like to die?

K: We're going to find out.

ES: Fine, good.

K: I mean, I don't want anybody to tell me because that means authority.

ES: Well, it means the dead, who can't speak.

K: Not only that. The whole Asiatic world believes in reincarnation, as you know, and in the Christian world it's resurrection and all that. To find this out, one must investigate to find if there is any permanent thing in me that reincarnates, that in me is reborn, resurrected, one must inquire into whether anything is permanent. Permanent? Nothing is permanent. The carpets in this room will go. (laughs) All the structures, the technological things, all the things Man has put together are in flux.

ES: But you're not suggesting that the measure is permanent? You were born and you have lived and you will die, and this will take you a certain number of years.

K: Twenty years, thirty years, whatever it is.

ES: Is the measure real or are you real?

K: No, I'm not talking in terms of measure.

ES: So then if the measure isn't real but something external to you, do we have a right to say that you simply end?

K: I'm coming to that, we're coming to that. You know, the whole Greek world thought in terms of measurement and the whole Western world is based on measurement. And the Eastern world said measure is illusion and they went into other kinds of . . . (laughs)

ES: . . . measures.

K: Other kinds of measure which they then call immeasurable. Now, I am saying, sir, life, as we now live it, is a conflict. What we call love is pursuit of pleasure. What we call death is an avoidance, is fear, dread of it. And being afraid so completely of such an ending, we have reincarnation theory, various other theories, which give us great satisfaction, great comfort. And that is not an answer.

ES: No, it keeps us from seeing the reality.

K: So negate all that. So what have we? There must be the understanding of death. What is death? There is the physiological ending. We don't mind that. We all see death everywhere. But what human beings are concerned with is the psychological ending, the 'me' ending, the 'me' which says: I own this house, my property, my wife, my husband, my knowledge – I'm going to lose all that. And I don't want to lose it. The known is more attractive than the unknown, the known is the factor of fear.

ES: In a rational world.

K: So I have to understand what death means. Does it mean that there is a permanent entity? Call it the soul, the Hindus call it the *atman*, it doesn't matter what name you give it. A permanent entity that never dies, but evolves, is resurrected, incarnated in time. Is there such a thing as a permanent entity? Not a theory, not a speculative assertion that there is, or there is not, but to find out for oneself if there is a permanent entity, the 'me', that says I must survive, therefore I must have future lives, whether in heaven or – it doesn't matter. Is there such a thing? Which, psychologically, is what thought has put together as the 'me'.

ES: I cannot conceive of there being a permanent entity associated with what we call the 'me'.

K: No, obviously. Then is there a permanent 'me' apart from that?

ES: But can we then ask the question: is there something immeasurable about me apart from that?

K: Ah, the moment you say the 'me' is the immeasurable, then 'I' am back again.

ES: 'I' am back again, sorry. Apart from the self, a not-me.

K: I'm going to find out.

ES: Yes, now we must pursue that.

K: There must be a discovery of whether there is the immeasurable or not. Not just saying there is or there is not. One must come upon it, the mind must come upon it. So there is no permanent self, higher, lower, no permanency. What then is death? Physically, biologically, there is death.

ES: This we all understand, we see it all the time.

K: Everything goes. What one is afraid of losing is the psychological accumulation in relationship of every form, of image, knowledge, function. That takes the form of the 'me' which is going to evolve, then become more and more perfect until it reaches heaven or whatever you like to call it. We see

65

that is false. Then what is death?

ES: You are suggesting that we can discover the meaning of the words 'to live' by looking for the meaning of the words 'to die'.

K: They are related.

ES: They are unquestionably related. And most religious writers in history and comparative religion have said that in order to live one must die.

K: Sir, I don't read these books or any of these things. It is an actual *fact* that to live you must die; which means dying every day to all the accumulations you have gathered during the day, ending each day so that the mind is fresh, new, every day.

ES: Yes, now, in order that we might pursue the question of living by looking at the question of dying, and looking finally at the ultimate death where the body has disintegrated in the grave . . .

K: The body is important – it needs to be looked after, cared for – you know, all the rest of it.

ES: But bury it when it's dead.

K: Get rid of it, bury it. Burn it, that's simpler! (laughs)

ES: Now, suppose that we want to see what happens when one dies in order to see what happens when one lives.

K: Then I must first understand what it means to live, not what it means to die. One's life as it is, is a turmoil. As it is, it is chaos, a mess, with all kinds of ideals, conclusions, concepts, it's a mess. Now, if there is no order in this mess, I can't understand what death is because death is perfect order.

ES: Now, what do you mean, because order to me is something imposed from without?

K: I'm coming to that. Death is perfect order because it is the ending of disorder.

ES: All right, I understand.

K: So there must be the ending of disorder in my living. And the ending of disorder is to be aware choicelessly of what is disorder. What is disorder? My belief, my gods, my country, my saying this is better – you follow? – all this terrible violence. See it as it is, and when you see it as it is without separation you have energy – we went into that. Then, in perceiving disorder, there is order, which is harmony. Now having established that – establish in the sense of see it, realize, be it – then death is not separate from order. They are together. Order means the ending of disorder.

ES: Yes, and order means a consciousness of my presence within you, or of your presence within me, or of our oneness. But we must pursue the question of our becoming aware, of giving this undivided attention, of loving each other in which the 'each other' is eliminated. At present, this is a duality.

K: Look, sir, there is no you and me. I am not you and you are not me. There is that quality of choiceless awareness, that sense of attention in which the 'me' and the 'you' cease. You don't say it's unity. Unity implies division.

ES: Oh, but you're using 'unity' in the mathematical sense now. Oneness to me means the same as undivided attention. It doesn't mean, doesn't presuppose, division.

K: You see, we are discussing what it means to live, to love and to die. That is, the ending of disorder is the ending of death. There is great beauty in this. And in that state there is no you and me, there is no division. Then, in that state, you can find out what the immeasurable is.

Only then *can* you find out, not before, because then it becomes merely speculation or somebody *says* there is the immeasurable, there is no God or there is God. That has no value. It is only when there is this complete order – really mathematical order – born out of disorder: not a blueprint imposed on disorder; then you find out, then the mind discovers whether there is an immeasurable or not. Nobody can say yes or no about that. Because if you don't see it, if there's no perception of the immeasurable, then it becomes merely conceptual. And most religions live on the conceptual.

ES: Suppose we were to pursue this question of order, the next step, and were to say that peace, harmony – like the harmony of my fingers working together or the harmony of you and me in our dialogue – if we were to say that peace or harmony is the tranquillity that is associated with order and wanted to say 'what more do we mean by order than just orderliness?'

K: Ah, orderliness every housewife has!

ES: Yes, and can be in complete turmoil while having orderliness.

K: We are talking not only of outward order but of deep, inward order.

ES: Yes, now what does this deep, inward order – can I use the word 'ordination' rather than order?

K: Ordination. I don't know quite what . . .

ES: The ordination of one to another, then subtract the divisions.

K: If we understand by the word 'order' the sense of no conflict, no sense of me being greater than you, no comparison, no sense of ambition, greed – the real quality of mind that is not concerned with all this bilge, all this nonsense. Then that is order.

ES: Then that order and peace and tranquillity is energy in its fullness rather than the lack of energy. It's not activity. It is the fullness of energy, so it's dynamic.

K: Yes, and that is necessary, isn't it? Which means when there is that complete order, the mind is no longer in conflict, and therefore has an abundance of energy.

ES: And what has been done by you or by me as we related to each other in order to achieve this order?

K: You can't achieve it. Out of being aware of disorder, choicelessly, order comes naturally.

ES: But it is true that many people do not achieve order – and we were also asking the question: can we change disorder into order or can we change death into life, can we change hate into love, can we change blindness into seeing? These are the questions we've been dealing with and we haven't answered the question: can this change take place?

K: I, or you, listen to what is being said. You give your whole attention, not as a Catholic or this or that. Now in that state of attention, there is a transformation. You're no longer a Hindu, Buddhist or whatever it is. You're finished with all that, you are now a total human being. Then you go around talking about it – you follow? You're acting, you're an outsider operating on the world. You're not of the world but an outsider.

ES: Would you say that, in our conversation, that the closer we get to the truth, the less conscious you become of the fact that I am a Catholic priest? Does it matter?

K: Not in the least. But it's up to you.

ES: And it does not matter to me whether you are a priest or not. I haven't thought of that because of giving choiceless attention to you.

K: It makes this difference. For instance, I've met Hindus in India who have come to me and said, 'Why don't you put on Sannyasi robes?' You know, monk's robes. I said, 'Why should I?' 'To show that you are not of the world.' I said, 'Look, I don't want to show anything to anybody. This is revealed to me, that's good enough. If you want to come and listen, listen, but don't go by my garb, my gesture, my face, that's not important.' But to them it is important because they use that as a platform from which to attack or distract or take. But if you're not standing on any platform; if you don't belong to anything, why should I wear a collar, or no collar, or no shirt?

ES: As we pursue the question of what it means to live and to die, to be and to not be, to love and to hate – as we pursue those things – we must at the same time pursue the question of what it means to belong? Now, if you asked me, 'Do you belong to the Catholic church?' I would say, 'Of course not', because I am not a thing that can be possessed by anyone.

K: Quite.

ES: Nor is the Catholic church something that I possess, so I would not like to use the word belong. If we had a loving relationship with each other, could I say, 'You are *my* friend?'

K: Yes.

ES: No, I couldn't because that would connote belonging!

K: I see what you mean . . .

ES: I could not say you were my friend. We use the word all the time, but the word 'my' distorts what we see . . .

K: I'm questioning: why do we belong to anything at all?

ES: I don't think we can. If we are free, then we're not slaves and we don't belong to anything.

K: That is the main thing.

ES: Possessive relationship is irrelevant.

K: Not to belong to any organized, spiritual, religious group or belong to a party, this or that, because that encourages division.

ES: If I am or if I am free – they mean the same thing – then I'm not capable of being possessed by anyone, I don't belong. The word doesn't mean anything.

K: Not to belong means to stand alone.

ES: Belonging is in contradiction to what we've been saying the whole time. 'Not to belong' is the price one must pay for being and loving and seeing anything.

K: Yes, sir, but also it implies not to belong to any structure which human beings have put together.

ES: Yes.

K: Which means that you have to stand alone, outside, not belong to all these messes. Sir, when you have order, you don't belong to disorder.

ES: Now I think we're getting close to what we wanted to say, that to die is to live and not to belong.

K: Is that a concept or a reality?

ES: No, that's an experience, it's a reality, yes.

K: If it is real, it's something burning! It burns everything false!

ES: I see that. And of course we experience this all the time. What I'm saying is that if one can get over the fear of dying then one can understand and live with the fullness of this energy that we're talking about. I think by the same token, if one can get over the question of belonging or having in any way, one can get to the question that being is. And I wonder if this is being alone.

K: The danger of *being*, one has to go into that. What is it to be? You can put it into various categories. The category is not being.

ES: But when we were discussing the question of what it is to be and we pursued this through the question of dying and belonging and you said, 'to be is to be alone and . . .'

K: How can I, sir, if I die to my conditioning as a Hindu, how can I be a Hindu? It has no meaning!

ES: Fine, but having died to . . .

K: See what happens, sir. I discard, I throw away the garb of Hinduism or Catholicism, whatever it is, and what takes place? I am an outsider. I'm an outsider in the sense that I may say I love you, but I'm still an outsider because there is a state of disorder to which human beings belong and the man who is outside just doesn't belong.

ES: Unquestionably. Or may not have a sense of belonging, or cannot use the word 'to belong'. I cannot use the word 'belong'.

K: There is no relationship.

ES: There is no relationship.

K: Now, when there is no relationship between disorder and order, what is the state of the mind which is not that disorder?

ES: And you were suggesting that the state of the mind is one of being alone.

 K: Alone in the sense that it is not contaminated, it is really innocent. It is really innocent in the sense that it cannot be hurt. After all, the root meaning of that word is not to be hurt. So though it may live in the world, it is not of the world.

ES: In the sense of conflict and turmoil.

 K: All the messy stuff. That is absolutely necessary to find out more – not more in the sense of something more – but that state is absolutely essential to discover whether the immeasurable is or not.

ES: Yes, I think this is true, so that we do, in a sense, find seeing and loving and being in being alone. One disassociates oneself from disorder.

 K: In observing disorder, in being aware choicelessly of disorder, order comes. You don't belong – there is order.

ES: Order. And as we pursued the question of the meaning of order or harmony or tranquillity or peace, we found ourselves with the same answer, but this is to be in the first place, this is to love in the first place, this is to see in the first place.

 K: Order, sir, is one of the most extraordinary things because it's always new. It isn't order according to a pattern, it is a living thing. Virtue is a living thing. It isn't: 'I am virtuous'. You can never say I'm virtuous because if you say that you're not virtuous. But virtue is a living thing like a flowing river, it is alive, and therefore in that state something beyond measure takes place.

ES: And it is at that moment that one discovers the immeasurable.

 K: Yes, not discover: it is there. You see, discovery and experience are rather unfortunate words because most human beings want to experience something great, their lives are shoddy, petty, full of anxiety and they say, for God's sake, give me greater experience, something more! Therefore you have these groups that meditate and so forth, they're searching for that, whereas they have to bring order in their lives first, and then what takes place is something quite beyond measure.

ES: So if we are pursuing the question of measurelessness . . .

 K: You can't pursue it.

ES: And you can't discover it. Fine, this is good. You cannot pursue

it, you cannot discover it, and it's not good to use the word
'experience' about it – all of this we put aside. When one comes
upon it . . .

K: You leave the door open, sir.

ES: You leave the door open.

K: And let the sun come in. And if the sun comes in, it's all right, if
it doesn't, it's all right. Because the moment you pursue it you
close the door.

ES: Good, the very pursuit is . . .

K: Then the very search for truth is the closing off, the blocking
of truth.

What Future Does Man Have?

David Bohm, FRS

Krishnamurti: I thought we should talk about the future of Man. As things are, from what one observes, the world has become tremendously dangerous. There are terrorists, wars, and national and racial divisions, some dictators who want to destroy the world and so on. Also, religiously there is tremendous separation.

David Bohm: And there is the economic crisis and the ecological crisis.

K: Problems seem to be multiplying more and more. So what is the future of Man? What is the future not only of the present generation but of the coming generations?

DB: Well, the future looks very grim.

K: Yes, if you and I were quite young, and knowing all this, what would we do? What would be our reaction? What would be our life, our way of earning a livelihood and so on?

DB: I have often thought about that. I have asked myself, 'would I go into science again?' And I am not at all certain now because science does not seem to be relevant to this crisis.

K: No, on the contrary it is helping to . . .

DB: . . . make it worse. Science might help but in fact it isn't.

K: So, what would you do? I think I would stick to what I am doing.

DB: Well, that would be easy for you.

K: For me, quite easy. You see, I don't think in terms of evolution.

DB: I was expecting we would discuss that.

K: I don't think there is psychological evolution at all.

DB: We have often discussed this, so I understand to some extent what you mean. But I think that people new to this are not going to understand.

K: Yes, we will discuss this whole question, if you will. But why are we concerned about the future? The whole future is now.

DB: Well, in some sense the whole future is now but we have to make that clear. This goes very much against the whole traditional way of thinking.

K: Yes, I know. Mankind thinks in terms of evolution, continuance, and so on.

DB: Maybe we could approach it in another way. That is, evolution seems in the present era to be the most natural way to think. So I would like to ask you: what objections do you have to thinking in terms of evolution? The word has, of course, many meanings.

K: Of course, we are talking psychologically.

DB: Yes, now the first point is: let's dispose of it physically.

K: An acorn will grow into an oak.

DB: Yes, also the species has evolved; for example, from plants to animals and to Man.

K: Yes, we have taken a million years to be what we are.

DB: You do not doubt that that has happened?

K: No, that has happened.

DB: It may continue to happen. That is a valid process.

K: That is evolution. Of course, that is a valid, natural process.

DB: It takes place in time and therefore in that region the past, present and future are important.

K: Yes, obviously. I don't know a certain language, and I need time to learn it.

DB: It also takes time to improve the brain. If the brain was small when it started out, it got steadily larger, and that took a million years.

K: Yes, and it becomes much more complex and so on. All that needs time, all that is movement in space and time.

DB: So you will admit physical time and neurophysiological time.

K: Absolutely, of course, any sane man would.

DB: Now, most people also admit psychological time, what they call mental time.

K: Yes, that is what we are talking about. Whether there is such a thing as psychological tomorrow, psychological evolution.

DB: Now, at first sight I am afraid this will sound strange. It seems I can remember yesterday, and there is tomorrow, I can anticipate.

It has happened many times, you know that days have succeeded each other. So I do have the experience of time, from yesterday to today to tomorrow – right?

K: Of course, that is simple enough.

DB: Now what is it that you are denying?

K: I deny that I will be something, become better.

DB: But there are two ways of looking at that. One way is: will I intentionally become better because I am trying? Or some people feel that evolution is a kind of natural, inevitable process, which is sweeping us along like a current, and we are perhaps becoming better or worse, or something else is happening to us.

K: Psychologically.

DB: Yes, which takes time but which may not be the result of my trying to become better. It may or may not be, some people may think one way, some another. But are you denying that there is a kind of natural psychological evolution like the natural biological evolution?

K: I am denying that, yes.

DB: Well, why do you deny it?

K: First of all, what is the psyche, the 'me', the ego, and so on, what is it?

DB: Well, the word 'psyche' has many meanings. It may mean the mind, for example. Do you mean that the ego is the same thing?

K: The ego, I am talking of the ego, the 'me'.

DB: Yes, now some people think of evolution as a process in which the 'me' will be transcended, that it will rise to a higher level. So there are two questions. One is: will the 'me' ever improve? And the other question is: supposing we want to get beyond the 'me', can that be done in time?

K: That cannot be done in time.

DB: Yes, now we have to make it clear why not.

K: I will, we will go into it. What is the 'me'? If the word 'psyche' has such different meanings, the 'me' is the whole movement which thought has brought about.

DB: Why do you say that?

K: The 'me' is the consciousness, my consciousness, the 'me' is my name, form and all the various experiences that I have had, remembrances and so on. The whole structure of the 'me' is put together by thought.

DB: Well, that again would be something which some people might find hard to accept.

K: Of course, we are discussing it.

DB: Let us try to bring it out. Because the first experience, the first feeling I have about the 'me' is that it is there independently and that the 'me' is thinking.

K: Is the 'me' independent of my thinking?

DB: Well, my own first feeling is that the 'me' is there independent of my thinking, and it is the 'me' that is thinking.

K: Yes.

DB: Just as I am here and can move my arm or head, I can think. Now is that an illusion?

K: No, because when I move my arm, there is an intention to grasp or pick up something, which means that first it is the movement of thought. That makes the arm move and so on. My contention – and I am open to this being challenged – is that thought is the basis of all this.

DB: Yes, your contention is that the whole sense of the 'me' and what it is doing is coming out of thought. What you mean by thought, though, is not merely intellectual.

K: No, of course not. Thought is the whole movement of experience, knowledge, and memory. It is this movement.

DB: It sounds to me as if you mean the consciousness as a whole.

K: As a whole, that's right.

DB: And you are saying that this movement is the 'me' – right?

K: The whole content of that consciousness is the 'me'. The 'me' is not different from my consciousness.

DB: Yes, well, I think one could say that I am my consciousness, for if I am not conscious I am not here. Now, is consciousness nothing but what you have just described, which includes thought, feeling, intention?

K: . . . intention, aspirations . . .

DB: . . . memories . . .

K: . . . memories, beliefs, dogmas, the rituals that are performed, the whole of that, like a computer that has been programmed.

DB: Yes, everybody would agree that certainly is in consciousness, but many people would feel that there is more to it, that consciousness may go beyond that.

K: Let's go into it. The content of our consciousness makes up the consciousness.

DB: I think that requires some clarification. The ordinary use of the word 'content' is quite different. If you say that the content of a glass is water, the glass is one thing and the water is another. The glass contains the water, so the word 'content' would suggest that something contains it.

K: All right, consciousness is made up of all that it has remembered, beliefs, dogmas, rituals, nationalities, fears, pleasures, sorrow.

DB: Yes, now if all that were absent would there be no consciousness?

K: Not as we know it.

DB: But there would still be a kind of consciousness?

K: A totally different kind.

DB: Well, then I think you really mean to say that consciousness, as we know it, is made up . . .

K: . . . is the result of the multiple activities of thought. Thought has put my consciousness together – the reactions, the responses, the memories, the extraordinary complex intricacies, subtleties – all that is, makes up, consciousness.

DB: As we know it.

K: As we know it. The question is whether that consciousness has a future.

DB: Does it have a past?

K: Of course, remembrance.

DB: Remembrance, yes. Why do you say it has no future then?

K: If it has a future it will be exactly the same kind of thing. The same activities, same thoughts, modified, but the pattern will be repeated over and over again.

DB: So are you saying that thought can only repeat?

K: Yes.

DB: But there is a feeling that thought can develop new ideas, for example.

K: But thought is limited because knowledge is limited, if you admit that knowledge will always be limited.

DB: Now, why do you say knowledge is always limited?

K: Because you as a scientist are experimenting, adding, searching. You are adding, and after you some other person will add more.

77

So knowledge, which is born of experience, is limited.

DB: Some people have argued that it isn't. They would hope to obtain perfect or absolute knowledge of the laws of Nature.

K: The laws of Nature are not the laws of human being.

DB: Well, do you want to restrict the discussion then to knowledge about the human being?

K: Of course, that's all we can talk about.

DB: All right. So are we saying that Man cannot obtain unlimited knowledge of the psyche? Is that what you are saying? There is always more that is unknown.

K: Yes, there is always more that is unknown. So once we admit that knowledge is limited then thought is limited.

DB: Yes, thought depends on knowledge and knowledge does not cover everything. Therefore thought will not be able to handle everything that happens.

K: That's right. But that is what the politicians and all the other people are trying to do. They think that thought can solve every problem.

DB: You can see in the case of politicians that knowledge is very limited. And when you lack adequate knowledge of what you are dealing with you create confusion.

K: So then as thought is limited, our consciousness, which has been put together by thought, is limited.

DB: Now, can you make that clear? That means we can only stay in the same circle.

K: The same circle.

DB: You see, if you compare with science, people might argue that although my knowledge is limited I am constantly discovering.

K: What you discover is added on, but is still limited.

DB: It is still limited. That's the point. I think one of the ideas behind the scientific approach is that although knowledge is limited I can discover and keep up with the actuality.

K: But that is also limited.

DB: My discoveries are limited and there is always the unknown that I have not discovered.

K: That is what I am saying. The unknown, the limitless, cannot be captured by thought because thought in itself is limited. So do you and I agree to that, not only agree but see it is a fact?

DB: Well, perhaps we could bring it out still more. That is, thought is limited, even though there is a very strong predisposition, feeling, tendency, to feel that thought can do anything.

K: But it can't. See what it has done in the world!

DB: Well, I agree that is has done some terrible things but that doesn't prove that it is always wrong. You see, maybe you could always blame that on people who have used it wrongly.

K: I know, that is a good old trick! But thought *in itself* is limited, therefore whatever it does is limited.

DB: And you are saying it is limited in a very serious way.

K: That's right, in a very, very serious way.

DB: Well, could we bring that out, and say what that way is?

K: That way is what is happening in the world. The totalitarian ideals are the invention of thought.

DB: Yes, we could say that the very word 'totalitarian' means they wanted to cover the totality but they couldn't – and the thing collapsed.

K: It is collapsing.

DB: But then there are those who say they are not totalitarians.

K: But the thinking of the democrats, the republicans and the idealists and so on is also limited.

DB: Yes, limited in a way that is . . .

K: . . . very destructive.

DB: . . . that is very serious and destructive. Now in what way could we bring that out? You see, I could say, 'OK, my thought is limited but this may not be all that serious'. Why is it so important?

K: That is fairly simple: because whatever action is born of limited thought must inevitably breed conflict. Dividing humanity geographically into nationalities and dividing humanity religiously and so on has created havoc in the world.

DB: Yes, let's connect that with the limitation of thought. That is, my knowledge is limited. Now how does that lead me to divide the world?

K: Aren't we seeking security? We thought there was security in the family, security in the tribe, security in nationalism. So we thought that there was security in division.

DB: Yes, that seems to be how it has come out: take the tribe, for example; one may feel insecure and then say, 'with the tribe I am

79

secure'. That is a conclusion. And I think I know enough to be sure that is so but I don't. Other things happen that I don't know of which make that very insecure. Other tribes come along.

K: No, the very division itself creates insecurity.

DB: It helps to create it but I am trying to say that I don't know enough to know that – I don't see that.

K: One doesn't see it because one has not looked at the world as a whole.

DB: Well, the thought that aims at security attempts to know everything important. As soon as it knows everything important it says, 'this will bring security' – yet not only are there a lot of things it doesn't know but one thing it doesn't know is that this very thought is itself divisive. It's going to be divisive, because I define an area that is secure, divided from another area.

K: It is divisive because in itself it is limited. Anything that is limited must inevitably create conflict.

DB: Well, you mean any thought that is . . .

K: If I say I am an individual, it is limited. I am concerned with myself, that is very limited.

DB: Yes, we have to get this clear. You see, if I say this is a table, which is limited, it creates no conflict – right?

K: No, there is no conflict there.

DB: Now when I say this is 'me', that creates conflict.

K: The 'me' is a divisive entity.

DB: Let's see more clearly why.

K: Because it is separative, it is concerned with itself; and the 'me' identifying with the greater, the nation, is still divisive.

DB: Yes, well, I define myself in the interest of security so that I know what I am as opposed to what you are and I protect myself. Now this creates a division between me and you.

K: We and they and so on.

DB: We and they. Now that comes from my limited thought, because I don't understand that we are really closely related and connected.

K: We are human beings.

DB: Yes, we are all human beings.

K: All human beings have more or less the same problems.

DB: But I haven't understood that. My knowledge is limited, I think that we *can* make a distinction and protect ourselves and me and not the others. But in the very act of doing that I create instability, insecurity.

K: That's right, you create insecurity. So if we see that, not merely intellectually or verbally, but actually feel it, that we are the rest of humanity, then the responsibility becomes immense.

DB: Well, how can you do anything about that responsibility?

K: Then I either contribute to the whole mess, or keep out of it. That is, to be at peace, to have order in oneself. I will come to that, I am going too fast.

DB: You see, I think we have touched upon an important point. We say the whole of humanity, of mankind, is one, and therefore to create division there is . . .

K: . . . dangerous.

DB: Yes, whereas to create division between me and the table is not dangerous because in some sense we are not one. Now mankind doesn't realize that it is all one.

K: Why, why?

DB: Well, let's go into that. This is a crucial point. It is clear it doesn't, because there are so many divisions, and not only between nations and religions but between one person and another.

K: Why is there this division?

DB: Well, the first thing, at least in the modern era, is the belief that every human being is an individual. This may not have been so strong in the past.

K: That is what I question. I question altogether whether we are individuals.

DB: That is a big question because . . .

K: Of course. We said just now that the consciousness which is 'me' is similar to that of all other human beings. They all suffer, they all have fears, they are all insecure, they have their own particular gods and rituals, all put together by thought.

DB: Yes, well, I think this calls for some clarification. There are two questions here. One is, not everybody feels that he is similar – most people feel they have some unique distinction.

K: What do you mean by 'unique distinction'? Distinction in doing something?

DB: There may be many things. For example, one nation may feel that it is able to do some things better than another, one person has some special things he does, or a particular quality.

K: Of course, you are more intellectual than I am. Somebody else is better in this or that.

DB: He may take pride in his own special abilities or advantages.

K: But when you put that away we are basically the same.

DB: You are saying that these things you have just described are . . .

K: . . . superficial.

DB: Now, what are the things that are basic?

K: Fear, sorrow, pain, anxiety, loneliness, all the human travail.

DB: But many people might feel that the highest achievements of Man are the basic things.

K: What have we achieved?

DB: For one thing people may feel proud of the achievements of Man in science, art, culture and technology.

K: We have achievements in all those directions, certainly we have vast technology, communication, travel, medicines, surgery . . .

DB: It is really remarkable in many ways.

K: There is no question about that. But what have we achieved psychologically?

DB: You are saying that none of these achievements has affected us psychologically?

K: Yes, that's right.

DB: And the psychological question is more important than any of the others because if the psychological question is not cleared up the rest is dangerous.

K: If we are limited psychologically, then whatever we do will be limited, and the technology will then be used by our limited psyche.

DB: Yes, the master is this limited psyche and not the rational structure of technology, and in fact technology then becomes a dangerous . . .

K: . . . instrument.

DB: So that is one point: that the psyche is at the core of it all, and if the psyche is not in order then the rest is useless.

K: If the house is in order . . .

DB: Then the second question is this: although we are saying that there are certain basic disorders in the psyche, or a lack of order which is common to us all, and that we may all have a potential for something else, are we really all one? Even though we are all similar, that doesn't say that we are all the same, that we are all one.

K: We said that in our consciousness we all have basically the same ground on which we stand.

DB: Yes, but the fact that human bodies are similar doesn't prove they are all the same.

K: Of course not, your body is different from mine.

DB: Yes, we are in different places, different entities and so on. But I think you are trying to say that consciousness is not an entity which is individual . . .

K: That's right.

DB: . . . the body is an entity that has a certain individuality.

K: That all seems so clear.

DB: It may be clear, but I think . . .

K: Your body is different from mine, I have a different name from you.

DB: Well, we are different – though of similar material, it is different, we can't exchange bodies because the proteins in one body may not agree with those in the other. Now many people feel that way about the mind, saying that there is a chemistry between people which may agree or disagree.

K: But if you actually go deeper into the question, consciousness is shared by all human beings.

DB: Yes, but the feeling is that the consciousness is individual and that it is communicated as it were . . .

K: I think that is an illusion because we are sticking to something that is not true.

DB: Well, do you want to say that there is one consciousness of mankind?

K: It is all one.

DB: It is all one. That is important because whether it is many or one is a crucial question.

K: Yes.

DB: Now, it could be there are many who are then communicating and building up the larger unit. Or do you think that from the very beginning it is all one?

K: From the very beginning it is all one.

DB: And the sense of separateness is an illusion – right?

  K: That is what I am saying over and over again. That seems so logical, sane: the other is insane.

DB: Now, people don't feel, at least not immediately, that the notion of separate existence is insane, because one extrapolates from the body to the mind, one says it is quite sensible to say my body is separate from yours, and inside my body is my mind. Now are you saying that the mind is not inside the body?

  K: That is quite a different question. Now just a minute, let's finish with the other first. If each one of us thinks that we are separate individuals psychically, what we have done in the world is a colossal mess.

DB: Well, if we think we are separate when we are not separate then it clearly will be a colossal mess.

  K: That is what is happening. Each one thinks he has to do what he wants to do, fulfil himself. So he is struggling in his separateness to achieve peace, to achieve security, a security and peace which is totally denied by that.

DB: Well, the reason it is denied is because there is no separation. You see if there were really separation it would be a rational thing to try to do. But if we are trying to separate what is inseparable the result will be chaos.

  K: That's right.

DB: Now that is clear but I think that it will not be clear to people immediately that the consciousness of mankind is one inseparable whole.

  K: Yes, sir, an inseparable whole, absolutely right.

DB: Many questions will arise if you once even consider the notion, but I don't know if we have gone far enough into this yet. One question is: why do we think we are separate?

  K: Why do I think I am separate? That is my conditioning.

DB: Yes, but how did we ever adopt such a foolish conditioning?

  K: From childhood this is mine, this is *my* toy, not *yours*.

DB: But the first feeling you get is to say it is mine because I feel I am separate. Now, it isn't clear how the mind which was one came to this illusion that it is all broken up into many pieces.

  K: I think it is again the activity of thought. Thought in its very nature is divisive, fragmentary, and therefore I am a fragment.

DB: Thought will create a sense of fragments. You can see, for example, that once we decide to set up a nation we will be separate, think we are separate from another nation, and from that all sorts of things, consequences, follow that make the whole thing seem independently real. We all have a separate language and a separate flag and a separate this and that, and we set up a boundary. And after a while we see so much evidence of separation that we forget how it started and say that was always how it was and we are merely proceeding from what was always there.

K: Of course. That's why, I feel if once we grasp the nature of thought, the structure of t'iought, how thought operates, what is the source of thought, and therefore see it is always limited, if we really see that then . . .

DB: Now, what is the source of thought, is it memory?

K: Memory, the remembrance of things past, which is knowledge, and knowledge is the outcome of experience and experience is always limited.

DB: But thought also includes, of course, the attempt to go forward, to use logic, to take into account discoveries and insights.

K: And, as we were saying some time ago, thought is time.

DB: Yes, all right, thought is time. That requires more discussion too, because you see the first experience is to say that time is there first, and thought is taking place in time.

K: Ah, no.

DB: For example, if we say that movement is taking place, the body is moving, and this requires time.

K: To go from here to there needs time, to learn a language needs time, to paint a picture takes time.

DB: To grow a plant needs time. We also say to think takes time.

K: So we think in terms of time.

DB: You see the first point that one would tend to look at is to say that just as everything takes time, to think takes time. And you are saying something else, which is: thought is time.

K: Thought is time.

DB: That is, psychically speaking, psychologically speaking. Now, how do we understand that? That thought is time. You see it is not obvious.

K: Would you say that thought is movement and time is movement?

DB: You see, time is a mysterious thing, people have argued about it. We could say that time requires movement. I could understand that we cannot have time without movement.

K: Time is movement, time is not separate from movement.

DB: Now, I don't say it is separate from movement, but to say time is movement, you see if we said time and movement are one . . .

K: Yes, we are saying that.

DB: Yes, they cannot be separated. That seems fairly clear. Now there is physical movement which means physical time – right?

K: Physical time, hot and cold, and also dark and light, sunset and sunrise, all that . . .

DB: The seasons, yes. Now then we have the movement of thought. Now that brings in the question of the nature of thought. You see, is thought nothing but a movement in the nervous system, in the brain? Would you say that?

K: Yes.

DB: Some people have said it includes the movement of the nervous system but there might be something beyond.

K: What is time, actually? Time is hope.

DB: Psychologically speaking.

K: Psychologically, I am talking entirely psychologically for the moment. Hope is time, becoming is time, achieving is time. Now take the question of becoming: I want to become something psychologically. I want to become non-violent, take that for example. That is altogether a fallacy.

DB: Well, we understand it is a fallacy but the reason it *is* one is that there is no time of that kind. Is that it?

K: Yes. Human beings are violent: and Tolstoy and people in India, have been talking a great deal of non-violence. The fact is we are violent and the non-violence is not real. But we want to become that.

DB: Yes, but again it is an extension of the kind of thought that we have with regard to material things. If you see a desert, it is real and you say the garden is not real, but in your mind is the garden that will come about when you put water there. So we say we can plan for the future when the desert will become fertile. Now we have to be careful: we say we are violent but we cannot by similar planning become non-violent. Now why is that?

K: Why? Because the non-violent state cannot exist when there is violence. That's an ideal.

DB: Well, one has to make it clearer because in the same sense the fertile state and the desert don't exist together either. You see, I think that you are saying that, in the case of the mind when you are violent, non-violence has no meaning.

K: That is the only state, not the other.

DB: That is all there is, the movement towards the other is illusory.

K: Yes, all ideals are psychologically illusory. The ideal of building a marvellous bridge is not illusory. You can plan a bridge but to have psychological ideals . . .

DB: Yes, if you are violent and continue to be violent while you are trying to be non-violent . . .

K: . . . it has no meaning and yet that has become such an important thing. So I question both becoming 'what is' and becoming away from 'what is'.

DB: 'What should be', yes. Well, if you say there can be no sense to becoming in the way of self-improvement, that's . . .

K: Oh, self-improvement is something so utterly ugly. We are saying that the source of all this is a movement of thought as time. Once we have made time important psychologically all the ideals, such as non-violence, achieving some superstate and so on, become utterly illusory.

DB: Yes, when you talk of the movement of thought as time, it seems to me that that time is illusory.

K: Yes.

DB: We sense it as time but it is not a real kind of time.

K: That is why we asked: what is time? I need time to go from here to there. I need time if I want to learn engineering, I must study it, that takes time. That same movement is carried over into the psyche. We say, I need time to be good, I need time to be enlightened.

DB: Yes, that will always create a conflict. One part of you and another. So that movement in which you say, I need time, also creates a division in the psyche. Between the observer and the observed.

K: Yes, that's right. We are saying that the observer is the observed.

DB: And psychologically, therefore, there is no time.

K: That's right. The thinker is the thought, there is no thinker separate from thought.

DB: All that you are saying, you know, seems very reasonable, but I think that it goes so strongly against the tradition we are used to that it will be extraordinarily hard, generally speaking, for people to really understand . . .

K: Of course, most people want a comfortable way of living: 'let me carry on as I am, for God's sake, leave me alone.'

DB: Yes, that is the result of so much conflict that people are wary.

K: But conflict escaped from or unresolved still exists, whether you like it or not. So this is the whole point: is it possible to live a life without conflict?

DB: Yes, that is all implicit in what has been said. The source of conflict is thought or knowledge, or the past.

K: That's right. So then one asks: is it possible to transcend thought? Or is it possible to end knowledge? I am putting it psychologically, not . . .

DB: Yes, knowledge of material objects and things like that, scientific knowledge, will continue.

K: Absolutely, that must continue.

DB: But what you call self-knowledge is what you are asking to end, isn't it?

K: Yes.

DB: On the other hand people have said, even you have said, self-knowledge is very important.

K: Self-knowledge is important but if I take time to understand myself, that is, if I say I will understand myself eventually by examination, analysis, by watching my whole relationship with others and so on, all that involves time. And I am saying there is another way of looking at the whole thing without time: which is, when the observer is the observed. In that observation there is no time.

DB: Could we go into that further? I mean, you say, for example, that there is no time but you still feel that you can remember an hour ago that you were somewhere else. Now in what sense can we say that there is no time?

K: Time is division, as thought is division. That is why thought is time.

DB: Time is a series of divisions of past, present, future.

K: Thought is divisive in the same way. So time is thought. Or thought is time.

DB: Yes, well, it doesn't exactly follow from what you said.

K: Let's go into it.

DB: You see, at first sight one would think that thought makes divisions of all kinds, with the ruler and with all kinds of things, and also divides up intervals of time, past, present and future. Now it doesn't follow just from that that thought is time.

K: Look, we said time is movement. Thought is also a series of movements. So both are movements.

DB: Yes, all right. Thought is a movement, we suppose, of the nervous system and . . .

K: You see, it is a movement of becoming. I am speaking psychologically.

DB: But whenever you think, something is also moving in the blood, in the nerves and so on. Now when we talk of a psychological movement, do you mean just a change of content? What is the movement, what is moving?

K: Look, I am this, and I am attempting to become something else psychologically.

DB: So that movement is in the content of your thought?

K: Yes.

DB: So if you say, 'I am this and I am attempting to become that', then I am in movement. At least I feel I am in movement.

K: Say, for instance, I am greedy. Greed is a movement.

DB: What kind of a movement is it?

K: To get what I want, to get more. It is a movement.

DB: All right.

K: And I find that movement painful, suppose. Then I try not to be greedy. The attempt not to be greedy is a movement of time, is becoming.

DB: Yes, but even the greed was becoming.

K: Of course. So is it possible, this is the real question, is it possible not to become? Psychologically speaking.

DB: Well, it seems that this would require that you should not be anything psychologically. That is, as soon as you define yourself in any way then . . .

K: No, we will define it in a minute or two.

DB: I meant, if I define myself as greedy, or say I am greedy or I am this, or I am that, then either I will want to become something else or to remain what I am – right?

K: Now can I remain what I am? Can I remain not with non-greed but with greed. And greed is not different from me, greed is me.

DB: Yes. That will require clarification – the ordinary way of thinking is that I am here and I could either be greedy or not greedy.

K: Of course.

DB: As these are attributes which I may or may not have.

K: But the attributes *are* me.

DB: Yes, now again that goes very much against our common language and experience.

K: Of course.

DB: But instead we are saying that I am my attributes, which suggests that the thought of attribution creates the 'me', right? The sense of 'me'.

K: All the qualities, the attributes, the virtues, the judgements, the conclusions and opinions are 'me'.

DB: Well, it seems to me that this would have to be perceived immediately as obvious.

K: That is the whole question. To perceive the totality of this movement instantly. Then we come to the point of perception: whether it is possible to perceive – it sounds a little odd, and perhaps a little crazy, but it is not – is it possible to perceive without all the movement of memory? To perceive something directly without the word, without the reaction, without the memories entering into perception?

DB: That is a very big question because memory has constantly entered perception. It would raise the question of what is going to stop memory from entering perception?

K: Nothing can stop it. But if we see that the activity of memory is limited, in the very perception of that limitation we have moved out of it into another dimension.

DB: Well, it seems to me that you have to perceive the whole of the limitation of memory.

K: Yes, not one part.

DB: You can see in general that memory is limited but there are many ways in which this is not obvious. For example, many of our reactions that are not obvious may be memory but we don't experience them as such. Suppose, say, I experience 'me' as being there presently and not as memory. That is the common experience. Suppose I want to become less greedy: I experience greed and I experience the urge to become as an actuality; it may be the result of memory but I say this 'me' is the one who remembers, not the other way around, not that memory creates 'me'.

K: All this really comes down to whether humanity can live without conflict? It basically comes down to that. Can we have peace on this Earth? The activities of thought never bring it about.

DB: Yes, it seems clear from what has been said that the activity of thought cannot bring about peace; it inherently, psychologically, brings about conflict.

K: If we once really see that, our whole activity would be totally different.

DB: But are you saying then that there is an activity which is not thought, which is beyond thought? And which is not only beyond thought but which does not require the cooperation of thought? That it is possible for this to go on when thought is absent?

K: That is the real point. We have often discussed this, whether there is anything beyond thought. Not something holy, sacred – I am not talking of that. We are asking: is there an activity that is not touched by thought? We are saying there is. And that activity is the highest form of intelligence.

DB: Yes, now we have brought in intelligence.

K: I know, I purposely brought it in! So intelligence is not the activity of cunning thought.

DB: Well, intelligence can use thought, as you have often said.

K: Intelligence can use thought.

DB: Thought can be the action of intelligence – would you put it that way?

K: Yes.

DB: Or it could be the action of memory?

K: That's it. Or it is the action born of memory, and memory being limited, thought is therefore limited, and has its own activity which then brings about conflict.

DB: I think this would connect up with what people are saying about computers. Every computer must eventually depend on some kind of memory, which is put in, programmed. And that must be limited – right?

K: Of course.

DB: Therefore when we operate from memory we are not very different from a computer; the other way around perhaps, the computer is not very different from us!

K: I would say a Hindu has been programmed for the last five thousand years to be a Hindu, or in this country you have been programmed to be British or a Catholic or a Protestant. So we are all programmed to a certain extent.

DB: Yes, now you are bringing in the notion of an intelligence that is free of the programme, it is creative perhaps.

K: That's right. That intelligence has nothing to do with memory and knowledge.

DB: It may act in memory and knowledge but it is has nothing to do with it.

K: It can act through memory, etc. That's right. Now, how do you find out whether this has any reality, and is not just imagination and romantic nonsense, how do you find out? To come to that one has to go into the whole question of suffering, whether there is an ending to suffering. As long as suffering and fear and the pursuit of pleasure exist there cannot be love.

DB: Yes, well there are many questions there. The first point is that suffering, pleasure, fear, anger, violence and greed are all the response of memory. They are nothing to do with intelligence.

K: Yes, they are all part of thought and memory.

DB: As long as they are going on it seems to me that intelligence cannot operate in or through thought.

K: That's right, so there must be freedom from suffering.

DB: Well, that is a very key point.

K: That is really a very serious and deep question: whether it is possible to end suffering, which is the ending of 'me'.

DB: Yes, again, it may seem repetitious but the feeling is that 'I' am there and 'I' either suffer or don't, 'I' either enjoy things or don't. Now I think you are saying that suffering arises from thought, it is thought.

K: Through identification, attachment.

DB: So what is it that suffers? It seems to me that memory may produce pleasure and then when it doesn't work it produces pain and suffering.

K: Not only that. Suffering is much more complex, isn't it? What is suffering? The meaning of the word is to have pain, to have grief, to feel utterly lost, lonely.

DB: It seems to me that it is not only pain but a kind of total, very pervasive pain.

K: Suffering is the loss of someone.

DB: Or the loss of something very important.

K: Yes, of course. Loss of my wife, of my son, brother, or whatever it is, and the desperate sense of loneliness.

DB: Or else just simply the fact that the whole world is going into such a state. It makes everything meaningless, you see.

K: What a lot of suffering all the wars have created! And this has been going on for thousands of years. That is why I am saying we are carrying on with the same pattern of the last five thousand years or more.

DB: Yes, and one can easily see that the violence and hatred of war will interfere with intelligence.

K: Obviously.

DB: But some people have felt that by going through suffering they become purified, like going through a crucible.

K: I know; that through suffering you learn, you are purified, through suffering your ego vanishes, is dissolved. It isn't. People have suffered immensely, from so many wars, with so many tears, and from the destructive nature of governments, unemployment, ignorance . . .

DB: . . . ignorance of disease, pain, everything. What is suffering really? Why does it destroy or prevent intelligence? What is actually going on?

K: Suffering is a shock – I suffer, I have pain, it is the essence of the 'me'.

DB: Yes, the difficulty with suffering is that it is the 'me' that is suffering, and this 'me' is really being sorry for itself in some way.

K: My suffering is different from your suffering.

DB: It isolates itself, it creates an illusion of some kind.

K: We don't see suffering is shared by all humanity.

DB: Yes, but suppose we do see it is shared by all humanity?

K: Then I begin to question what suffering is. It is not my suffering.

DB: Well, that is important. In order to understand the nature of suffering I have to drop this idea that it is my suffering because as long as I believe that I have an illusory notion of the whole thing.

K: And I can never end it.

DB: If you are dealing with an illusion you can do nothing with it. You see, we have to come back. Why is suffering the suffering of the many? At first, it seems that I feel toothache, or else I have a loss, or something has happened to me, and the other person seems perfectly happy.

K: Happy, yes. But he is suffering too in his own way.

DB: Yes, at the moment he doesn't see it but he has his problems too.

K: Suffering is common to all humanity.

DB: But the fact that it is common is not enough to make it all one.

K: It is actual.

DB: Are you saying that the suffering of mankind is all one, inseparable?

K: Yes, that is what I have been saying.

DB: As is the consciousness of Man?

K: Yes, that's right.

DB: That when anybody suffers the whole of mankind is suffering.

K: The whole point is we have suffered from the beginning of time and we haven't solved it.

DB: But what you have said is that the reason we haven't solved it is because we are treating it as personal or as in a small group, and that is an illusion. And any attempt to deal with an illusion cannot solve anything.

K: Thought cannot solve anything psychologically.

DB: Because you can say that thought itself divides. Thought is limited and is not able to see that this suffering is all one. And in that way divides it up as mine and yours.

K: That's right.

DB: And that creates illusion, which can only multiply suffering. Now, it seems to me that the statement that the suffering of mankind is one is inseparable from the statement that the consciousness of mankind is one.

K: Sir, the world is me, I am the world.

DB: You have often said that.

K: Yes, but we have divided it up into the British Earth and the French Earth and all the rest of it!

DB: Do you mean by the world, the physical world, or the world of society?

K: The world of society, the psychological world, primarily.

DB: So we say the world of society, of human beings, is one, and when I say I am that world, what does it mean?

K: The world is not different from me.

DB: The world and I are one, we are inseparable.

K: Yes. And what that requires, is real meditation, you must feel this, it is not just a verbal statement, it is an actuality. I am my brother's keeper.

DB: Many religions have said that.

K: That is just a verbal statement; they don't keep it, they don't do it in their hearts.

DB: Perhaps a few have done it but in general it is not being done.

K: I don't know if anybody has done it, we human beings haven't done it. Our religions have actually prevented it!

DB: Because of division, every religion having its own beliefs and its own organization?

K: Of course, its own gods and its own saviours. So after all this, is that intelligence actual? You understand my question? Or is it some kind of fanciful projection, hoping that it will solve our problems? It is not to me, it is an actuality. Because the ending of suffering means love.

DB: Now before we go on, let's clear up a point about 'me'. You have just said 'it is not to me'. Now in some sense it seems that you are still defining an individual. Is that right?

K: Yes, I am using the word 'I' as a means of communication.

DB: But what does it mean? Let's say there are two people, 'A' who sees the way you do and 'B' who does not. That seems to create a division between 'A' and 'B'.

K: That's right, but 'B' creates the division.

DB: Why?

K: What is the relationship between the two?

DB: Well, 'B' is creating the division by saying, 'I am a separate person', but it may confuse 'B' further when 'A' says, 'it's not that way to me' – right?

K: That is the whole point, isn't it, in relationship? You feel that you are not separate, and that you really have this sense of love and compassion, and I haven't got it. I haven't even perceived or gone into this question. What is your relationship to me? You have a relationship with me but I haven't any relationship with you.

DB: Yes, I think one could say that the person who hasn't seen is, psychologically, almost living in a dream world, and therefore the dream world is not related to the world of being awake.

K: That's right.

DB: But the fellow who is awake can at least perhaps awaken the other fellow.

K: You are awake, I am not. Then your relationship with me is very clear. But I have no relationship with you, I cannot. I insist on division and you don't.

DB: Yes, in some way we have to say that the consciousness of mankind has divided itself, it is all one, but it has divided itself by thought. That is why we are in this situation.

K: That *is* why – all the problems that humanity has now, psychologically as well as in other ways, are the result of thought. And we are pursuing the same pattern of thought, and thought will never solve any of these problems. So there is another kind of instrument, which is intelligence.

DB: That opens up an entirely different subject, and you also mentioned love and compassion as well.

K: Without love and compassion there is no intelligence. And you cannot be compassionate if you are attached to some religion, like an animal tied to a post.

DB: Well, as soon as your self is threatened then it cannot . . .

K: Of course. But you see, the self hides behind . . .

DB: . . . other things, such as noble ideals.

K: Yes, it has immense capacity to hide itself. So what is the future of mankind? From what one observes it is leading to destruction.

DB: That is the way it seems to be going.

K: Very gloomy, grim, dangerous and if one has children what is their future? To enter into all this and go through all the misery of it all? So education becomes extraordinarily important. But now education is merely the accumulation of knowledge.

DB: Every instrument that Man has invented, discovered or developed has been turned toward destruction.

K: Absolutely. They are destroying Nature, there are very few tigers now.

DB: Forests and agricultural land are being destroyed too.

K: Nobody seems to care.

DB: Well, most people are just immersed in their plans to save themselves but others have plans to save humanity. I think also there is a tendency toward despair implicit in what is happening now in that people don't think anything can be done.

K: Yes, and if they think something can be done they form little groups and little theories.

DB: Well, there are those who are very confident in what they are doing and those who . . .

K: Most Prime Ministers are very confident. But they don't really know what they are doing.

DB: But most people don't have much confidence in what they are doing.

K: I know. But if you have tremendous confidence, I may accept your confidence and go with you. So what then is the future of mankind? I wonder if anybody is concerned about it? Or is each person, or each group, concerned only with its own survival?

DB: Well, I think the first concern has almost always been with the survival of the individual or the group. That has been the history of mankind.

K: And therefore perpetual wars, perpetual insecurity.

DB: But this, as you said, is the result of thought making the mistake, on an incomplete basis, of identifying the self with the group, and so on.

K: Sir, you happen to listen to all this, you agree to all this, you see the truth of all this. Those in power will not even listen to you, they are creating more and more misery, the world is becoming more and more dangerous. What is the point of you and I agreeing and seeing something true? This is what people are asking: what is the point of you and I seeing something to be true and what effect has it?

DB: Well it seems to me if we think in terms of the effects, we are bringing in the very thing that is behind the trouble – time. That is, the first response would be we must quickly get in and do something to change the course of events.

K: Therefore form a society, foundation, organization and all the rest of it.

DB: You see, our mistake is to feel that we must think of something, and that thought is incomplete. We don't really know what is going on, and people have made theories about it, but they don't know.

K: No, but if that is the wrong question, then as a human being, who is mankind, what is my responsibility, apart from effect and all the rest of it?

DB: Yes, we can't look toward effects. But it is the same as with 'A' and 'B', that 'A' sees and 'B' does not. Now suppose 'A' sees something and most of the rest of mankind does not. Then it seems, one could say mankind is in some way dreaming, it is asleep.

K: It is caught in illusion.

DB: And the point is that, if somebody sees something, his responsibility is to help awaken the others out of the illusion.

K: That is just it. I mean this has been the problem. That is why the Buddhists have projected the idea of the Bodhisattva, who is compassionate, the essence of all compassion, and who is waiting to save humanity. It sounds nice, it is a happy feeling that there is somebody doing this. But in actuality we won't do anything that is not, both psychologically and physically, comfortable, satisfying, secure.

DB: Well, that is basically the source of the illusion.

K: How does one make others see all this? They haven't time, the energy, even the inclination, they want to be amused. How does one make 'X' see this whole thing so clearly that he says, 'all right, I have got it, I will work, and I see I am responsible', and all the rest of it. I think there is the tragedy of those who see and those who do not.

Who Is the Experiencer?

Iris Murdoch, philosopher and novelist.

Iris Murdoch: I have a lot of questions so I will just start with one
of particular interest and see where we go.

It is about the word 'experience' which you sometimes use in
your writings as representing something that you think we
should in some sense overcome. You seem to connect the idea
of experience with the notion of preconceived attitudes or
dogmas or beliefs which impede a kind of being that you would
connect with a creative present existence. I don't entirely
understand this. It seems to me impossible to entirely . . .

Krishnamurti: . . . wipe out experience.

IM: Yes, to discount or escape from experience. I would like just to
stick to the term 'experience' because perhaps there is a
particular sense you want to attach to it. It is such a very general
word, it seems to describe the continuity of consciousness that
is simply characteristic of being human. Perhaps you could say
something about that.

K: I don't quite know what you mean by experience. One can
experience what one desires.

IM: You mean imagining it?

K: Yes. Also, one can experience according to your conditioning. If
I am a devout Buddhist, I can experience the state of that
consciousness which was supposed to have been Buddha's.

IM: Well, that is a rather special sort of experience, isn't it?

K: Yes, but I am just questioning what we mean by experience. Say
I experience anger. Is there a difference between the experience
and the experiencer?

IM: Well, this is a difficult question of usage because the word 'experience' in English describes something fairly vague. It can mean something momentary, either, 'I had a strange experience yesterday', or it can mean the continuity of your conscious life and your relationship to your past. But I think what you mean by it is something that, as it were, collects your past. At one point I think you have described desire as experience, whereas you say that love is not experience.

K: Love cannot be experience.

IM: Could you explain what the distinction is?

K: Could we go into the question of who experiences the whole thing, anything, whether it is the experience of something imagined, or the experience of one's past tradition and images, and so on?

IM: You are asking, who is the experiencer?

K: Yes, who is experiencing?

IM: This is also a difficult question, isn't it. If one were to ask a passer-by in the street he would say the 'individual'.

K: Yes, 'I' am experiencing.

IM: These experiences belong to 'me'.

K: I had an experience of an accident this morning in a car. I experience so many things.

IM: But then, if one were to pursue the matter beyond that kind of answer, one might say well of course one must distinguish between different kinds of experience. I can think of, say, three kinds immediately: there is the experience of my past life, we say of somebody, 'he is an experienced man', meaning he has a lot of experiences of a particular kind, and then we would also say that experience is just the continuity of my consciousness, going away into the past.

K: Or the continuity of one's consciousness. What do you mean by the word 'consciousness'?

IM: Well, let's pursue the matter in this way; one would say consciousness differs at different times. And the meaning of the word 'experience' I would think would differ, depending on whether you were talking about just ordinary life. Let's put it this way: partly you were sort of imposing yourself on the world and saying 'I am doing this, I am doing that', and this would be perhaps experience. But also there might be an experience where you aren't really present.

K: That's it, that's just it. Where the experiencer is not, is there an experience that you can then remember and say, 'this is it'?

IM: Well, I would think that people have what I would call selfless experience when, for instance, they are looking at a great work of art.

K: Yes.

IM: I am not sure whether one could say this if they are with somebody they love very much. I think these two cases are very different. What do you think?

K: I would like first to go into the question, if I may, of *who* is experiencing all this? Whether it is ordinary things, or the most complicated forms of experiences, or so-called spiritual experiences. Who is it that is always experiencing? Is the experiencer different from the experience?

IM: Well one would normally say so, wouldn't one, because one may believe in the continuity of an individual person.

K: Yes, that is what is commonly held. Now we are going to question that: is the thinker different from his thoughts?

IM: Again, we would usually say so because one could say, 'I order my thoughts'. This assumes that I am deciding, that I collect my thoughts.

K: Yes, but is that I, who orders his thoughts, different from his thoughts? He may order them, he may discipline them, he may control them, he might say, 'this is right, this is wrong, this must be done, that must not be done', but is the controller, the person who disciplines, brings order, different from the things that he is ordering?

IM: Well, let's make a distinction here between ordinary language in a law court where somebody is held responsible for something they have done. They can't say, 'well I am a different person now', or something like that. This is the ordinary sense of the continuity of the individual and somebody being the subject. But leaving that aside, one doesn't have to be a philosopher or hold a religious view to think that one is divided, a divided person.

K: That's it.

IM: And there are times when one part of you disapproves of another part.

K: The dualistic process . . . is there a difference between – we come back to the old question – the good and the bad?

IM: Well, nothing could be more fundamental, yes, I mean this seems to me the nature of the real world.

K: I know. The real world is division: we have divided the good and the bad, and the thinker from the thought, the experiencer from the experience.

IM: Yes, this would follow in that if you condemn yourself for doing something then you are divided.

K: 'I should not', 'I must', 'I will become', and all the rest of it, this breeds division in oneself. I would like to ask again, if I may, is that experiencer different from the thing he is experiencing or the thinker different from his thoughts?

IM: Well, if this is an appeal to how I think about myself, I would say – leaving aside the common-sense, the ordinary-language view – sometimes yes and sometimes no. I mean sometimes one is consciously judging oneself, dividing oneself, sometimes there is nothing except a single being or something.

K: A single movement. So is not the experiencer the same as the experience?

IM: Well, it sometimes seems so.

K: So when we say, 'I am envious', there is a division, then 'I' try to control or rationalize my envy, to justify or suppress it and so on, but the 'I' *is* envy, not separate from it.

IM: Well, I would have thought that it is and it isn't. From what I have read and understood there are two things that you say; and I don't understand how they connect or harmonize. One of the things that I liked very much was this: if I think that I am envious, say, the word 'envy' suggests something bad so I may want not to be envious. If I see this, I must start, not with a kind of ideal self that doesn't exist but in my real being, which is the envious person. I feel great sympathy with this. But then you also say that there is no process involved here, I must *be* good, not become good, and that the idea of becoming good is in some way an illusion.

K: That's right.

IM: Perhaps you could explain this, I mean it seems to me that in the first case you are suggesting that I must start from a point that is a long way from my conclusion, my conclusion being to become unenvious. In the second case you are saying that there is no process of becoming.

K: For me there is no psychological becoming at all.

IM: Yes, this is what I don't understand.

K: Let us go into it. First of all let's come to this point: we have divided the good from the bad both in the world and in ourselves. Right?

IM: But you don't dispute, you don't object to this?

K: I don't refute it, I am just looking at it. Is the bad related to the good or is the good totally divorced from the bad, so that they are not related at all? If they are related the good will still be part of the bad.

IM: Well, if you are asking me if I agree with that, I am not sure. It seems to me we think about good and bad in several different ways, don't we? We think of bad grading into good as if it were a spectrum, with goodness here and badness there.

K: Yes, continuing into the bad.

IM: A continuing. We also think of good – if we think of it as perfection – as being really outside the world altogether.

K: Not as perfection – I mean being good, whole, good health, a good man, the word 'good' in that sense.

IM: Let's say 'a good man' then.

K: Is that good part of the bad? Does the good know the bad? Is the good the outcome of the bad? If it is the outcome then it is still part of the bad. It's like a child being born; it's still part of the mother.

IM: Yes, some people would say that they are opposites that exist in relation to each other.

K: Now, I ask: are they opposite? Or are they totally unrelated?

IM: Well, there is a very clear difference between a bad man and a good man. So in that sense they are very different. On the other hand in a human being good and bad grade into each other, and sometimes you don't know which is which.

K: No, that is what I am questioning, that is what I would like to discuss with you. I mean to me the good is totally divorced from the bad, just as love is not related to hate.

IM: Yes. I mean in the ordinary fallen human condition of course love often occasions hate.

K: Of course.

IM: Whereas you say that love is not related to hate, that it is an entirely different kind of concept.

K: Totally. Love has no feeling about hate, it has no relation to hate, it does not encompass or embrace hate.

IM: Wait a minute. Let me ask a supplementary question. Would you say the same about love and desire?

K: Yes, I would.

IM: You regard desire as something connected with psychological becoming?

K: Yes.

IM: Whereas love is . . .

K: . . . something entirely different.

IM: Now, how does this different thing come to one? I might say now, 'why should it concern me?' What am I to do about it?

K: It is simple enough. There is conflict. Desire always brings conflict, but love can never bring conflict. Love has no conflict, it has no sense of conflict.

IM: You are using the word 'love' in an ideal sense, which is unusual.

K: No, the brain is the entire centre of desire, feeling, anxiety, pain, loneliness. The consciousness is all that, the beliefs, fears, sorrow, loneliness, anxiety, the whole . . .

IM: . . . the psychological being.

K: Yes, the psychological structure, confusion. That is the brain. And love is not part of the brain because it is something outside that.

IM: Yes, this comes back to your saying you don't experience love in the way in which you experience desire.

K: I can't experience something that is so.

IM: In ordinary parlance we speak of a 'jealous' love or something like that. But that is not what we are talking about. We are talking about some sort of absolute – I can't think of the right word here – love. But suppose I dearly love somebody in one might say not a bad way but in a good way, as it were, would you want to say that this is not part of any psychological process in my mind?

K: No, I would say: if when I say I love you there is any tinge of attachment, jealousy, any shadow of conflict, then it is not the real thing.

IM: Yes, all right. I was brought up as a Christian, so there is a lot of the Christian way of looking in me, although I don't believe in

God or the divinity of Christ. But in Christianity there would be an idea of divine or perfect love, which is something that we don't normally achieve perhaps at all.

K: I don't see why not. Because if I am not jealous, I won't be jealous. When there is no sense of attachment to another person, that doesn't mean lack of love.

IM: Well, in what we would call in ordinary parlance a virtuous love, where you are not hurting anybody else by loving this person, and you are not possessive, unreasonable and so on, there is attachment. I mean inevitably if the person dies . . .

K: Wait a minute, that is a different question. Why are we attached to anything? If I am attached to this house . . .

IM: I would, I think, take a different view of the notion of desire. I would think that becoming good – to use this phrase that perhaps you would want to exclude – is a matter of purifying one's desires, of having 'good' desires, desiring something that is good. Now in loving somebody I would have felt that the element of desire was present.

K: Let's look at desire. What is desire?

IM: Well, there again one would say there are low desires and there are high desires.

K: Yes, but what is the origin, the beginning of desire? Why has desire become such an extraordinarily important part of our life?

IM: Desire is certainly connected with the future.

K: With the future.

IM: It is connected with time.

K: Of course, with time.

IM: Because I desire something that is absent. Let's take examples. I might desire to be frightfully rich, or I might desire to study a subject and become good at it.

K: Good at the piano.

IM: Well, let's say good at mathematics, to acquire knowledge.

K: Yes, of course.

IM: And I might say I love my subject, I love what I am studying.

K: No, what I am asking is: what is desire? How does it come about? Why does it control us so strongly? After all a monk, or one of the Indian sannyasis, their whole idea is to suppress or to transmute desire.

IM: Well, transmute, yes. I would rather use the word 'transmute'.

K: To transmute means that there is an entity who transmutes it.

IM: Yes, and there is a process of transmuting, and a discipline or a training, or something like that.

K: Which is only a subtle form of suppression, a subtle form of organizing desire, or saying desire for God is good.

IM: Or desire for riches is bad.

K: And desire for possessions is bad. So we are not discussing the objects of desire, whether it is God, or power, whether to become a rich man or a prime minister, but what is desire? How does it take shape in us?

IM: Well, whether there can be love without desire I am not sure. If one thinks perhaps of some kind of perfect love the notion of desire would have changed so much that perhaps you would have to exclude it. At a more ordinary but good level, if I desire to become well educated or something . . .

K: Yes, that is a different matter.

IM: . . . there is a tension between a condition that exists and a condition that does not exist.

K: But I am not asking about the desire to become a good human being, or a good scholar, and so on, but about desire itself.

IM: I think I would evade or reject this question because I don't see how one could explain what desire was without thinking of different kinds of desire.

K: I say I desire a house, I desire this or that, so many desires. But what is the movement of desire, the origin of it? Because we have either suppressed, transmuted, escaped from, or totally controlled it. But again who is the controller? Who says this is good desire, this is bad desire, this must be pursued because it is helpful, the other is not and so on. It is still desire. Desire for God, or desire for money, it is still desire.

IM: And if someone says one is good and the other is bad, you would come back to saying, all the same it is desire?

K: Yes, desire is important to understand, not good desire and bad desire.

IM: I am not sure that I would be able to understand it without using that distinction. But let's shift our ground slightly, there is something *behind* what you are saying.

K: You said just now desire involves time.

IM: Yes. Well, all right. I am going to withdraw that now and modify it by saying that I think that there might be some kind of desire which does not involve time but where you are completely united with the object of your desire. This is something found in Christian mysticism, that if you desire God and are united with God – not that I know what that would mean – then your desire is fulfilled and becomes perfect love.

K: Yes, but whether it is the desire of a man who says, 'I must become a very rich man, a powerful man', or the desire of a man for God and unification with God, it is still desire.

IM: But you speak of desire as if it were something that you want to overcome or set aside.

K: No, I want to understand the movement of it, the process of it, the intolerable burden or the pleasure of it.

IM: Yes, it is not always a burden, is it? If, for instance, you are hungry and know that you are going to have a good meal shortly, the intention of desire is pleasurable.

K: Yes, that's understood.

IM: But there is something *behind* what you are saying which I can't get at.

K: I will go into it. Desire exists only when there is identification with sensation.

IM: By sensation you don't mean . . .

K: I see a lovely house, I want it, there is a desire for it.

IM: You don't mean that there is an actual physical concomitant but that there is a kind of imagery.

K: Both.

IM: You imagine yourself in the house, something like that.

K: Sensation, then thought creating the image of my owning the house, then desire begins.

IM: Yes, all right. There is a kind of sensory aspect.

K: Thought then gives that sensory aspect an image.

IM: But if one says one desires to be educated, it doesn't mean you are thinking about it all the time or having sensations about it.

K: Of course not.

IM: It means you are carrying on your life. There would be perhaps moments when you have a sensory experience of desire. You imagine what it would be like when your education is better.

K: The moment that sensation is given shape by thought, it becomes desire. That is all I am saying. I am not saying good, bad and all the rest of it, but desire *per se*.

IM: But you say that love is different from desire.

K: Love is different: love is not pleasure, love is not desire.

IM: Yes, all right. This introduces another topic that I will just mention and put aside. I am also concerned with what you feel about motivation and energy. I think desire is a source of energy. And good desire is a source of good energy, but let's take this idea of love being different. There seems to me a contrast between a process and something that is not a process.

K: Love is not a process.

IM: It is not a process. And you used some term like creative being, which is to do with the present. And you would connect this with the possibility of love and truth?

K: Yes.

IM: Whereas desire is something restless which is outside.

K: Restless. But that doesn't mean that love is static.

IM: No, static is probably the wrong word here. What would you say?

K: It's alive, it isn't just a . . .

IM: It is creative and . . .

K: It is not exclusive. I may love you but I also have this feeling of love. It is not just identified with one person.

IM: But the feeling of love is quite a different feeling from the feeling of desire.

K: Naturally.

IM: So you are not excluding the sensory aspect?

K: No, wait a minute, let's go into it slowly. As we said just now, the brain is part of the senses, part of reactions, action, responses, beliefs, faith, fear, all that is the centre here, which is my consciousness. The content of my consciousness is all that, God, no God, my knowledge, my failure, my depression, my anxiety. Now in that there is a great deal of confusion, contradiction, fear, and all the rest of it. Is love part of that?

IM: I don't know. You tell me.

K: To me, personally, it is not.

IM: But then if there is a human condition, a state of creative being, which is love and a person is sometimes in this condition, are you suggesting that at that moment all the psychological stuff which that person consists of and has collected is somehow absent?

K: Yes, absent.

IM: But he still must know what the object of his love is.

K: No, just a minute. I might love *you*. But love is not exclusive, it is not limited.

IM: Yes, though in a sense it is and it isn't, because I mean if one loves a person, you love that person and not another one. But it doesn't mean that you exclude anybody.

K: Love is not exclusive.

IM: No, but it is selective, if one can put it that way. One doesn't love everybody. Perhaps God does . . .

K: No, I don't want to attribute love to God or to somebody . . .

IM: I am using God as a figure of speech. There is an ideal love perhaps.

K: No, I wouldn't use the word ideal. I strongly object to ideas, ideals and all that nonsense. I see – definitely – that love has no relationship to hate, love has no relationship to jealousy, it is not attached. It is not desire, it is not pleasure.

IM: Well, let's say that you are interested in another person. I mean, after all people come to you.

K: I care.

IM: Yes. But I ask, do you think there are certain times in one's life when one is – it is difficult to find the word here – when one is expressing or being love? Should this be every moment of one's life?

K: I am not at all sure that it cannot be there all the time.

IM: Yes, good. And you think . . .

K: You see, can love exist where there is self-centred interest? That is the real question.

IM: No, it would be imperfect love. Let's leave out imperfect love which is not love.

K: All right. When there is self-interest can the other exist? Obviously it cannot, because self-interest is very, very small.

IM: You won't let me use the word 'perfect' or 'ideal', so I'll use love in your sense. All right. Love then excludes self-interest.

K: Where there is self-interest the other is not.

IM: Yes, well, something that I very much want to find out, and everybody wants to find out, is how to change, how to move out of the state of being envious.

K: This is really an interesting question. I am envious. There is no difference between 'I' and envy. 'I' am envious, envy is me.

IM: Yes, as we were saying earlier, the person is . . .

K: I mean envy is me, I cannot act on envy because it is me.

IM: Yes, but you can become less envious.

K: But it is still me.

IM: Go on.

K: So there is no question of suppression, transmutation, or escaping from it, it is me.

IM: So what do I do next?

K: If it is me I watch it, watch it very, very carefully, not trying to act upon it.

IM: So there is a you who is watching the envy?

K: No, in watching, there is no you. When you are watching a bird, for instance, there is no you.

IM: Well, watching a bird is quite different from other kinds of watching.

K: Of course. Is there a watching without the word, without condemning, without agreeing, rejecting or resisting, just watching?

IM: Well, there can be such watching, but it is difficult. Wait a minute. We have got this envious person, oneself, one is envious. Then one is aware of the envy, one watches it, just watching.

K: Watching.

IM: Or being it if you like, put it in another way. Consciously being your envy. Would you accept that form of words?

K: You are envy.

IM: I mean, when you do something enviously, thoughtlessly, you are not watching. But then there are moments perhaps when you are attending to it.

K: That is what I am saying. Look, you are watching a precious, intricate jewel. You are looking at the extraordinary delicacy, the bright light and the beauty of the jewel.

IM: Yes, in this case you are looking at envy.

K: Then I see the whole movement of envy, which is comparison and so on. So I watch it without any thought interfering with my watching. That requires a great deal of attention, not concentration, real attention in which the self is not.

IM: But are you not making a judgement?

K: No.

IM: You are watching without judgement.

K: Yes, I express no values. I don't say you must or must not have envy, it is immoral, or anything of that kind. Human beings have lived with envy for thousands of years.

IM: But then is not the result of this attention that your envy disappears?

K: Watching with attention, watching is attention.

IM: Yes, I like the word attention. You attend, you would say, in some non-evaluating way, you are not making a moral judgement. You are not saying, 'I ought not to be envious'.

K: Oh, no, that would be too . . .

IM: But is not, I won't say the purpose, but certainly the result of this attention, that the envy dissolves?

K: Yes, because in attention there is no self at all.

IM: Yes, good. OK, I understand this state of being.

K: You can watch it, you know. It's great fun.

IM: I mean this connects with my question about how do I change. This is, to use old-fashioned language, a spiritual discipline – no, you don't like the word discipline!

K: The word 'discipline' really means to learn. Not to compartmentalize but to pursue. To learn watching, not memorize the things watched, but to see the whole implication of envy, comparison, and all the rest of it.

IM: But does this happen only when you are meditating – to use a word you yourself use – or should it happen all the time?

K: All the time, if you are watching. Which means you don't let a single thought slip by without knowing what it is.

IM: Yes, and this would co-exist with one being a ticket collector or whatever one's job in life is, though the idea of living at different levels, or in different states, must I think come in. But there would be a state of your being which was this constant attention.

K: But you see you also introduced the word meditation.

IM: Yes, it is a word that you use yourself.

K: I know. I use that word but, you see, meditation is a very complex business. In meditation there is no meditator at all.

IM: Yes.

K: But what we do is to say 'I must meditate, I must follow a system to meditate, there must be practice', which is all desire, wanting to *achieve* a certain state.

IM: Yes, this seems to me in a sense unavoidable. I was taught a system of meditation a long time ago, and I have practised it to some extent, something like meditation, only in a very feeble sort of way. But it does seem to me that there is something that is trying to do it better.

K: Now when you use the word 'better' that means more, therefore measurement comes in.

IM: There is no 'more', since you say of meditation that there is no duality, there is no subject.

K: Absolutely not.

IM: And I would say that something like this happens in the experience of art.

K: The moment you say 'experience' you are already . . .

IM: All right. I mean, if I am looking at a great picture – if I am really looking – I am not there. The picture is there.

K: That's all. When you are really looking at something there is the absence of the self.

IM: And this would be an image of love too, wouldn't it?

K: There is no image in love. Of course not, an image is put together by thought.

IM: I think that would be so in a certain way of loving, in unselfish love . . . this is difficult to talk about because love happens in time and you have to struggle and think and plan and do things for somebody you love. But you would be really selfless in all that you were doing, I mean there would be somebody there doing . . .

K: Of course.

IM: . . . but the self would be absent, the object of attention would be present. But it seems to me you have to try. You have given me the end but not the means.

K: Let's look at it. The means is the end, the two are not different.

IM: May I just quote a remark by Kafka? He said that there is no way, there is only the end. What we call the way is just messing about. Yes, I see and I don't see, as it were.

K: Let's try something else. You see change implies future, as you pointed out. From *this* to *that*.

IM: Yes, and imagining the future.

K: What is the future? The future is a continuity of the past, modified through the present, it is a movement.

IM: All right.

K: So the future is in the present. Now, if I am learning a language, I need the future, I need time, I need discipline, etc. Now *there* it is all right, but psychologically, inwardly, subjectively, the past, which is 'me', my memories, my experiences, all the past, is being modified in the present and proceeds to the future – right? This is the whole movement of our evolution, of our psychological well-being, or not well-being, and so on. So the present is in the future because what I am now will be what I am tomorrow, unless I change now – right? So the present contains the past and the future is now. Now the present is what I am.

IM: Yes, in a sense there isn't anything else, but go on.

K: That's what I am, my memories, all that. And there is no future unless I continue. Now, is there an end to that?

IM: You mean, is there an alternative state of being?

K: Yes, ending this whole movement of becoming, struggling, achieving.

IM: Of course philosophers have always been worrying about the difference between being and becoming, and in Platonism and in Christian theology, being is real and becoming is unreal. And I feel something of this in what you say. But I don't want to mislead myself by thinking about anything else. I am trying to picture what you are speaking of would be like. Let's say you are spending your time learning a language and you don't know the irregular verbs today, next week you will know the irregular verbs. And this is human life and unavoidable and proper and quite right.

K: Quite right.

IM: However during this time you are also attending to everything that you do.

K: Of course. I am paying attention to everything I do now. So the now contains all time.

IM: You are picturing a possible human state . . .

K: No, I am not picturing. I am just saying see what has happened to the human psyche: it has always moved in this direction, the past, modifying the present, and the future. This is the chain in which we are caught. I won't even use the word 'caught'. This is what we are.

IM: Yes, the word 'caught' though suggests there is a possibility of freedom, which is another word you use. Freedom that is connected with truth and with love. And so somebody comes to you saying, 'Well I am in this trap, how do I get out of it?'

K: If you are in a trap let's look at what the trap is first before you want to get out of it.

IM: Well perhaps this is an irrelevant point but I don't want to get out of the trap in the sense that I don't want to stop wanting next week to know the irregular verbs.

K: Of course.

IM: That goes on. But what I also want, say, is to achieve a state of being which is selfless.

K: Yes, which means what? Be careful. You desire it, you have a concept of the future.

IM: Yes, I mean I know that I am not selfless now but I would like to become selfless.

K: Therefore let's understand what the self is. You can't change or rather break down the self without understanding the movement of the self, you cannot just invent a goal.

IM: But where one was looking at one's envy, for instance, we agreed that one result of this attention would be that the envy would disappear. So the self is changing.

K: It is not the ending of envy but the attention that matters.

IM: Well, supposing I attended to my envy but just went on behaving enviously, with complete consciousness of what I was doing. Would that be a good state?

K: Then, you see, *you* being conscious – that is still part of the self.

IM: Well, this is not postulating a kind of condition that is totally unlike the human condition. One is imagining a state in which human beings might be.

K: Yes, we are human beings, we live in this constant conflict, pain, sorrow and all that. This is our life, this is our condition. But one day you come along and tell me, look, there is a different way of living. You do not have to be everlastingly in this business. And you listen to him, you find out. You may say it is rubbish and drop it; there must be a relationship between the speaker and yourself.

IM: Like now, I am asking you, of course.

K: You tell me envy is not love, and envy cannot be put aside. So watch it, look at it, see it and let it unfold. Don't condemn, transmute or deny it or escape from it. Just watch it, which means give your whole attention to it.

IM: But would this not result in my inhibiting it?

K: No, I am bringing it out.

IM: All right, let me put it another way. Wouldn't it be good for me to inhibit my envy?

K: No, it will come up again if I inhibit it.

IM: Yes, all right. But meanwhile it might be better.

K: Ah, I don't want a meanwhile!

IM: Well, yes, but you seem to me to exclude the element of training oneself. I mean you don't like the word discipline.

K: Discipline comes from the word 'disciple' – one who is learning. Learning, not memorizing, learning to see the beauty of that jewel. I haven't looked at the jewel, I have always condemned it, rationalized, etc, but now there is only watching that jewel.

IM: Yes, but what you are watching in the case of a jewel is something pictured as absolutely precious. If I am looking at my envy, it is the opposite of a jewel, it is something bad.

K: No, I don't condemn it. There is no spirit of condemnation, judgement or evaluation, just watching it. I watch my son. I don't say, 'by Jove, he shouldn't be this, he shouldn't be that'. I just watch him. Say, for instance, when I look at a picture, I watch it, I see all the light, the proportions, the darkness . . .

IM: Looking at a picture is a good example for me in trying to understand what your fundamental idea is here. But it still troubles me that you are suggesting a kind of ideal mode of being in which you are connected with reality. There remains the fact that one is not in this state, one is sunk in illusion, one is full of illusion.

K: That's all. Now I am in illusion. I am illusion, I live in illusion, my thinking, my belief, faith, is illusion. The word illusion comes from 'ludere', to play. So I am playing with illusions.

IM: Why should I bother? Put it in another way. Why shouldn't I just watch my illusion? If I am a clever person I can watch my envy and be amused by it and continue to behave enviously.

K: All right, carry on. But there is conflict in it, a certain sense of agony, there is pain.

IM: If you saw somebody that you loved in a state of illusion, wouldn't you wish that person to change?

K: I would go and talk to him.

IM: Well, then you are suggesting that he should change, you are suggesting moral values.

K: No, I would say to him, look, why do you have these illusions?

IM: Well, to call them illusions is already to make them . . .

K: Don't even call it illusion. Somebody believes in God or in some other thing.

IM: Well, let's stick to the case of envy because that's fairly straightforward. Somebody is absolutely consumed with envy; 'oh, he's got that, he's better than me', and so on. You watch somebody like that and say, 'look, why waste your energy and anxiety on something that is not deeply, really, important. You should not be doing it.'

K: That is if they are willing to listen. The moment they are willing to listen to you, you have already helped them.

IM: All right, yes. But then you have taught them something.

K: Ah, no, there is no pressure, I don't want him to change.

IM: Well, I know all good teachers refuse to call themselves teachers.

K: You see, conflict is the real root of all this.

IM: But supposing somebody was in a completely harmonious state, with lots of what we call vices, supposing they are envious, jealous, violent, angry, couldn't they be a harmoniously connected person? Supposing they are very successful in everything they do, would you say that this was impossible?

K: No, you can't be harmonious if you are being violent with your right hand while being harmonious with your left hand.

IM: Yes, I agree with that. I think people assume rightly that an evil man is in a state of conflict and that a good man is harmonious.

K: A good man has no conflict.

IM: Yes, and an evil man has conflict. Well, this suggests then that somewhere the evil man has made a kind of mistake, there is something unreal about what he believes about the world. So in making the distinction between good and bad one is making a distinction between . . .

K: Yes, you can see for instance that in a man who is a terrorist, who kills for the fun of killing, there is something wrong with him. I don't call him evil or good, there is some kind of aberration going on in the poor chap.

IM: So what you want to produce is a harmonious personality?

K: No, is it possible to end all conflict within oneself? That is the real root of the question. All conflict.

IM: And you would be prepared to drop the words 'good' and 'bad' and use the words 'harmony' and 'disharmony'?

K: I wouldn't use 'harmony' or 'disharmony' because the moment there is no conflict you are whole, there is a holistic way of living.

IM: Yes, but you are still talking about good and evil in the sense in which we normally understand them. You referred to the terrorist, a very evil man, not just an envious man but somebody who is cruel.

K: Yes, somebody who kills.

IM: Then one would want this person to change.

K: If he will listen, if he will change, so much the better. But they generally don't listen.

The conversation continued later the same day.

IM: I am still trying to formulate some fundamental question that I can't quite get a grip on at the moment. Perhaps I could ask one or two different kinds of question.

The idea of duty is a fundamental one in most moral systems, philosophers argue about it but there it is. People are taught duties when they are growing up, that they ought to tell the truth for instance. You shy away from the idea of duty.

K: I feel 'responsibility' is better than 'duty'.

IM: Well, all right, a sense of responsibility would be a sense of duty under some circumstances – one could extend the two ideas in different directions – but you would rather call it a sense of responsibility?

K: Yes, because responsibility implies care, affection, a sense of communication with the other person, not doing something because you are obliged or told to do it, but being responsible. If I undertake to build a house, I am responsible for building a house. If I am responsible for my children, I would be responsible completely, not only until they leave home, but I would see that they live properly, are brought up not to kill.

IM: There would be no limits to responsibility.

K: No limits to responsibility.

IM: Yes, one does perhaps connect duty with very definite things which have to be done. On the other hand, if you take something like a duty to tell the truth, that's something fundamental.

K: Telling the truth is part of my responsibility. I wouldn't be dishonest to myself.

IM: Well, don't let's worry then about the word 'duty'. But this is a case where one's dealing with a continuing aspect of human life. Would you say that by being such an everyday notion, part of the decent moral continuity of a society's life, it is essentially different from what we were talking about this morning, from the real thing, and from love?

K: Yes, I would consider it to be different.

IM: But I don't quite see where the division comes between what we would call ordinary goodness or moral behaviour and this fundamental thing.

K: Could we start by asking why we are fragmented, why we look at life and all our actions, whatever it is, always in fragments, business, religion, love, hate? It is all so broken up. Why do we do this?

IM: Well, life has to be dealt with every day.

K: Yes, but why should I accept that life has to be dealt with in this way?

IM: You seem to feel that we should have some kind of completely unitary selflessness, which would then be indivisible.

K: Yes, that's it.

IM: But then words like 'truth' and 'love' . . .

K: . . . are one. If there is love there is truth, there is beauty.

IM: Yes, this is so, if one is looking at it in a philosophical sense.

K: No, in an actual sense, I mean if I really love there is beauty in it; and then I can't be dishonest.

IM: I feel that beauty is a more difficult concept in this regard. What worries me is the point of connection between the truth that is love, the fundamental truth, and ordinary conceptions of truth, as in tell the truth.

K: Suppose I have lied. I acknowledge that I have lied, I acknowledge that I have been angry. That is honesty, that is truth in the ordinary sense of the word. I don't cover up my lie with lots of phony stuff. I say I have lied, I have been angry, I have been brutal. I think we are so trained to cover up this kind of thing, to escape from it, and so not being terribly honest to oneself.

IM: Yes, well, how does this connect with – one of the things which I think you are very much concerned with – overcoming conflict and overcoming separatist thinking? You make distinctions between desire and love, for instance, and you then bring truth into the centre by saying that love is truth.

K: Yes, of course.

IM: But this doesn't seem to me to connect very easily with ordinary moral life, and this is where my idea of purifying desire, or something like that, would come in. It looks as if one would have two judgements of morality, you would say that he is a good man in the ordinary sense of the word, but he is an imperfect man in your sense of the word. And isn't it important for you, I am thinking of you as someone wishing well to men, isn't it important for you to make connections?

K: Yes, I see that. Look, I would first ask myself, or I would ask my friend, why are we fragmented?

IM: You want to go back to a metaphysical question first. You feel that we must be right at the beginning all the time.

K: Of course, you have to start from there all the time.

IM: Yes, I like this too, in a way, what you want is something new that is not the acquired collection of what one has already.

K: I have asked the students in many of our discussions: why is it we are fragmented like this, broken up, what has gone wrong with us? After millions of years we are still fighting each other, killing each other, we are angry – you follow? What is wrong?

IM: Well, there is a sense of conflict or fragmentation, which is bad, which means fighting, but there is also ordinary discursive reason and how we set about getting to know things, which isn't necessarily bad.

K: Yes, I use my reason to see why the world is divided into these things like nationalities and religions. You know what is happening in India with the Sikhs, or with the Jews and the Arabs. Why, why do we accept this way of living?

IM: I think there is a kind of empirical, ordinary answer to this that we can try and stop it by doing all sorts of things, like people do when they talk to other people.

K: But we don't, the fact is we've never done it, we haven't stopped this division. I mean if I had a son with an Arab woman and a son with an Israeli woman, what am I to do, they will fight!

IM: You wouldn't deny then that part of what you want to communicate is something that would have practical effects on politics?

K: It has practical effects, yes. On politics, religion, daily life. But I would say, look, don't let's start with theories, let's start with why we human beings throughout the world are so broken up, so divided.

IM: But that seems to me partly an empirical question in that you could say we could find out why a certain religion held certain views at a certain time and separated off. One could study Christianity in this way. But there is a sort of metaphysical question here, which I would think is partly unanswerable. I mean it is like saying: why are there human beings? One must say, well I don't know. I mean people who believe in God would say that God created the world.

K: And the scientists have different reasons.

IM: If you exclude the empirical answer, you are asking a kind of metaphysical question which in a way can't be answered.

K: I think it is fairly simple. I would like to ask: is it that thought itself is fragmented?

IM: I think thought itself *is* fragmented and it seems to me in a sense unavoidably so. I mean, what we are doing now – using a natural language and concepts and using words which we have learnt to understand and so on – is something which depends on a spreading out of interest to the world in many different ways. The word 'discursive' covers this kind of notion that the intellect has to spread itself out, it has to emerge into language and so on. It can't be one, which many philosophers want. They want to think there is a 'one'. But you don't seem to me to allow – let me put it this way – the redemption of the world, I mean the bringing of the world into the centre, into goodness, into truth, love.

K: I say, yes, that must be.

IM: Well, yes, but then one can't get rid of all fragmentation. One has got to redeem it, if you see what I mean.

K: All right, let's redeem it. Now why are human beings like this? Let's redeem *that*. Not explaining intellectually, but there is the fact, the daily fact, that there is such conflict, such violence. Why?

IM: There are historical reasons why there is, for instance, a conflict in Ireland. But you are thinking of much deeper things.

K: Yes, much deeper things.

IM: Well if somebody asks me that, I would say I can't answer the metaphysical question but what I can ask is why ought it not to be so. And this uses the word 'ought' which you don't want. We have a conception of goodness from which we spread, as it were, all kinds of thought and action into the world – this is putting it very badly.

K: I understand.

IM: Hoping that gradually we can make the world better and remove conflict in the superficial and in the deeper sense too.

K: We have lived on this earth, according to the scientists, for at least two or three million years. We are still at it. Just look at what is happening.

IM: Yes, and who can say what the future holds?

K: The future is what we are now. If we don't do something now we will be exactly the same tomorrow.

IM: But what we can do now is really something very limited. We can do something to ourselves and we can do something to a small number of people.

K: But when you say ourselves, we are the world.

IM: And we can also take part in politics, which is a way of doing something in the world.

K: But I am the rest of the world, because my consciousness is like the rest of mankind.

IM: Yes, you mean that if you can do it other people can do it.

K: If I change I affect the rest.

IM: Well, there is also the fact that one has a very limited amount of time in which to achieve such insight.

K: That's why I say don't let time interfere with this question. I am a human being. My way of life, my way of thinking, my action, is comparatively like the rest of mankind. There may be outward differences, but deeply I am the rest of mankind, I am mankind.

IM: Except that you are a very unusual person.

K: No, I am mankind because we all suffer, we all go through a hell of a time. So I am the rest of mankind, I am humanity. That is real love.

IM: Somebody may say, all right, but you are just you, you are by yourself – I mean you may be showing what is a human potential.

K: Come and join me, come and join me.

IM: Yes, well.

K: Let your petty little nationalisms and all the rest of it go and join me, let's be free and look at the world differently, and not always keep in conflict with each other. With every husband and wife, this is happening every day.

IM: But I can't help putting the problem in terms of how much influence one can have. If one is going to teach people – don't let's think of you and me now – but if anybody wants to influence people in order to bring about the end of this conflict, they have to involve themselves in persuasion, in politics. And many people would say, many people do say nowadays, that to worry about your own soul and whether you are selfless or not is a waste of time, you must simply go and help other people, go and stop them suffering.

K: See what is happening with those people who are helping and those people who are helped. Very little is happening. Hitler wanted to help. Buddha said, mankind suffers, there must be an end to suffering. And look what has happened: suffering is going on.

IM: I keep wanting to turn this round a bit so that I can get a bit more light. When you speak of overcoming conflict, of overcoming suffering . . .

K: . . . not overcoming, ending . . .

IM: . . . ending, yes. Is this anything like what a Buddhist would think of as Nirvana?

K: From what I have discussed with people, Nirvana apparently means a state in which the self is not. The self in the sense of all the turmoil. Come to that point, don't discuss what Nirvana is, you will find out.

IM: I would understand something like this as meaning that one is in a selfless condition and the denial of the world is the meaninglessness of all these other things.

K: They have done that, denied the world. But I don't say deny the world. On the contrary, you have to live there.

IM: Yes, if one thinks of Plato's image of the cave, you are in the darkness and then gradually you move out into the light. He also speaks about coming back into the cave, by which I think he means that you find some kind of liberation for yourself but then have to liberate everybody else as well.

K: That's the point. You know there is the whole notion of the Bodhisattva – I won't go into that. But if you change fundamentally, won't it affect mankind?

IM: You will affect a certain number of people.

K: No, look, Christianity has affected many millions.

IM: Yes, certainly. I was about to say there are cases, like the life of Christ – whether Christ really existed as an historical person or not – the image of Christ has changed people's lives.

K: I am saying that they have changed through propaganda. Also, Buddhism has affected the whole of Asia. I say, 'let a few of us work at this – then we will change the world'.

IM: I think we have had great teachers who have had a great deal of influence, who have, as far as I can see, advocated a kind of selflessness not unlike what you are speaking of.

K: Yes, freedom, freedom from the self.

IM: What is one to do? It doesn't seem to me . . .

K: What is one to do? That requires sitting down, talking about it, going into it – right? Naturally. And breaking down barriers between us.

IM: We have come perhaps to a slightly different kind of question: a question about influence.

K: I don't want to influence anybody. That is the worst thing to happen, because if I influence you somebody else can come along and influence you too in another direction. But if you see something for yourself it is clear.

IM: Yes, that again is something which we agree about, that you have to do the thing yourself. It is no good being told by somebody else.

K: Therefore no propaganda, no programming.

IM: This is something which I think theologians are now realizing – that you can't have God thrust upon you. I mean whatever the spiritual life is, it is something you have to discover for yourself.

K: In the spiritual world there is no authority. But now everything is that. People want authority, they want some kind of security in authority.

IM: Well, I don't myself see any answer to the problem of how the discovery of spiritual truth, whatever this may be, can change the world. You perhaps have more hope for the world than I have.

K: No, I am neither pessimistic nor optimistic, but I see that unless there are a few of us who radically change the whole psychological structure that we are now we will be going downhill all the time. That's all.

IM: Well I agree with that too. If the world lost people who are concerned with what you are concerned with I think that it would in some way lose its centre.

K: But there are very few people who are concerned to be totally free from all this.

IM: But then, to put it somewhat bluntly, you want there to be more such people, but at the same time you reject traditional methods, for instance, ideas of duty, of asceticism and so on, which have been part of the training, as it were, of people who perhaps achieve this state.

K: Why should I be trained? If I see something to be true I stick to it. Why should I be trained?

IM: Yes, but you have probably had a gift of grace, of what a Christian would call grace, which a lot of people haven't had. What you achieve easily would be very, very difficult for the majority of people.

K: Perhaps that may be. But after all there must be . . . all right, if you use the word grace, all right. Be in a state to receive that, which means don't be selfish, don't have conflict, have some kind of inward silence.

IM: I agree entirely with that. Yes, don't let's argue about the question of influence or politics, because I understand your position there. I feel it is perhaps important to try in certain ways to influence one's surroundings, but I know that this is full of difficulties. I would rather in a way stick to the question we were worrying at earlier. It is partly to do with the question of time and fragmentation. That is, that time is fragmentation.

K: Yes, that's it. To be free of time, that means no movement forward.

IM: To be free, and in the truth and love, and not to be acquiring and not to be planning. If one had this kind of insight, or however you would put it, would one know that one had it?

K: I think one wouldn't know but it would show in your actions, in your daily life.

IM: But it seems to me that you are thinking in terms of two entirely different planes. And I am wanting to connect the two.

K: No, there is the physical plane.

IM: And also the psychological plane. That is what we are talking about.

K: Why should there be division of the psychological plane? Why should there be a superior psychology or lower psychology, it is a whole psychology?

IM: Yes. I mean, some kind of – I introduced the word – redemption . . .

K: It doesn't matter, I understand.

IM: . . . of the psychological hurly-burly of one's mind could happen it seems to me in a quite ordinary way. And people wouldn't be puzzled by it, it would just be a natural function.

K: You see, to be redeemed by whom? If I look to you to be redeemed I am lost.

IM: I am not thinking of being redeemed in the Christian sense. By 'redeemed' I mean that something which is fragmented is drawn in. I am using an image of a centre and of outlying parts. I am all the time trying to discover just where this divide is that you make between, say, the life of a very good man in the ordinary sense, an ordinary very virtuous man who is being very unselfish in the ordinary sense and has done a lot of good to people and so on, between that kind of life and the life of truth.

K: Ah, that is totally different.

IM: Well, why is it totally different?

K: Of course it is.

IM: I mean it seems to be a metaphysical remark to say it is totally different.

K: I know.

IM: You don't mind that?

K: I don't mind. After all, the self is a very subtle, cunning thing, it can hide under prayers.

IM: Oh, absolutely.

K: It can hide under every little action thinking it is noble, I am helping mankind, I am influencing it for the good.

IM: I am really a remarkable person admired by everybody – in brackets, as it were.

K: To understand what the self is requires such observation, such daily looking at it, not just saying, 'I am free at one moment', and saying that is it, it demands such attention to everything that you are doing.

IM: You think that if somebody was entirely absorbed in outward action, as it were, it wouldn't be in truth?

K: That is a most dangerous thing.

IM: So a certain amount of fundamental quietness could be compatible with leading an active life?

K: That silence is not the product of thought.

IM: Yes, OK, that's good.

K: That silence is not to be cultivated.

IM: Yes, I think I believe in that silence too.

K: Silence, quietness, inside there is no movement.

IM: And this would connect with what you say about living in the present and timelessness?

K: Yes. You know meditation is an extraordinary thing. I have talked to people who meditate, Tibetan, Hindu, Buddhist, Zen, you know all the rest of it – it is all a conscious deliberate effort. And it isn't something you do for the 'love' of it – you can 'love' and yet be selfish. I mean meditation in the sense of meditating without conscious effort.

IM: Yes, I think any means that one adopts towards goodness is likely to become a barrier.

K: Absolutely.

IM: It is likely to because one seeks idols, we are idol worshippers.

K: Then it is finished, that is not meditation.

IM: I mean if one seeks consolation in the feeling that you are doing something. But nevertheless doing it could help you.

K: No, I have talked to people who have spent years doing this – please, I mean it – a man came to me who was about seventy, much older than I was, and he said, 'I have spent twenty-five years in the jungle, wandering about begging and I have deceived myself all along'.

IM: Well, he should be congratulated, I suppose.

K: I know, that shows something.

IM: He was prepared to say something that people don't often admit.

K: To be really quiet is something you can't cultivate, you can't get it by practice. It is in your daily life that you have to be quiet.

IM: It comes by a gift perhaps.

K: Otherwise what is the value of your quietness if your daily life is not affected, if your daily life isn't without conflict?

IM: Well, of course, I want constantly to say that the connection with one's daily life is a fundamental idea. I mean if somebody claimed to have this quietness but behaved badly in ordinary life I would be sceptical.

K: I know, so would I.

IM: I think my own thoughts on this subject are influenced by Plato and I feel perhaps that something that you are insisting on, which he also insisted on, is the absolute separateness of this idea of the timeless and eternal. That it is quite separate from what we ordinarily think of as goodness, which is a kind of idolatry.

K: Yes, idolatry.

IM: And he uses the image of destroying idols. If you destroy images, you destroy idols and you move on. But he pictures life as a pilgrimage in a way in which I think you don't.

K: If I have no images in myself about anything, there is no self in that.

IM: You are really picturing what many spiritual people have thought of as the end of the journey, except that you want to insist that of course one is already in a sense potentially at the end.

K: One has to be careful of that too because the Hindus believe there is God, the *atman* inside and that gives you a chance to peel off your ignorance and then you will be as God! That is an

127

assumption. I don't want to assume anything.

IM: I wouldn't call it an assumption, because it is something I agree with.

K: But it is an assumption, an idea.

IM: Yes, this is a metaphysical or religious assertion – only you wouldn't want to use the word 'religious' because that might be misleading.

K: I am only suggesting that it is a concept that has been cultivated, which has been traditional and that has no meaning, because, look, I have this concept of 'God in me' and then I go off and kill somebody.

IM: Yes, anything involving the *idea* of a God is of course already in a sense an idol.

K: That is all I am saying. We are idol-worshippers, whether made by the hand or the mind.

IM: For you, there is the absoluteness of the division – and perhaps I see what you mean, I am not quite sure – between the ordinary process of life and this being-in-the-truth that is something which lives in the present in the way in which something eternal must live in the present. You must insist on it being quite separate from the worldly idols.

K: Absolutely, of course. After all Man's search has been for eternity. They make an idea of it . . .

IM: . . . which is not continuation of time, it is quite different.

K: It is the ending of time.

IM: Yes, well, I think, by thinking about Plato, I have come to some understanding of what you have been saying. Oh dear, thank you very much.

Is the Brain Different from a Computer?

Asit Chandmal, *computer specialist and consultant, and* **David Bohm**.

Krishnamurti: Asit and I have been talking about the nature of computers. I have also met several experts from America and India and as far as I understand, computers can perform some of the same functions as thought. They can learn, they can correct themselves, they can beat chess masters, they have their own artificial intelligence. They can be programmed and the more astute, clever and informed the programmer, the greater the capacity of the computer. It can also solve problems quicker than the human brain. Thought creates its own intelligence and computer intelligence is perhaps equal to that of the intelligence that thought has created. And just as the computer is programmed, so are we programmed, to a certain extent, to be Catholics, Protestants, Hindus, Buddhists and so on.

Now, what is true intelligence? There is the artificial intelligence of the computer and perhaps the intelligence created by thought is also artificial. So what is intelligence that doesn't belong to either? If the computer can do almost all the things that thought can do then what happens to Man? Man has lived by thought, has created this world of thought, not Nature, but the economic, social, religious world and the problems which thought has created, thought cannot solve. It may solve economic problems, it may solve our social problems, but I question whether it can ever solve the psychological problems. So if the computer takes over the activities of thought, and it can diagnose, correct itself, learn and so become more and more and more informed and function on its knowledge, as human beings do, what then is Man? That's the real question. Man has lived on memory, on experience, on

129

knowledge, all of which the computer can have because it can learn, correct itself and increase its knowledge, and perhaps discover new things. So what is going to happen to Man? You carry on from there.

David Bohm: Perhaps we should first discuss whether this is true. Because not everyone who works with computers accepts all this. For example, it doesn't look likely that computers will solve economic or political problems because these are connected with psychological problems. I think there is no doubt the computer can do a great many things which thought is doing, and can do many more, but whether it can do the whole of what thought is doing is not clear. You see, it is in the nature of thought itself that in order to carry out a logical train of thought it is necessary to make certain assumptions and categories and axioms, or whatever you want to call them, and the mathematician Goedel has shown that it is not possible to get a closed set of assumptions. If you say the assumptions are complete they will be inconsistent. In order to be consistent they must be incomplete, so there are more and more of them. The system is open rather than closed. The problem is this: a certain set of assumptions may be consistent in a certain context but if you want the computer to go outside that context, to run everything, then it is necessary to change the assumptions as you go along.

Asit Chandmal: Goedel's theory is a limitation on computers, and my contention is that the same limitation applies to the human brain.

DB: Well, in the human brain we can change the assumptions when we find they are not working.

AC: I'll explain what I mean. I am not saying that computers will ever become omniscient or omnipotent or become God and solve all problems. I am saying that whatever human thought can do computers can do. And human thought itself has tremendous limitations. Goedel's theorem, quite rightly, is a limitation on any logical system.

So two questions arise: one is, does the human brain also operate in the same way, making assumptions, extrapolations, using deductive, inductive logic and therefore having the same limitations as those imposed on the computer by Goedel's theorem? That's the first question. The second is: at what point do these limitations start applying to these very large computer systems? Do they, before these limitations start applying, get to a point where they are already performing much better than human brains? And the third point is that essentially, I think, what Goedel says is that a system on its own cannot be consistent and complete, there is no finite system. But if the system is unable to tackle a certain set of problems because you run into contradiction or incompleteness, you could have other computer systems tackling those problems.

DB: But they will run into the same problems.

AC: Yes, they will. But this is the way human beings function at the moment. The human brain has a limitation. Say I don't know much about medicine, I can go to a human brain who knows a great deal about medicine and together we try and solve my medical problems. But his brain also has limitations. So what I am saying is that computers do have limitations but so do human brains.

DB: Well, I question that. You see, I think people may actually happen to work that way but it is not necessary that they should. People may work in terms of fixed assumptions but there is no reason why they should do so, except out of habit or tradition. When you see an assumption is not working, then you can see the contradiction. Whether a computer can see contradiction I don't know.

AC: I think that could be done. You could programme a computer and show that there are no self-contradictory assumptions within it. But you would still have the other problem, incompleteness, but the consistency problem could be dealt with.

DB: Well, no, because you see there would always be new situations where any set of assumptions would fail to be consistent. You see, any set of assumptions is consistent in some limited context, but in some new context it may fail.

AC: Are you saying that the human brain doesn't operate that way?

DB: No, I think that the computer is a sort of tremendous simplification of the human brain, but I think the human brain is infinite, while the computer is finite.

AC: I am not clear on that. The human brain is programmed.

DB: Partly.

K: Yes, programmed.

AC: You are born with a set of programmes, right? The inherited programmes, for example, your heart starts functioning. The child is obviously programmed to learn – a six-month-old baby can't speak English or can't play chess; twenty years later it can, so obviously some programming process takes place.

DB: Well, it is not certain that any programme has made it learn. You see that is an assumption. It is very hard to prove a thing like that.

K: You said just now that the human brain is infinite, and personally I think it is. But just a minute. For that infinite to move, work, live, thought must come to an end.

DB: Well, we have to look at that and say what thought is. You may say there is a certain kind of thought that is programmed but there may be a more open kind of thought that is not.

AC: Is there such a thing? I would question that.

DB: Well, how could you show that there is or there isn't?

K: I think what he is saying is, since the brain is infinite . . .

AC: Which is also an assumption, we don't know.

K: No, I wouldn't call it an assumption. I think we can prove it.

AC: Let's keep it open, as an assumption.

K: For the moment let's call it an assumption; and you are saying there may be a different kind of thought that is not born of knowledge.

DB: Also, not limited by knowledge.

K: And that also.

AC: If one says there may be a different kind of thought not limited by knowledge, one would need to define thought. Or there might be a different kind of operation of the brain that is not limited by thought.

K: I would like to introduce another word, 'insight'. Right, sir? Insight is not the result of thought.

AC: Before we come to insight – let me put it this way: would you be comfortable with the use of the word 'thought' in another form? Thought is knowledge, memory. I am uncomfortable with any other sense and therefore we have chosen the word 'insight'. I think this is an important issue.

K: It is an important issue.

AC: The issue being that thought can never act except out of knowledge and memory. Because if that is so then the implication is that the computer can do this, and do it much better. And then what happens to human beings? Then it becomes very important to find the other thing.

K: Yes, now wait a minute. Thought is really the reaction or response to or the outcome of memory, knowledge, experience. It is a material process. We agree to that. So let's go into the question of intelligence first and then come back. From what Asit and others have said, the computer, by being programmed, and learning and discovering for itself new axioms and so on, has its own artificial intelligence.

DB: I wonder if it has intelligence in that sense.

K: They say it has.

AC: In the sense of the computer having done several things that five years ago nobody would have imagined it doing. There are examples which for most people would mean that it has discovered or invented new things or is capable of thinking. It has certainly demonstrated that it can find novel proofs for various theorems which nobody has thought of before. And the process of discovery can be defined as something that you have not been taught, nobody else has thought of, and you think of it. That is a reasonably good definition.

Then there is the Turing test – a human being in one room with a computer terminal and a computer in another room. And you converse on the terminal and don't know whether it is the computer responding or a human being. If you can't make out who is responding, then Turing argued, and most people accept it, that this is a valid test showing that the computer can think. There is the example of a grandmaster playing chess with a computer and not knowing whether he was playing against a computer or a human being, and as far as he was concerned it had passed the Turing test. There are other examples like this. This was some years ago and the rate of growth in the technology is so phenomenal that by now there must be many other examples. Inevitably by the end of the century you will have a computer capable of carrying on conversations on virtually everything and nobody will know the difference.

So if this is so, and computers are much faster and have more infallible memories than human beings, then two things could happen. One is that one might abdicate more and more the thinking functions to the computer, just as children do with calculators and forget how to multiply. Now will that atrophy the mind? One doesn't know. If it does, then the consequence is very dangerous. However, even if it doesn't atrophy the human mind, what is left of it if computers can outperform it, is there anything left at all? Are we in fact an endangered species, which so far has survived by using and improving the brain, but now something else is going to be much better than it, so will the species die out?

DB: I think there are two issues: one, that the computer will take over all these more mechanical functions of thought. I think that formal logic is mechanical, and I am not surprised that a computer can do it better than a man, because any form of logic consists of making certain assumptions and coming out with whatever that implies. As long as the assumptions are fixed, then the computer should eventually, even now perhaps, do it better than any human being.

AC: Yes, you agree that the computer can probably even now do a much more rigorous logical analysis of a situation given certain assumptions. So the question arises: is it only in the irrational area that the brain might be better than a computer? If I may put it that way!

DB: Well, only when the assumptions are not fixed. You see, as long as you can fix the assumptions the computer will work out all the consequences, but when you come to an area where the assumptions can't be fixed then I am not convinced that the computer can handle that.

AC: How do you mean by the assumptions not being fixed? When do human beings change assumptions? For example – let me try and give an example if I have understood you correctly. I try to run from here to Los Angeles and I find I can't do it, so I make the assumption that I can't run from here to Los Angeles and I try and catch a bus. Is that an example of an assumption? Can we give a better example?

DB: You see, I think there has been a tendency in modern mathematics to treat mathematics as nothing but formal logic. I think that is a very backward step, which is mechanical, and it is not surprising that eventually the computer will do this better. I think mathematics is more of an art form than a form of logic. Basically in mathematics you have an equation, you say A equals B, but it is only interesting when A is not equal to B. You assert the quality of things that are different. What that means is that it becomes interesting just when logic has broken down, when this indicates a new implicit structure which you perceive. So I think the interesting point about mathematics is not logic but proof, which is never perfect anyway because you can't be certain of it. But as you have pointed out, what mathematicians do regularly, and what a lot of what people do, is mechanical, and I am very ready to agree to that.

AC: What do human beings do with the human brain that is not mechanical?

DB: Well, what I just said, when the logic breaks down and you discover some new implications that no computer could discover unless it was told that was the sort of thing it should look for.

K: I would say, Asit, that insight is not mechanical.

AC: Insight being the ability or the process of seeing instantly through a problem. So no process or thought or logic is used.

K: Yes.

AC: It is not intuition, it is insight.

K: No, it is insight. That is not based on knowledge, not based on experience, remembrance, it is not involved in time. It is an insight, immediate perception, action. That's not mechanical.

AC: Are you also saying that in order for that to take place the mechanical must come to an end?

K: Obviously.

DB: Well, you can't be dominated by the mechanical. You see, the computer is controlled entirely by the mechanical, although you may make it more and more subtle.

AC: But the key point Krishnaji is making is that there is such a thing as insight that has nothing to do with knowledge, memory, experience and thought.

DB: I wouldn't say nothing, I would say that it is not based on assumptions made by thought.

K: That's right.

AC: Now in order for insight to take place, my question is: does this process have to come to an end?

DB: I think the mechanical, logical process must come to an end.

AC: It must come to an end. Now, if that is true intelligence, why do we continue in this mechanical process, why doesn't it come to an end?

K: That's a different question altogether.

AC: It is a different question. But this is why I have got so interested in computers. We only function in this, it doesn't come to an end.

DB: Unless you pull out the plug!

AC: Let me make my point clear. We are caught in this process, we are not coming out of it into insight. We only know this.

K: Yes, we are programmed to that.

AC: And the computer will be able to do this much better. So what is left of us?

K: That is what we are asking, the same thing.

DB: The more mechanical features of thought really can be done by a computer.

K: That's all.

DB: And many of these features which people thought were not mechanical are; a lot of mathematics is mechanical. You see, I think proofs are mechanical, they are merely worked out from the assumptions to the conclusions.

AC: Would you say Einstein's theory of relativity was something different from a child proving a theorem for the first time?

DB: It wasn't a proof, you see, there is no way to prove it. The perception, the insight of a need for relativity was a flash of perception, and from there on he began to work it out. And a lot of that was mechanical.

K: Insight is and working it out is mechanical.

DB: Well, relatively so anyway. You may need a bit more insight as you work it out.

K: Quite.

AC: So you are saying that the concept of relativity comes about through insight, a Beethoven symphony comes about through insight. And actually writing it out and playing it is mechanical. But there is this process of insight.

K: What are you trying to say, Asit?

AC: My point is that this obviously happens extremely rarely. How many Einsteins or Beethovens are there? Because almost all of us are caught in a process that the computer can do much better.

DB: I think the rarity is irrelevant. You see, it just happens that people tend to be caught in the mechanical. But the fact that it is rare doesn't make it less significant.

AC: No, but what I am saying is that for most people in this world, the only thing they have which makes them really function is their brains. That is the reason they have dominated this earth as opposed to any animal species. And if there is going to be another species that has a better brain in this sense . . .

DB: Well, I am not sure that it will.

K: That is an assumption. Asit, let's get something that is clear and simple. As far as I can make out – correct me, please – as we now use it thought is mechanical, based on experience, knowledge, memory.

DB: And logic.

K: And logic. From that there is action. From that action you learn, which is the same process going on. That is mechanical. And the machine can do that far better than us.

AC: Yes.

DB: There is a limit to that in the sense that any mechanical system being limited, and reality being unlimited, there must be some check by a human being who is beyond the mechanical, because at some stage the computer may do something disastrous . . .

AC: Well, so do human beings!

K: Of course.

DB: That's because human beings are imitating computers!

AC: What I am saying is – I am repeating myself: the computer is not going to be perfect but neither are human beings. But in the case of Einstein and Beethoven, I wouldn't say they have insight, they have partial insight. Look at their lives!

K: Of course, that's understood.

K: So we are saying, thought is mechanical because of what it is based on. And is there thought which is not mechanical?

DB: Perhaps there is.

K: There is, that's what we are inquiring into.

DB: Perhaps thought has become mechanical because it is being used wrongly.

K: Even if you used it rightly it is still not the other.

DB: No, but if you hold the assumption that it is absolutely fixed that is what makes it mechanical. Then it is like a machine. People have made assumptions about everything and say they are absolutely true, they are absolutely fixed. That makes thought mechanical. Now, intelligence does not make such fixed assumptions, but reads between the lines. So intelligence will gather information from all over without putting it into fixed categories. Thought is being mechanical because it puts information into predetermined, absolutely fixed, categories. That is what the computer does. In order to classify your information, it has to be gathered and put into categories, like here and there, now and then, before and after, inside and outside. Now if that is absolutely fixed the computer can . . .

K: . . . do it better.

DB: . . . do it better. But you see what happened, it seems to me, is that Man became a computer . . .

K: Became a computer!

DB: . . . and then he made another computer which . . .

K: You follow what he is saying?

AC: What he is saying is that human beings have become badly programmed by slow computers.

K: Therefore he has created a computer which will etc, etc . . .

AC: But are you also saying that a computer couldn't work in an unstructured situation?

DB: Unless there was some predetermined structure how could it work?

AC: That's what I am not sure about.

DB: I mean what could it do? It must be given some instructions.

K: It can learn.

DB: But only if it is given instructions before, it cannot learn from nothing.

AC: But is that different from human beings?

DB: Well, I think human beings have insight that can remove wrong structures, dissolve them and alter them. Of course, if you could make a computer with insight!

K: You see, the human being may have the capacity for insight. The computer has not that capacity because it is essentially programmed by a human mind that is itself limited.

DB: And also in the mechanical structure itself there is a limit to what it can do.

AC: Because it is a mechanical process, it is limited. In other words the question is: can you programme insight? Let us assume for the moment you can't. Come back to the human being. He is functioning as a computer, programmed as a computer. Now we are saying that he also has the capacity for insight.

K: The capacity. Yes, he may have the potential.

AC: If he doesn't have it he is doomed – would you agree?

K: Yes, of course.

AC: So it becomes very important to find this capacity.

K: That's right.

AC: How does it happen?

K: Now we are into quite a different question.

AC: Yes, but that is ultimately the question we keep coming to. It becomes vitally important to find that capacity. Especially because the computer is being developed so fast. Perhaps there was nothing so important two hundred years ago.

DB: It is hard to say. One doesn't know, every development rises up and reaches a curve and falls. I think there are no linear developments that go on for ever. The computer will go a long way but then it will probably reach a limit.

AC: At the moment it's kind of exponential . . .

DB: . . . on its way up but some day it is going to turn down.

AC: But leaving the timeframe out of it, it becomes vitally important to find this other capacity, if it exists.

K: Yes, sir. So what do we do?

AC: Now you are addressing a programmed slow computer to find the process of insight!

K: Yes, put it to the computer.

AC: You are telling me, find the process.

DB: You can't accept that that is all you are in the sense that you don't have a potential.

AC: I have the potential but how do I find, express that potential? Do you see the problem?

K: I see the problem.

AC: You are in fact asking a computer . . .

DB: It is not the same because if you asked a mechanical computer to have insight, that would be impossible.

AC: Yes, because it doesn't have the potential.

DB: It is limited.

AC: But you are asking a programmed system . . .

K: No, I am asking, as he pointed out at the beginning, whether there is that which is not programmed.

AC: There may be a process which is not programmed.

K: And that may be insight. And you are asking, as that insight is so important, how does it come about.

AC: How can it come about in a system that is operating in this manner?

K: Obviously, it cannot. If my mind, my brain, is programmed to function in a certain pattern, in a certain category and so on, all that has to stop. That is where the Hindus and meditation began. I am pretty sure of that. To stop the whole process of thought.

AC: May I ask you a question? You know me extremely well.

K: I hope so, I think so!

AC: Have you ever seen anything in the way that my mind operates which is different from a programmed, conditioned mind?

K: Yes.

AC: You have? I am asking this very seriously, sir. Because, all right, let me put it in another way: people operate only in this mode of the programmed, conditioned mind.

K: No, I am putting it differently. When you are not hearing with the sensory ear, but hearing inwardly, completely, in that state we are absolutely silent. When absolutely silent, then insight may take place. Perception in which there is no division as the 'me', the perceiver and the perceived – right? So the whole mechanical process of thinking, with its conflict, comes to an end.

DB: Well, as an interesting question, would you think that a computer has a division as the thinker and the thought?

K: Of course not. It can be programmed to say the observer is the observed!

DB: Well, I think the programmer is really the observer, isn't he?

K: Yes.

AC: I would like to say something about this. If a computer passes the Turing test, what is there to say that it doesn't have consciousness? What I am saying is that if there was a computer in the other room and a human being, and I am interacting from here, and I told nobody it was a human being answering on the computer, it would be fairly certain that the computer is at least thinking as well as that human being is.

K: Yes, mechanically.

DB: You see, you would have to have a much more subtle communication with it to determine whether the computer had insight.

AC: But how would you find out if I had insight or not?

DB: Well, that's a question.

AC: You see!

K: Oh, yes, you can.

AC: How, sir? If you could find out if I have insight . . .

K: Ah, not if you *have* insight. You may have the potentiality of it.

AC: Could you find that out by talking to me?

K: Oh, yes.

AC: Suppose you are talking to a computer.

K: I know what you are getting at.

AC: You might feel the computer has a potential, for instance. What I am saying is: what is consciousness? Why would you think that a computer doesn't have consciousness? If it prints out, 'I am conscious', why would you say it isn't? Why are we assuming – why should I assume, not you, that anything else exists?

K: No, I don't assume, because I have an insight and act on it.

AC: But I find that I don't have these insights.

K: Why?

AC: You must accept that.

K: No, why should I accept it?

AC: Because you see the way I live, sir.

K: No, you may have a partial insight.

AC: That's not insight.

DB: Why do you say it is not? I mean there would be a difference, the computer would not have a partial insight.

AC: What I am saying is this: if the computer passed the Turing test and says, 'I am conscious', what reason do you have to say it is not? In what way would it be different from a human being if it passed the Turing test?

DB: Suppose you were having a discussion of this kind with the computer . . .

K: Is it taking it all in?

DB: . . . the question is, what answers will the computer come up with?

AC: I am assuming that the computer has passed the Turing test.

DB: But the Turing test is not good enough because we could say that the full test for a human being is: does he have insight?

AC: But actually that is my question. How would you assume, how would you define insight?

K: I wouldn't ask a human being whether he has insight. That, I think, would be a wrong question. But I would ask: does the mechanical process of thinking ever stop? Or is the brain perpetually occupied?

AC: For most human beings it is perpetually occupied. Now, supposing a human being were to say, yes, it stops? What then?

K: Wait a minute. It may stop because it is very tired, or for various reasons, lack of oxygen and so on. That is not insight.

AC: The computer can do that.

K: Of course it can.

AC: So how would you find out if I have insight, sir?

K: But are you putting the right question?

AC: My question is: how do you know a human being has insight? How will you find out?

K: Both of you have said that Beethoven and Einstein had partial insight.

AC: Yes, but what I would argue is that what they did nobody had done before, what they did was extremely rare. There are, I think, four billion people on earth today, and there have been a lot in the past, and something happened to Einstein and Beethoven – that's all I am willing to say. I am not even willing to say that they had partial insight, I don't know what happened. How can one know?

K: I think one can observe it in oneself.

AC: Sir, may I ask you another question? If you understand something can you teach it to another human being?

K: If the other human being is willing to listen. To listen.

AC: In other words if the process by which Beethoven composed his symphonies and Einstein had his flashes of perception had been understood by them they could have explained it to another?

K: I think so.

AC: They obviously couldn't and didn't.

K: Insight can't be something totally disharmonious, a lack of harmony, it must be your whole way of life, your behaviour, everything must be as a whole. When that wholeness takes place there is immediate insight. I think that is how it operates. Would you agree to that?

DB: Yes, everything has to be together.

K: The decks have to be cleared!

AC: You are saying it is an integral process, it is not fragmented. Now I am asking you, and let us assume that you have this insight . . .

K: That's a different matter.

AC: If you understand the process . . .

K: Ah, not the process!

AC: I think we'll get it clear if I find the right word. If you find the conditions under which insight can come into being.

DB: There are no conditions.

AC: OK.

K: You see, you can answer it yourself, old boy.

AC: So I'll try to clarify it. Are you saying it just happens?

K: No, it is not by chance, not by calculation.

AC: Not by calculation, not by conscious effort. As you said in your books, it comes uninvited.

K: Uninvited in the sense that you see the problem, if there is a problem, and you don't analyze it, you see it as a whole.

AC: Now I am saying to you, sir, that I am unable to see it as a whole, help me. What would you do?

DB: Could I ask you a question here: is the computer talking?

AC: It is, you see. (laughs) I am asking you literally to programme me to have insight; I am!

DB: But the computer can't do this.

K: I don't know, perhaps it will, when it reaches its peak. (laughs)

AC: I agree that the computer can't do it, I am willing to accept that. I am saying that a human being can't do it either!

K: I am not sure, sir.

DB: But if the computer is saying this, it could just be the programme, couldn't it?

143

AC: I accept that the computer can't do it.

DB: No, but I am putting another question, on this very statement. You see we are doing, as it were, the Turing test now. You have said that you are a computer. So it's up to us to talk with the computer to see if it can answer the question.

AC: OK, I am willing to state that I am not a computer, I am the potential. I will have a completely open mind on this because I want insight, I really do. And I am saying, can you help me, can you teach me, can you show me? Is there any way you can do this? That's what I am saying.

K: Let us say that you have got quick insight into many things – I come to you and say, look, I would like to have that capacity. I may have the potentiality but I would like it to flower. What would be my question? That I would like to have it? When I ask that question it becomes mechanical. I don't know if you follow what I mean?

AC: I follow that.

K: So don't ask the question. When you ask that question, you are asking for a system, for a method – wait, wait – for some kind of information that you can manipulate, that you can organize, that you can categorize, and all the rest of it. Now if you asked a question without any of that; would you ask it?

AC: Yes.

K: No, wait!

AC: Sir, my question is very simple, give me an insight into insight for a moment. That is all. I don't want a system just to be able to repeat it.

K: I understand your question.

DB: You see, I think you are approaching it in the way a computer would. If the computer wanted an insight it would ask how and what to do to get it. It is just the question the computer *would* ask!

K: You follow what he is saying?

AC: I follow completely. In fact, sir, it is confirming what I am saying, that I can operate only like a computer. That is what I am saying.

K: Therefore don't operate like a computer. (laughter)

AC: Then my next question is, show me. This is the only thing I know, sir!

K: David, can you teach me – seriously, can you teach me a thing that you have grasped immediately, something whole? Can you inform me about it, teach me so that I can learn it?

DB: Not through a series of steps.

K: Can you convey that to me? That you have seen something as a whole and therefore acted as a total human being without any conflict, etc, etc. You act from *there*. And I come to you as your disciple, as whatever, and I say, please, inform me about it, tell me – whatever words you use – I want to capture the feeling of that, something instantly taking place. Right? That's what you are asking.

Now, wait a minute, we are going to inquire into this. What is the state of my mind that is asking this question? It is wanting something, it is grasping for something, it says, if I could have that my problems would be solved.

AC: That's one state. But I am not in that state right now. Shall I tell you the state I am in? Here is a man whom I have seen in daily life for many years and he has been talking about it for so long and obviously he has something and I want a glimpse of it, not so that my problems will be solved but I am really deeply interested, curious, deeply serious. He has been talking of it for so long, he is living it, he is doing it, what is it, why is it escaping me? That's the state I am in, not that I want to solve my problems.

K: No, again, what is the state of your mind when asking this question? What is the state of my mind when I go to David – I am going to call you David, for a long time I haven't – I go to David and say, look, you have this insight, you see things as a whole, I can't. I am not asking to have an insight in order to solve my problems, I am not interested in that. But I want to learn or comprehend or feel the quality of a mind that is whole. Do you see what has happened? I have reached a certain point in myself to ask that question. I don't know if I am making it clear?

AC: OK.

K: It is not mechanical. I have dropped the mechanical. Right? I have dropped it because I am much more interested in this, the mechanical is in abeyance.

AC: Yes, I think that is it. I might not have dropped it, but . . .

K: . . . it's in abeyance, it's down in the basement. Right?

AC: I am not sure about that.

K: You are getting what I am talking about? Is your mind free, not functioning mechanically, when you are asking the question?

AC: I am not sure.

K: Are you asking this question mechanically . . .

AC: No.

K: . . . or non-mechanically? Wait, stay. I go to him and I say, sir, I am quite sure I am not asking this question mechanically.

AC: I can't make that statement. I really don't know whether I am asking it mechanically, I really don't know.

K: Because I want to capture that.

AC: That I want to do.

K: I want to understand what that thing is, so my mind is absolutely not knowing.

AC: Yes.

K: Ah – not knowing, not expecting, not wanting!

AC: How can you say not wanting, not expecting?

K: Of course. Not expecting something from him. I come to him and say, sir, I want to understand this insight that may transform everything, etc.

AC: Isn't that expecting, wanting?

K: No, I want to *understand* it, to *feel* it, the contours of it, the smell of it.

DB: I think we should make it clear that there is a difference between expecting and what you are saying. You see, expecting would be to *already* have some feeling about what it is, right?

K: Of course, I am not expecting something.

AC: OK, in that sense I am not.

K: I don't know what it is.

AC: I don't know, I really don't.

K: So, therefore I am not waiting, as he says, not expecting.

AC: I am not, when I come to you.

K: Are you coming mechanically or non-mechanically?

AC: I don't know, sir.

K: Well, find out, sir. Is your question born out of mechanical response?

AC: No.

K: No, therefore I go to David – I am very clear on this – I see he has got this quality of insight, very strongly. He takes decisions, he does things without the operation of thought entering into his decisions, right? When he sees something it is not thought out, he sees non-mechanically but works it out mechanically.

AC: It can be supported by thought.

K: Supported by thought. So I am asking the question, knowing all this, I say, what is this insight? I am already in communication with it. You understand, sir?

DB: Why do you say you are already in communication with it?

K: Because my mind is free of the mechanical.

DB: Yes, well, that is the essence of insight. You are saying that insight is natural if the mind is not mechanical.

K: It is not mechanical, it is not born out of knowledge, it is not of time, it is immediate perception. And the computer can't do this. My brain is mechanical, has been mechanical for a million years, and David tells me, your brain is infinite. I see that immediately. David said that just now. When he said that I said, 'by Jove, it is so'.

AC: That was insight.

K: Nothing to do with logic.

AC: Yes, you saw it.

K: Not saw it. The infinite . . .

AC: It happened absolutely instantaneously.

K: Yes.

AC: My reaction is: I don't know, why do you say that? Prove it.

K: Which is mechanical.

AC: Yes, absolutely.

K: Which means what? You are listening with the sensory ear, which is mechanical.

AC: Yes.

DB: The sensory ear.

AC: I am saying that, sir, I am saying that I am doing that. And I see somebody else having insight and so I say . . .

K: Wait. You see, if David tells me, meditate, if he says make the mind quiet, if he says it is necessary to have an absolutely quiet brain in order for insight, which is non-mechanical, to take place, all those are time-binding. I don't know if you follow?

AC: Yes.

K: I dispense with all that. Then he said 'infinite'. Right?

AC: Yes, I saw your eyes light up. But you say you dispense with all that. That is certainly the process of insight.

K: When he said 'infinite', why didn't you jump?

AC: I explained why. My reaction is still like that; if you tell me the mind is infinite, I will still ask: why do you say that, could you prove it? I don't see that it is infinite.

K: Which means what? The mechanical brain is tremendously active.

AC: Yes.

K: Argument, logic, reason, opposing opinions, and so on. It is moving, moving. You are functioning with that programme.

AC: Yes.

K: Pull the plug out!

AC: You are right, we are back to that point.

K: Of course we are back to that point. David tells me one thing, which is, the brain is infinite. Because it is infinite it is not personal.

AC: I gather that intellectually. *You* have an insight that the brain is infinite. Somebody says the brain is infinite, you have an insight. And then you move from that, from insight to insight. Your process – please let me call it process – is moving from insight to insight.

K: Yes, sir.

AC: My process is moving from logic, it may be bad logic or good logic, observation, all that. Now I am saying that this stream and that stream . . .

K: . . . can't go together. Absolutely.

AC: And I can see that this stream creates a lot of problems. And so obviously most of the time when I want this insight it is to be free of problems. You are telling me, you are in this stream, jump out of it.

K: You can't. No, you can't jump out of it.

AC: End it.

K: Ah!

AC: That's what you are saying.

K: Pull the plug out!

AC: I am saying deeply, subconsciously as well as consciously, that I can't do it. It is the only thing I know. It would be almost tantamount to committing suicide.

K: Of course, of course, of course.

AC: You are saying drop the only thing you know: and I am saying that I would like to do it but I can't.

K: No, we must go back. David is telling me, as the brain is infinite, it's not personal, it's not your brain or my brain, that is very clear. It is not *your* brain, it is not *my* brain, right?

AC: Yes.

K: Therefore it is nothing to do with persons.

AC: Yes.

K: Do you see that very clearly? Wait, see it *immediately*!

AC: No, sir, the difference is – please let me explain this. I start by saying *if* the brain is infinite the rest of what you say follows. Whereas you are saying it is *obvious* that the brain is infinite, this is *obvious*.

K: Ah! Because when he said that I was listening to him. I wasn't arguing about it. I can argue afterwards. When he made that statement I was on top of it.

AC: I know.

K: Why? Analyze it. Why? I was listening, my mind was listening, inquiring, looking and David drops a stone in that and . . .! You are not listening, you are arguing, is this so, and so on.

AC: When you say you were listening, did you examine that statement at all?

K: No, I didn't examine it, it is so. From that immediately the brain is not personal. Because it is infinite, the brain can never be personal. Mechanical thought says, it is *my* brain.

AC: I follow that, sir. What you are saying is: insight is perception or listening without any examination, any analytical process at all.

K: Of course.

AC: But then how do you *know* it is so?

K: Because from that insight you can argue logically.

AC: If you couldn't argue it logically wouldn't it still be there?

K: There would be nothing there.

AC: It wouldn't be there?

K: No.

AC: So you are saying you see something and you can support it with logic?

K: Yes.

AC: So why isn't it called logic?

DB: If you start with logic, you are starting with your past assumptions that are wrong. You see the difficulty. When you start from insight, you start from something new, a new perception, from there you can go on to reason with that new perception. But if you start from logic, you must start from what you already know, which is always wrong, fundamentally.

K: Yes, of course.

AC: I won't accept this so easily.

K: This is simple.

DB: Well, it's bound to be wrong.

K: You said just now that thought is limited, thought is mechanical, logic is mechanical, right?

AC: Yes.

K: So with logic you can't come to the other. Once you have that insight, thought can operate logically.

AC: My point is: you are at the top of a mountain, you can climb down it, I am at the bottom. Now, either there are parallel paths and there is no meeting point at all, or if you can come down logically to this point I could climb up logically to that point.

K: It's nothing to do with logic, insight has nothing to do with logic.

AC: But you say you can support it by logic.

DB: I think you could say it could be unfolded logically to communicate. It's not really identical with the insight. Logical expression is a way of communicating *about* insight.

K: Yes, that's right.

AC: I am saying – please correct me if I am wrong – you cannot communicate it logically.

K: Logically you cannot communicate it, because logic is thought.

DB: You see, I think that insight changes the basis on which you reason. One begins by reasoning on a false basis, that's the normal basis; that is, from where you are you can't get anywhere. There is no way to get from where we are to anything else, but if you have an insight then that is no longer so, and your reasoning is coming from insight, not from what you already know.

AC: In fact if you have insight there is no need to reason it out, you have it. The reasoning process would be there only when you were trying to communicate something about it.

DB: Also to apply it. If you want to apply your insight to make a computer, for instance. From your insight, say, into gravitation, then you might use reason for something.

K: So we started out by saying that thought is mechanical. The computer is mechanical. What thought can do the computer can do, up to a certain point. But thought being mechanical, can never capture that which is non-mechanical. And insight is non-mechanical, totally non-mechanical. Now *listen* to that, don't argue. You have argued enough now to say thought is mechanical, computers are mechanical; whatever thought can do, up to a certain point the computer can do, it can learn, relearn, adjust, it can do all the kinds of thing that thought can do, based on knowledge and so on. We both agreed to that. David tells me it is perfectly right up to that point. But that doesn't bring about insight, he tells me. So I say, all right. I don't say, what am I to do? The moment I say, what am I to do, you are back in the cycle. Right? He tells me that. He says, see that very clearly and don't move away from that. We have argued about this mechanical process sufficiently. We can go into much more detail and so on but we have got the principle of it. Right? That's all. Don't move from there. Don't say, what is insight? If you don't move, it's there. I don't know if I've conveyed this.

AC: *Now* I am beginning to see what you are saying. Are you saying, *see* the mechanical process of your mind and just *see* it, that's all, and don't *move* from it, *see* it?

K: See it, see it completely. You can add little bits here and there, but you see thought is mechanical. The moment you move away from that it becomes mechanical. If you see that, stop there.

AC: Yes, any movement away from it is . . .

K: You see, movement is time, we have discussed this. Movement is time. If there is no movement of knowledge – after all, the ancient Hindus had this idea of Vedanta. Vedanta means to end knowledge. But we say, how am I to end it, and I'll practise this and do this and do that, which is still the same wheel going round and round.

[After a long pause] I think this is exactly what happened when the brother died, there was absolutely no moving from that.[1]

[1] This refers to his grief at the death of his much-loved brother, Nitya, in 1925.

151

AC: From that sorrow?

 K: From that sorrow, that shock, that feeling. Which means K didn't go after comfort, didn't go after reincarnation, didn't go after masters. I don't know if you follow?

AC: Yes, sir.

 K: There is no other path except that.

AC: The mind stayed with death, then.

 K: Yes, see what happens if you stay with death, its vitality.

Is There an Eastern Mind and a Western Mind?

Pupul Jayakar, author and former cultural adviser to Indira Gandhi.

Pupul Jayakar: Krishnaji, there is a strange phenomenon happening in the world today where the East reaches out to the West to find sustenance, and the West reaches out to the East for – in inverted commas – wisdom to fill some vacuum which exists. Would you say that there is an Indian mind that may have the same directions, or the same elements of sorrow, greed, anger, etc, as the Western mind, but where the ground from which these spring is different?

Krishnamurti: Are you asking whether Eastern thought, Eastern culture, the Eastern way of life, are different from those of the West?

PJ: Well obviously the Indian way of life is different from the West because the two are differently conditioned. But in a sense they complement each other.

K: In what way?

PJ: In the sense that the East, or more specifically India, lacks perhaps the precision for turning an abstraction into concrete action.

K: Are you saying that in India they live more in abstractions?

PJ: Yes, they are not so much concerned about action on the environment, action as such.

K: What would you say they are concerned with?

PJ: Today, of course, a great change is taking place and it is very difficult to say what the Indian mind is. Because at one level the Indian mind is now looking for the same material comforts . . .

K: . . . progress in the technological world, and applying it in daily life.

PJ: Yes, technological progress and consumerism. That has percolated very deep into the Indian spirit.

K: So what ultimately is the difference between the Indian mind, Indian culture, and the Western culture?

PJ: Perhaps, in spite of this material overtone, there is still a certain edge to the delving process, if I may put it that way – delving into the self, delving into the within, insights into things. For centuries the Indian mind has been nurtured on a ground of this feeling. Whereas, from the time of the Greeks, there has been a movement in the West away from that towards the outer, the environment.

K: I understand. But the other day I heard on television a well-known Indian say that nowadays technology in India is humanizing the Indian mind. I wonder what he meant by that – 'humanizing'? Instead of living in abstractions, theories, the complexity of ideation and so on, technology is bringing them down to earth?

PJ: Perhaps it is necessary to some extent.

K: Obviously it is necessary.

PJ: So if these two minds have a different essence . . .

K: I question that very much – whether thought is ever East or West. There is only thought, it is not Eastern thought or Western thought. The expression of thought may be different in India and the West, but it is still the process of thought.

PJ: But is it also not true that what the brain cells contain in the West and perhaps the centuries of knowledge and so-called wisdom of the East have given a content to the brain that make the East and West perceive in a different way?

K: I wonder if what you are saying is accurate. I would like to question it, if I may. I find when I go there, there is much more materialism now than there used to be – more concern with money, position, power and all that. Of course there is overpopulation and all the complexity of modern civilization. Are you saying that the Indian mind has a tendency towards an inward search, much more so than the West?

PJ: I would say so. Just as the Western mind has . . .

K: . . . a technological concern . . .

PJ: . . . not only technological but environmental . . .

K: Yes, environmental, economic and so on, ecological.

PJ: The outer. There is the inner environment and the outer environment. Put that way I would say that the outer environment has been the concern of the West and the inner environment has been the concern of the East, of India.

K: But that has been the concern of a very, very few people.

PJ: But it is only the few people who create the culture. How does culture come into being?

K: That is a question that we should discuss. But before we go into that, is there really a distinction between Eastern thought and Western thought? I would like to establish that. Or is there only this extraordinary phenomenon of the world being divided into the East and the West?

PJ: But what has divided it?

K: Geography, first; then politics, economics. India has a much more ancient civilization – if I can use that word – than the West. All that is the Indian mind – if you can use the word 'mind' with regard to all that. The Western world is much more concerned, as far as I can see, I may be mistaken, with worldly affairs.

PJ: But what turned it in that direction?

K: It is a much colder climate, and all the inventions, all the modern technology come from the northern part of the world, the northern people.

PJ: Yes, but if it was only climate then Africa, equatorial Africa, would have the same mind.

K: Of course it is not only climate. The whole so-called religious way of life in the West is very different from the East.

PJ: That's what I am saying. Somewhere along the line people of one racial stock seemingly divided.

K: Divided, yes, from Sumeria and so on.

PJ: And the direction in which the West turned was the discovery of their dialogue with nature, out of which arose technology, all the great scientific truths. India also had a dialogue with nature but of a different kind.

K: So are you saying that the Eastern mind, the Indian mind, is more concerned with religious matters than the West? Here in the West it is all rather superficial, though they think it is rather deep. And in India, tradition, literature and everything say that the world is not so important as the understanding of the self, the universe, the highest principle, Brahman.

PJ: The swiftness with which the mind can start the inquiry is perhaps different from the West, where inquiry, the great insights, have been in different directions.

K: Of course. But, here in the West, doubt, scepticism and questioning in religious matters are absolutely denied. Faith is all important here. In Indian religion, in Buddhism and so on, doubt, questioning, inquiry become all important.

PJ: So out of this today somehow both the cultures are in crisis.

K: Yes, of course. Would you say not only cultures, but the whole human consciousness is in crisis?

PJ: Would you distinguish human consciousness from culture? In a sense they are the same.

K: No, basically they are not different.

PJ: So the very root of the crisis is making the East and West search some way away from themselves. They feel an inadequacy so they turn to the other culture. It is happening in both of them.

K: But you see, Pupulji, I am asking whether in their search away from their materialistic outlook, if I may use that word, they have not been caught by all kinds of superstitious, romantic, occult ideas, with these gurus that come over here, and all the rest of it. What I want to find out is whether the crisis in human consciousness can not only be resolved, without war destroying humanity, but also whether human beings can ever go beyond their own limitation. I don't know if I am making myself clear?

PJ: Sir, may I just say this? The outer and the inner are like the material and the search within, two mirror images of these two directions in which Man has moved. The problem really is that if Man has to survive, the two have to be . . .

K: . . . they must live together.

PJ: Not live together, but a human culture must come into being that would contain both.

K: Now, what do you mean by that word 'culture'?

PJ: Isn't culture everything that the brain possesses?

K: That is, would you say the training and refining of the brain? And the expression of that refinement in action, behaviour, relationship, and also a process of inquiry that leads to something totally untouched by thought? I would say – *that* is culture.

PJ: Would you include inquiry in the field of culture?

K: Of course.

PJ: Isn't culture a closed circuit?

K: You can make it that way, or you can break it and go beyond.

PJ: As we understand it today, Krishnaji, it is our perception, the way we look at things, our thoughts, feelings, attitudes, the operation of our senses. You could keep on adding to this.

K: Yes, the religion, faith, belief, superstition.

PJ: The outer and the inner, which keeps on growing. It may be growing but it is all growing within that contour. And when you talk of a search that is in no way connected with this, would you include that search, inquiry, observation in the field of culture?

K: Of course. Would you say, I am just trying to clarify the matter, that the whole movement of culture is like a tide going out and coming in, like the sea going out and coming in? And human endeavour is this process of going out and coming in, and never inquiring whether that process can ever stop? What I mean is: we act and react. That's human nature, act and react, like the ebb and flow. I react, and out of that reaction act, and from that action react, back and forth. Now I am asking whether this reaction of reward and punishment can stop and take a totally different turn? We function, we live, and our reactions are based on reward and punishment. Physically, psychologically and in every way. And that's all we know, deeply. Now I am asking whether there is another sense of action that is not based on this action and reaction?

PJ: Yes, and this action and reaction is an impulse of the brain cells.

K: It is our conditioning.

PJ: It is the way the brain cells respond, and the way they receive through the senses.

K: Our question is really: what is culture?

PJ: What is culture, and we went into that. It can be expanded much further, but it still remains within the same field.

K: The same field, but you can enlarge the field.

PJ: Would you say then that culture is that which is contained in the brain cells?

K: Of course, all our past memories.

PJ: Is there anything else?

K: Now this is a difficult question because one must be very careful. If there is something else – if – then that something else can operate on the brain cells that are conditioned. Right? If there is something else in the brain, then the activity of that can bring about freedom from this narrow, limited culture. But is there something else within the brain?

PJ: But even physiologically they are saying nowadays that the operation of the brain cells uses a very minute portion of its capacity.

K: I know. Why?

PJ: Because conditioning limits it, and it has never been free of the processes that limit it.

K: Which means that thought is limited.

PJ: Yes, it has put all its eggs in one basket.

K: Thought is limited. And we are all functioning within that limitation, because experience, knowledge and memory are always limited. So thought is limited.

PJ: What place have the senses in the perceptive process in this?

K: That raises another question, which is: can the senses operate without the interference of thought?

PJ: As they operate today, Krishnaji, they seem to have one root. The movement of the senses is the movement of thought.

K: Therefore it is limited.

PJ: So when you ask is it possible for them to operate without the interference of thought, what does one do with a question of that type?

K: I am inquiring, with a lot of hesitation, and a certain amount of scepticism, whether the brain, which has evolved through thousands of years of experience, untold sorrow, loneliness, despair, and all the rest of it, and of search to escape from its own fears through every form of religious endeavour, whether those brain cells can ever change, bring about a mutation in themselves. Otherwise, a totally different new culture cannot be.

PJ: If they don't bring about a mutation in themselves and there is nothing else . . . you see this is a paradox.

K: I understand your question. It is also an everlasting one. I mean the Hindus raised it long ago, many centuries ago – you probably know much more about it than I do – they raised this question which is: is there an outside agency, God, the highest principle and so on. Whether that can operate on the conditioned brain.

PJ: Or can it awaken within the brain? There are two things. One is an outside agency or energy operating; or is there from within the brain cells, the untapped portion of the brain cells, an awakening that transforms?

K: Let's inquire, let's discuss it. Is there an outside agency, let's call it that for the moment, that will bring about a mutation in the brain cells which are conditioned?

PJ: The problem is that energy really never touches the brain cells. There are so many obstacles one has built that the flow of energy from nature never seems to touch and create.

K: Now, what are we two discussing?

PJ: We are discussing the possibility of a human culture that is neither of India nor of the West, which contains all mankind, if I may say so.

K: Humanity that is not Western or Eastern.

PJ: And where the division between the outer and the inner ends. And insight is insight, not insight into the outer or insight into the inner. Now for that to come about something has to happen in the brain.

K: Yes, I say it can happen. Without the idea that there is an outside agency that will somehow cleanse the brain that has been conditioned, or the inventing, which most religions have done, of an outside agency. Instead, can the conditioned brain awaken to its own conditioning and so perceive its own limitation, and stay there for a moment? I don't know if I am making my point clear. You see we are all the time, are we not, trying to act on the assumption that the doer is different from that which is being done. Suppose I realize, for example, that my brain is conditioned and so all my activity, my feelings, and my relationships with others are limited. I realize that. And then I say that limitation must be broken down. So I am operating on the limitation. But the 'I' is also limited, the 'I' is not separate from the other. Can we bridge that, see that the 'I' is not separate from the limitation which it is trying to break down? Both the limitation of the self and the limitation of the conditioning are similar, not separate. The 'I' is not separate from its own qualities.

PJ: And from what it observes.

K: With one part observing the other part.

159

PJ: When you say that all the time we are trying to do something . . .

 K: To operate on the other. Our whole life is that, apart from the technological world. I am this and I must change that. So the brain is now conditioned in this division of the actor being different from the action. And so that conditioning goes on. But when one realizes that the actor is the action, then the whole outlook changes altogether. Let's come back for the moment. We are asking, Pupulji, are we not, what brings about a change in the human brain?

PJ: That is really the crucial point. What is it that makes it end?

 K: Yes, let's go into it a little bit more. Man has lived on this earth for a million years, more or less. And psychologically we are as primitive as we were before. We have not basically changed very much, we are killing each other, we are seeking power, position, we are corrupt, with everything that human beings are doing in the world today, psychologically. What will make human beings, humanity, change all that?

PJ: Great insight.

 K: Wait. Insight. Now is so-called culture preventing all this? You understand my question? Take Indian culture, a few people, great thinkers in India, have gone into this question. And the majority of people just repeat, repeat, repeat. It is just tradition, a dead thing. They are living with a dead thing. And here, too, tradition has tremendous power . . .

PJ: Yes, because it is the other way – a few have great insights into science.

 K: So looking at all this, what will make human beings bring about a radical mutation in themselves? Culture has tried to bring about certain changes in human behaviour. And religions have said, behave this way, don't do this, don't kill, but they go on killing. Be brotherly, and they are not brotherly. Love one another, and they don't. These are the edicts, the sanctions, and we are doing quite the opposite.

PJ: But cultures have collapsed really.

 K: That's what I want to find out. Whether it has collapsed and it has no value at all any more, and so Man is now at a loss. If you go to America, for example, they have no tradition. Each one is doing what he likes, he is doing his thing! And they are doing the same thing here in a different way. So what will bring about a mutation in the brain cells?

PJ: What you are saying is that it doesn't matter whether the Indian matrix is different from the Western matrix, the problem is identical – the mutation in the human brain.

K: Yes, that's it. Let's stick to that. I mean, after all, Indians, even the poor Indians suffer as they suffer here – loneliness, despair, misery, all that, it is just the same as here. So let's forget the East and West and see what prevents this mutation taking place.

PJ: Sir, is there any other way but perceiving the actual?

K: The actual. That is what we have been maintaining for sixty years, that the 'what is', the actual, is more important than the idea of the actual. Ideals, concepts and conclusions have no value at all because you are away from the fact, from what is going on. Apparently that is tremendously difficult because we are caught up with ideas.

PJ: But in perceiving the actual there is no movement in the brain.

K: That's all I am saying. If one observes very carefully, facts in themselves bring about a change. I don't know if I am making this clear. Human sorrow is not Western sorrow or Eastern sorrow. It is human sorrow. And we are always trying to move away from sorrow. Now, could we understand the depth and the meaning of sorrow? – not understand intellectually but actually delve into the nature of sorrow – and sorrow is not yours or mine. So what is impeding or blocking the human brain from inquiring deeply within itself?

PJ: Sir, I want to ask one thing: you used the word delving, you used the words inquiring into oneself – both are words connected with movement. Yet you say the ending of movement is . . .

K: Of course. Movement is time, movement is thought, the ending of movement – can that really end, or do we think it can end? After all, the people who have somewhat gone into this kind of thing, both in the past and the present, have always divided the entity that inquires and that which is to be inquired into. That's my objection. I think that is the major block.

PJ: So when you use the word inquiry, do you use it as perception?

K: Perception, observing, watching. Now we will go into that in a minute. But I want to come back to this, if I may: what will make human beings alter – very simply put – the way they behave? Very simply put. This appalling brutality, what will change all this? Who will change it? Not the politicians, not the priests, not the people who are talking about the environment, the ecologists and so on. They are not changing human beings. Who will change it, if Man himself will not change, who will change it? The church has tried to change Man and hasn't succeeded. Religions have tried, throughout the world, to humanize, or make Man more intelligent, more considerate, affectionate and so on, they have not succeeded. Culture has not succeeded.

PJ: But you say all this, Krishnaji, but that in itself does not bring Man to the perception of that.

K: So what will make him? Say, for instance, you and another have this perception, I may not have it, so what effect has your perception on me? Again, if you have perception and power, position, I worship you or kill you. Right? So I am asking a much deeper question: I really want to find out why human beings, after so many millennia, are like this – one group against another group, one tribe against another tribe, one nation against another nation. The horror that is going on. A new culture, will that bring about a change? Does Man want to change? Or does he say, 'things are all right, let's go on. We will evolve to a certain stage eventually.'

PJ: Most people feel that.

K: Yes, that's what is so appalling about it. Give me another thousand years and we will eventually all be marvellous human beings, which is so absurd. And in the meantime we destroy each other.

PJ: Sir, may I ask you something? What is the actual moment, the actuality of facing the fact?

K: What is a fact, Pupul? We were discussing this the other day with a group of people here: a fact is that which has been done, remembered, and that which is being done now. Being done now, acting now, and that which has happened yesterday, and remembrance of that fact.

PJ: Or even the arising of a wave of fear, horror, anything.

K: Wait a minute. Let us be clear when you say, 'what is the fact?' The fact of yesterday, or last week's incident, is gone, but I remember it. There is remembrance of something pleasant or unpleasant that happened, a fact that is stored in the brain. And what is being done now is also a fact coloured by the past, controlled by the past, shaped by the past. So can I see *this whole movement as a fact*?

PJ: Seeing it as a fact . . .

K: The whole movement – the future, the present, the past.

PJ: Seeing it as a fact is seeing it without a cliché.

K: Without a cliché, without prejudice, without bias.

PJ: Or without anything surrounding it.

K: That's right. Which means what?

PJ: Negating, first of all, all the responses that arise.

K: Negating the remembrances. Just keep to that for the moment.

PJ: The remembrances that arise out of . . .

K: . . . the fact of last week's pleasure or pain, reward or punishment. Now is that possible?

PJ: Yes, that is possible because the very attention itself . . .

K: . . . dissipates remembrance. Which means: can the brain be so attentive that the incident that happened last week is ended, and not carried on in remembrance? My son is dead, and I have suffered. But the memory of that son has such great strength in my brain that I constantly remember it. So can the brain say, yes, my son is dead, that is the end of it? Go into it a little bit more. My son is dead. I remember all the things, etc, etc. There is a photograph of him on the piano or the mantelpiece, and there is this constant remembrance – flowing in and flowing out.

PJ: But the negating of that pain and the dissolving of this, doesn't it have a direct action on the brain?

K: That's what I am coming to. Which means what? My son is dead. That's a fact. I can't change a fact. He is gone. It sounds cruel to say it, but he is gone. But I am carrying him all the time, right? The brain is carrying him as memory, and the reminder is always there, I am carrying it on. I never say, he has *gone*, that's a *fact*. But I live on memories, which are dead things. Memories are not actual. And I am saying: the ending of the fact. My son is gone. It doesn't mean I have lost love, or anything. My son is gone, that's a fact.

PJ: What remains when that fact is perceived?

K: May I say something without being shocking? Nothing. My son or my brother, my wife, or whoever, is gone. Which is not an assertion of cruelty or denying my affection, my love. It is not denying the love *of* my son, but the *identification* of love *with* my son. I don't know if you see the difference.

PJ: You are drawing a distinction between love of my son and love . . .

K: . . . and love. If I love my son in the deepest sense of the word, I love humanity. It's not only I love my son, I love the whole human world, the earth, the trees, the whole universe. But that is a different matter.

So you asking a really good question, which is: what takes place when there is pure perception of the fact, without any bias, any kind of escape and so on? To see the fact completely, is that possible? When I am in sorrow over my son's death, I am lost, it is a great shock, it is something terrible that has taken place. And at that moment you can't say anything to the person. As he comes out of this confusion, loneliness, despair and sorrow, perhaps he will be sensitive enough to perceive this fact.

PJ: I come back always to this one thing: this perception of the fact, doesn't it demand . . .

K: . . . tremendous attention?

PJ: . . . a great deal of watching?

K: Watching, of course.

PJ: You can't tell a person who has just lost . . .

K: No, that would be cruel. But a man who says, my son is dead, death is common to all humanity, what is it all about . . .? A man who is sensitive, asking, inquiring, he is awake, he wants to find an answer to all this.

PJ: Sir, at one level it seems so simple.

K: And I think we must keep it simple, not bring in a lot of intellectual theories and ideas.

PJ: Then why do we – is the mind afraid of the simple?

K: No, I think we are so highly intellectual, it has been part of our education, of our culture. Ideas are tremendously important, concepts are seen as essential, it is part of our culture. The man who says, please, ideas are not very important, facts are, has to be extraordinarily simple.

PJ: You see, sir, what you are saying: in the whole field of Indian culture the highest is the dissolution of the self. And you talk of the dissolution of the fact, which is essentially the dissolution of the self.

K: Yes, but the dissolution of the self has become a concept. And we are worshipping a concept – as they are doing all over the world. Concepts are invented by thought, or through analysis and so on – people come to a concept and hold onto that concept as a most extraordinary thing.

So come back to the point: what will make human beings, throughout the world, behave? Not behave my way or your way. Behave in the sense of don't kill, don't be afraid, you know, have great affection and so on, what will bring that about? Nothing has succeeded. Knowledge hasn't helped Man. Right?

PJ: Isn't it because fear is his shadow?

K: Fear, and also we want to know what the future is.

PJ: Which is part of fear.

K: Yes, we want to know because – it is simple – we have sought security in so many things which have all failed. And now we say there must be security somewhere. And I question if there is security anywhere at all, even in God – which is a projection of one's own fears.

PJ: What is the action of this dissolution on the brain cells, on the brain itself?

K: I would use the word 'insight'. Insight is not a matter of memory, of knowledge and time, which are all thought. So I would say insight is the total absence of the whole movement of thought as time and remembrance. So there is direct perception. It is as though I have been going North for the last ten thousand years, and my brain is accustomed to going North, and somebody comes along and says, that will lead you nowhere, go East. When I turn round and go East the brain cells have changed. Because I have an insight that the North leads nowhere.

Wait, I will put it differently. The whole movement of thought, which is limited, is acting throughout the world now. It is the most important action, we are driven by thought. But thought will not solve any of our problems, except the technological ones. If I see that, I have stopped going North. I think that with the ending of a certain direction, the ending of a movement that has been going on for thousands of years, there is at that moment an insight that brings about a change, a mutation, in the brain cells. One sees this very clearly. But one asks, what will make humanity change?

What will make my son, my daughter change? They hear all this, they read something about it, from biologists and so on, psychologists, and they continue in their old way. Is the past tradition so strong? I have thought about myself for the last thousand years and I am still thinking about myself – 'I must fulfil myself, I must be great, I must become something.' This is my conditioning, this is my tradition. Is the past so tremendously strong? And the past is incarnating all the time. Is that part of our culture, to continue in our conditioning?

PJ: I would say that it is part of our culture.

K: Look at it. I have been watching this very seriously, how tradition is a tremendous stranglehold – not the tradition of superstition, I am not talking of that, but a continuity of something of the past that is moving, moving. The past carrying on with its own momentum. And we are that. Culture may be part of our hindrance, religious concepts may be our hindrance. So what is the brain to do? They are saying now that one part of the brain is old and the other part of the brain is something totally new, and that if we can open the door to the new there might be change. Because according to the specialists we are using only a very small part of our brain.

PJ: Obviously when there is attention the fragment has ended.

K: Yes, that's it. We can talk about it like this, ask what is attention, go into it, and at the end of it a listener says, 'all right, I understand all this, but I am what I am. I understand this intellectually, verbally, but it hasn't touched the depth of my being.'

PJ: But isn't it a question of that first contact with thought in the mind? I have a feeling, sir, that we *talk* about observing thought. That is an entirely different thing from the actual state of attention.

K: I understand that, but we are going away from the central issue. The world is becoming more and more superficial, more and more money-minded, power, position, fulfilment, identification, me, me, me. All this is being encouraged by everything around you. Now you who have travelled, who have also seen all this, what do you make of all this business? There are these extraordinarily intelligent, clever people, and the most stupid, neurotic people, the people who have come to a conclusion and never move from that, like the communists: the totalitarian world *is* that; they have come to a certain conclusion and that is final.

PJ: But those are all commitments that you can't touch. You can only touch the people who are not committed.

K: And who are the people who are not committed?

PJ: I would say that today that is the one sign of health.

K: Are they young people?

PJ: Today, as never before in the last twenty or thirty years, there are people who are not committed to anything.

K: I question that, I would really like to question that.

PJ: Really, sir, I would say so. On the one hand you see this tremendous deterioration of everything, on the other this movement away from a commitment. They may not know where to turn, they may not have a direction, they may . . .

K: But don't belong to anything.

PJ: They don't belong to anything.

K: There are people like that, I know. You see they become rather vague, they become rather confused.

PJ: Yes, because they translate into concepts. It is so easy to turn what *you* say into a concept.

K: Of course, of course.

PJ: And to have axioms that contain what you say. But a culture that is so living because it is only living on insight . . .

K: I wouldn't use the word culture.

PJ: But I am thinking of a human culture that perhaps will be the culture of the mind that dwells in insight. In such a state, if I may ask, what happens to all the civilizations that the world has seen and known?

K: Gone, like the Egyptian civilization.

PJ: No, they may have gone but they are still contained in the human race.

K: Yes, of course, it is the same.

PJ: But when you wipe out . . .

K: Which means, Pupulji, actually, what is freedom? Are we aware that we are prisoners of our own fantasies, imaginations, conclusions and ideas, are we *aware* of all that?

PJ: I think we are.

K: Pupul, if we are aware, attentive to all that, the thing is burnt up!

PJ: This is, of course, at some point where we can't . . . because you don't admit an in-between state.

K: No, that is impossible.

PJ: This is the whole problem.

K: It is like a man who is violent trying to be non-violent, in the in-between state he is violent.

PJ: No, not necessarily. Isn't that also a question of this whole movement of time?

K: Time and thought and so on, which is what? Limiting. If we first acknowledge, or see the fact that thought, in any direction, is limited, in any field – surgery, technology, computers and so on, and also thought inquiring into itself, thought being limited, your inquiry will be very, very limited.

PJ: The difference is, sir, I might see that, but the attention necessary for it to remain alive in my waking day is not there. It is the quantum, the capacity, the strength of that attention which . . .

K: You see, how do you have that passion? How do you have that sustained movement of energy which is not dissipated by thought, by any kind of activity? I think that only comes when you understand sorrow and the ending of sorrow, then there is compassion and love and all that. That intelligence is energy that has no depression.

PJ: You mean it neither rises nor falls?

K: No, how can it? To rise and fall you must be aware that it is rising and falling. Who is it who is aware?

PJ: But is it possible throughout the day to hold that . . .

K: It is there. You don't hold it, it is like a perfume that is there. That's why I think one has to understand the whole conditioning of our consciousness. I think that is the real study, real inquiry, to explore this consciousness which is the common ground of all humanity. And we never inquire into it; I don't mean inquire as a professor or a psychologist inquires, but we never say: yes, I am going to study, look into, this consciousness which is me.

PJ: No, one says that. I can't say that one doesn't, one does say that.

K: But one doesn't do it.

PJ: One does.

K: Partially.

PJ: I won't accept that, sir. One does it, one attends, one inquires.

K: So then what? Have you come to the end of it?

PJ: Suddenly one finds that one has been inattentive.

K: No, I don't think inattention matters. You may be tired because your brain has inquired enough, enough for today. There's nothing wrong with that. But you see again I object to this question of attention and inattention.

PJ: But that is the basic question in most of our minds.

K: I would not put it that way. I would say that where there is this total ending of something there is a new beginning that has its own momentum. It is nothing to do with me. That means one must be so completely free of the self. And to be free of the self is one of the most difficult things, because it hides under various rocks, behind various trees, various activities.

Is It Possible to End Fear?

Ronald Eyre, in his lifetime a writer and television producer.

Ronald Eyre: I would like to ask you about playfulness, which
matters to me more and more; knowing that if I tackle a piece of
work with a certain solemnity, it sort of destroys itself, but if there
is an element of playfulness in my approach, of letting it happen...
Krishnamurti: I wonder what you mean by that word.
RE: Well, you have an idea that you would like to carry out, so you
have the end in the beginning, you know what it is going to be.
What I mean by playfulness is allowing for things – thoughts or
notions – to come in that you hadn't expected.
K: Do you mean that when working you are concentrating, and
when that concentration is not focused, then the other things
come in?
RE: Yes, like many of us, I was brought up in a very puritanical way
to believe that effort was a fine thing. I believe I am having to
learn that effort is double-edged and can be oversolemn, it can
push you towards conclusions, blind and deafen you to all sorts
of things you should be seeing and hearing. I feel I need to sit
back and 'play' more. Does that make sense?
K: Letting other thoughts come in rather than having one
continuous effort and thought.
RE: And let it shift so that it shapes itself organically, maybe in a
direction you hadn't intended.
K: Would you say that distraction is necessary?
RE: It is distraction, isn't it. Perhaps one could call it mindful
distraction, but it is not merely being open to anything.
K: Not being empty-minded.
RE: That's right.

K: So concentration, with a sense of distraction of which you are aware.

RE: That feels quite important.

K: But when you are aware that it is distraction, is it distraction?

RE: Perhaps it is extremely subtle concentration. I feel also that an element of fear comes into it – that you may go wrong or something unwelcome may happen. Then it freezes you, and you think you are concentrating, but you are actually shutting out. Would you say that is correct?

K: Only partly. Can we discuss what concentration is and then come to the other? What do we mean when we say 'concentrate'? To focus one's thought?

RE: Focus feels as though your intention is maybe a little too much involved.

K: Yes, concentrate on what one is doing, don't let anything else come in.

RE: To be totally available to what one is doing is another way of putting it.

K: Yes, all right. What happens when one is so centred, focused? Aren't you shutting off every other form of thought, every other form of distraction, if we can use that word? So you build a wall around yourself and say, 'please, don't think of anything else, let's think about this.'

RE: When you said that you made a gesture that seemed slightly worried, you know, please don't bother me, I am concentrating on this. Although I certainly do that often, it seems to me to have fear in it and to be probably not so useful as an openness to something that merely, quietly, sets other things aside.

K: I am not sure.

RE: Ah, tell me more!

K: Could we begin by discussing what makes us concentrate? Having a motive, a direction, a purpose, intensified desire, which is will, and that says, 'this I must do, this is necessary'. I concentrate and therefore push aside every other thought that comes in. So I build a wall around myself for a moment, and that is a form of resistance. That is a form of – may I put it differently – a self-centred attempt to hold onto something, which then becomes fear.

RE: Yes, it seems clear that put like that this is a prelude to failure.

171

It's the thing that happens before you can't do it. So I am interested in the state beyond that in which you are really – let us say 'concentrating' again but perhaps there is another word – freely open and available for things to come in.

K: There is another word, which is 'attention'.

RE: Attention, that's better, yes.

K: But that is much more complicated. Not one is available, but to attend.

RE: In attention do you allow yourself to be surprised by things that come in to you?

K: I would like to discuss that a little. 'Attending' means giving all your energy, sensitivity, the whole nervous organism, so that not only your hearing, your eyes, but everything is tremendously alive. In that state of attention there is no centre as the 'me' attending. So there is no fear in that. I don't know if I am making myself clear.

RE: I understand, yes.

K: We have been trained from childhood to concentrate. Teachers say, 'concentrate, don't look out of the window'. But there is contradiction there, I want to look out of the window, so fear and effort begin.

RE: I think this is why I started talking about playfulness. I am interested in that very necessary and fearless attention you are talking about, which is not unserious but isn't solemn.

K: Attention is attention.

RE: It is just what it is. I am interested in the word 'play' because since childhood and professionally I have never tired of stories. That has been my burden and my pleasure, so I naturally work in the theatre, and tell stories to others and myself, or I write them. And then the word 'play', of course, happens to be the word given to these events and when I was in India making some films...

K: You have seen the statue of Shiva dancing?

RE: Absolutely. I wanted you to talk to me about that because it seems wonderful that the word 'play' should actually be the word to describe the way things are.

K: But dancing, playing football, golf and so on – why have those things now become important? Play is play. But when we play it is a release, away from concentration. That's what we are doing

– working all day in an office, nine to five, or whatever it is, and then going to a bar, seeking distraction through the cinema, this, that, the other, there is tremendous contradiction in that.

RE: None of that is play.

K: None of that is play, it is distraction. But suppose we drop the words 'distraction' and 'play' for the moment, then what happens?

RE: How do you mean?

K: I have been working in a factory and it is a terribly tiring, dirty, noisy, smelly job. I come home or go to a bar, and there I relax, have a drink and so on. I go home in that state of relaxation and my wife begins to quarrel, I get irritated and we keep that up between us. In between there is sex and all that, and I keep going on in the same way. So sex also becomes a distraction. You follow? The job, the whole thing forces me to distraction – the nightclub, and so on.

RE: Yes, I suppose I think of myself as very free-footed because I move from job to job. But in another sense I move from distraction to distraction, I actually move to another situation for comfort – if you take on a new job it feels comfortable temporarily, and then eventually it becomes its own straight-jacket and imprisons you, and you have to move from that prison. So I don't quite know – well, I know there must be an alternative!

K: You see in all this there is an element of fear. I am not doing my job properly, I drink too much, or there is too much sex, and I am losing my way. So this sets in motion a cycle of fear.

RE: Now we can't crack that cycle by *thinking* we can crack it, can we?

K: There is another question. Do we do anything that we love?

RE: Not much, if anything. (laughs)

K: If anything. One is forced by circumstances to specialize as a carpenter, a scientist or a writer. So gradually the brain itself becomes very narrow and limited. And that limitation itself becomes a bore. We want to break out of that, so then we go and play, there is beer, sex, nightclubs, golf, football.

RE: There is almost a process in each of these things. At the moment of change it is almost as though you are given a whiff of oxygen, of extra energy, but as soon as you get into the next phase of the distraction, beer, sex, or whatever it may be, it wears off and the oxygen then drains away.

K: So is there an energy that is not wasted at all? And therefore no fear?

RE: And can this energy ever be constantly available?

K: It is there.

RE: Is it there?

K: Of course. But I misuse it, I do something that I hate to do. I want to go for a walk on a lovely morning like this, but my wife says, let's go to church.

RE: Yes, that's right. So what are we frightened of then?

K: That is what I wanted to ask. Are we talking now, not of playing or not playing, but of the ending of fear, and therefore of living?

RE: Is it that we think we will die if we don't have the next diversion?

K: Of course, of course, there is this terrible fear of death.

RE: In many subtle forms.

K: Sir, I don't know if you want to go into all that.

RE: Please, I do, yes.

K: You see, this involves a becoming, not only a physical becoming – I am weak but I will get strong, I haven't done much running but I shall and will get physically fit. I make tremendous efforts towards that. They are all doing that nowadays, it is the fashion. Now, has that spilled over into the psychological realm? I don't know if I am conveying this.

RE: Yes, I understand. You mean we are not talking about the fear of death, we are talking in a way about trying to avoid the cycle of life.

K: Yes, so the whole way of living has become a movement of fear – fear of death, fear of losing a job, fear of my wife or husband, of not becoming successful. You follow? This whole way of living has become a process leading step by step to the ultimate fear of death.

RE: Yes, good, that's wonderful. All fear has these roots going back to the fear of death. If fear is to be absent at any moment it is a conquest of death.

K: No, the point is to understand living, the significance of living, not this perpetual battle, struggle, conflict, I must have more, be better, this constant measurement of myself with somebody else – he is famous so I must become famous, he is on television, I am not! This terrible sense of poverty; and in the attempt to be rich there is the burden of fear. I may never get rich because there is somebody much richer.

RE: So in a sense I see that these little prisons we inhabit one by one, these little distractions, are incomplete, there is something in us that knows they won't work. That is the cause of great misery. I mean, at least if you go into a place you think may be nice you are not deceiving yourself until it becomes nasty! There is something in us that knows that it doesn't work.

K: We know it doesn't work but we go on with it.

RE: Isn't that strange?

K: Like war, we know it is appalling, most wasteful, destructive. I heard the other day, when they had the D-Day celebrations, that twenty thousand young men were killed at the first attack. Twenty thousand! And the politicians pass over it.

RE: The problem is, isn't it, that if, for instance, you say you won't watch D-Day celebrations, or pour scorn on the whole thing of these memorials, you are considered to be disrespectful to those who died. But it's quite the opposite. I mean, it's infuriating! What you feel is, because I cared about those who died I don't want to have anything to do with the poppies. When I was making films about religion, I noticed that religions have obviously and frequently been used as havens from the fear of death. But one can't just stop there because anything, a house, a job or a distraction can be a religion in that sense, so the world isn't quite so tidy, is it? If we could say that only the religions are doing it we would feel free. But that isn't the case.

K: So what are we talking about?

RE: Well, about fear of death, I feel. Because I feel it to be pervasive and I can't understand why there is moment by moment in my life some sort of censor or judge...

K: Would you say death is part of play?

RE: Absolutely, in the sense that a good death is part of play.

K: What do you mean by a 'good death'?

RE: Well, perhaps it is like climbing something and maybe you fall off and don't care. That's what I mean by a 'good death'.

K: Say, for example, a very rich man who has got everything in life, writes books, and at the end of it says, 'I have had a jolly good life', and dies. And there are those who are paralysed or maimed and all those terrible ever-increasing cases in the world. To them, the invalids, the incurables, death may be an

175

extraordinary event. But are we talking about the fear of death or the fear of life, which makes us fearful of death?

RE: That's more like it.

K: So why are we afraid of life? What is the cause, what is the reason, what are the many reasons, that make one fearful of living?

RE: I wish I knew.

K: Let's discuss this. One reason is that from childhood I am forced to learn, memorize, and trained to meet, problems. One's brain has been conditioned to solve mathematical problems from childhood, college, university – problems, problems, problems. So the brain is conditioned to problems, and then when it meets one, its resolution of the problem makes it more complicated, the solution of it gives rise to ten other different problems. That is what the politicians are doing.

RE: Yes, as you describe it, our education seems to be a series of trial runs for solving problems. But the problem when it arises is never the problem that you have done the trial run on.

K: No, therefore what happens?

RE: You apply the rules you have learnt in the hope that they work.

K: They don't work.

RE: And they don't.

K: So that is one of the real problems of human beings, to approach a problem without having problems at all.

RE: Very good. In fact, I suppose the way you are taught defines the problem for you. But the problem may be quite different. So you can only solve the problems you have been taught to solve. You can only see as problems things that you have been taught to solve and there may be much greater and more terrifying things.

K: Therefore you approach a problem with a brain trained to problems. For instance, most religious people in the world believe in God and to reach the Godhead they believe you must torture yourself, fast, undergo every kind of denial – no sex, don't look around you, don't feel anything, control your desires. And we are conditioned to that. So to reach God I go through all that, and then I become a saint!

RE: It is crazy when you think about it. In Christian scriptures, for instance, there are numerous references to people who were outsiders, the prostitute and so on, but as the religion hardens in practice that goes, doesn't it?

K: It is crazy. So let's just look at it for a minute. We are afraid of living. Then we ask what is the significance, the meaning of life: and not finding any we invent – the philosophers, the specialists, the psychologists come in – we invent; and that invention becomes our security. I then hold onto that, fight for that, kill for that.

RE: It is like a poison, isn't it?

K: That's it, this is what is happening, sir.

RE: I will tell you a little story. When I came here for the first time there were two hours to wait and I was put in a room and shown videotapes of your talks. And after two hours I conceived quite a strong dislike for you.

K: Dislike, good.

RE: A strong dislike. Then I went with my dislike to have lunch, and heard a voice behind me say, 'you should try the grated carrot, it's very good', and that was you and we got on fine after that. Now the curious thing is that I was obviously manufacturing, I was trying to foresee what you were about. I was getting all sorts of notions and the effect of them was deeply depressing. And yet carrots and your presence were fine, I had no problem with that!

K: So we are discussing, aren't we, why life has become so meaningless. The tree or the tiger doesn't ask that question, it says, 'I am living'. If there is no conflict in one's life, no conflict whatever, one will never ask that question.

RE: The question of the meaninglessness of life.

K: The significance of life.

RE: Because implied in that question is an idea of some perfection that you ought to be having – which is another fiction. So we blunder from fiction to fiction.

K: From illusion to illusion, fantasy to fantasy, and so on. What makes human beings ask this question? It is because their own life has no meaning – going to the office from nine to five until you are sixty, with all the responsibilities, house, mortgage, insurance, the conflict in relationships and so on. And at sixty-five, seventy, eighty, you will pop off! And then you ask, what is the meaning of this? Next there is death. So then you say, 'I am going to die, I hope I will live next life.' That whole cycle begins: hope, despair, depression, fear. I have achieved so much in this life, what does it mean, coming to the end of it all? I was told of a man who was enormously rich, his cupboards were filled with gold, paper money of every description, especially Swiss. He was dying, and he said, 'as I can't take it with me, keep all the cupboards open so that I can look at it as I am dying.' Just think of it.

RE: What a last thought! I feel when we talk about death – we know it as the obscenity, as the thing that you may not talk about, in the last century it was sex, in this century we can't talk about death – I feel that the absence of really living with it, sitting with it, just makes our situation so impossible.

K: I am not sure it is that, sir. After all, death means total ending – all the memories, all the experiences, the knowledge, the attachments, the fears, the sorrows, the anxieties. Ending is like somebody cutting to pieces all the thread that you have gathered. We ought to discuss what ending is. Do we ever end? Or in the ending is there another continuity? What is ending? That is death. I may believe I shall be born again next life. I want to believe it, because it is comforting. It gives me great comfort to say, at least I have another chance.

RE: I see what you mean.

K: The whole Asiatic world believes in reincarnation. And some of that is accepted in the West now, books are written about it, people say, I believe in reincarnation.

RE: Yes, there is traditionally in this country a general belief in the afterlife.

K: In the Christian world they believe in a different form of it, resurrection and so on.

RE: This is a subtle way of keeping you quiet about what is going on now.

K: Yes, so there is death, ending, and there is living. The living has become so – we don't have to go into it that, we know it very well. And there is death waiting – not waiting – it is there, we are all going to pop off, die. That's the issue. There is a time interval, which may be five or fifty or a hundred years. And during that time interval I am living, acting, suffering, there is despair, all the rest of it. I haven't solved the problem raised by this way of living, found out whether there is a different way, in which there is no pain, no suffering. And then there is death, which is the ending of all that. Now, if there was no time interval, they would go together. Which means ending everything, everyday: your attachment; this is *my* school, *my* this, *my* that, you follow? That makes the brain so small, so limited.

RE: But our means of attachment are so extraordinary. For instance, one can congratulate oneself on getting rid of attachment A while B to Z line up to take over!

K: Yes, sir.

RE: It is an extraordinary, killing problem.

K: So is it possible to live without attachment?

RE: What do you think?

K: Oh yes, I think so. That is the only way to live, otherwise you go through hell. The only way is living so that life contains death, so that living is death. So that every day what you have collected, you put aside. If I am attached to this house, I know death will come and say, 'old boy, you can't be, this is the end of you', so I say, 'all right, I will be free of attachment to this house.' Be not attached.

RE: Unattached, and yet use the house. There is a problem here, because non-attachment can frequently take on forms of resistance.

K: You are completely free of it. Which means, I am living in this house, I am responsible for this house, for what is happening here, but also I am going to die. But while I am, this day, living, I am fully responsible.

RE: There must be something in us that thinks that life will hurt if we live it. It seems that while the mind will say, 'yes, I know that it's stupid to believe in whatever it is, relationships, drink or the job, as a haven', there must also be a subtle, quiet voice in the mind saying, 'the alternative is more terrifying'.

K: Yes. You see that's why one has to inquire, is there a becoming and therefore the ending of becoming is fear.

RE: The ending of becoming is fear – yes.

K: And is there psychological becoming at all? There is a becoming in the world in the sense that one is apprenticed to a master-carpenter and you gradually work with him until you become as good as he is. But that same attitude spills over, or is extended into, the other, the psychological, inner field – *I must*

become something. If I don't I am lost, I am a failure, I am
depressed, look, you have become something, I am nobody.

RE: That implies somehow that the later stage is preferable to the
earlier, that the master is preferable to the apprentice. I have a
feeling that the people I admire have, as well as their calendar age,
also stuck at another age. The people I really like have got that
curious, sort of wide-eyed thing. I am always a bit suspicious at the
thought of building up to anything, or a growth to something. And
any way that one tries to devise to break out of one's little prisons,
whatever it is, has fear written into it because it is just an idea.

K: Quite, so idea becomes fear.

RE: That's right. So the idea of liberation is fear. So we wait.

K: No.

RE: What do we do then?

K: We find out whether it is possible to end fear.

RE: To end fear.

K: Not a particular fear, but the whole tree of fear. And we are
trying to trim the fears.

RE: What is the axe? How do you get at it?

K: We will go into it. What is time? Not by the watch, the clock,
the sun rising, the sun setting.

RE: I think I can only understand time from something that is past.

K: Sir, you have said it. So time is that which has happened yesterday.

RE: That gives me the idea of time.

K: Yes, that which has happened yesterday, or a thousand
yesterdays, or the duration of the forty-five thousand years that
Man has supposed to have been on earth, which is in the present.

RE: Our thought is in the present and everything we know of the
past is in the present.

K: Yes, all that is in the present. And the future is the present.

RE: We assume there is going to be one and we make it into a
projection.

K: The future, tomorrow. And the past is now, in the present.

RE: That is how we must take it, yes.

K: That's so, an actuality. I remember meeting you last year, so
there is that duration of time, and the recognition, if I recognize
you, and the future is the same as now because I will meet you
again next year and say, 'hello, old boy'. So the future is also

now. The present contains the past, the present and the future. So there is no future. I don't know if you see this.

RE: Yes, I do see what you mean.

K: The future is what you are now.

RE: Yes, it is amazing how we inhabit this future, this invented future.

K: So the future is now. And if there is no breaking down now of the 'me', tomorrow I shall be exactly the same. So I question whether there is any psychological evolution at all.

RE: Yes, I do too.

K: There isn't any.

RE: There doesn't seem to be, except some fiction that somebody has invented.

K: So I see that for me there is no 'more' or 'better'. The better is future, is measurement, what I should be. And what I *should* be is an avoidance of what I *am*. So that creates a conflict. If I see actually, not theoretically or sentimentally, the actual fact that the whole of time is now and therefore there is no becoming, no ideal to be reached...

RE: That is such a radical thought. The feeling about it is that one has kind of heard it, it is familiar, but also desperately unfamiliar in challenging everything that one lives by. Tell me about this axe as well.

K: I am coming to that.

RE: Because I want to take it away!

K: Sir, what is change? If I change according to the future ideal, that ideal is projected by thought, in which time is also implied, thought is time. So if one really grasps the depth of this statement, or the feeling of *all time is now*, and there is therefore no tomorrow in the sense of I will be something tomorrow, there is an ending to conflict.

RE: Yes.

K: Which is an enormous factor. We have accepted conflict as a way of life, but now there is no conflict at all. That is, I have to understand change: I am this but if I don't change I will be exactly tomorrow what I am now. So I am asking whether there is psychological change at all? Or only 'what is', and the giving of attention to 'what is' is the ending of 'what is'. But one can't give total attention to 'what is' when you have an ideal.

RE: That's right.

K: I was once asked to speak to people at the United Nations. First of all, it is a contradiction in terms, United Nations. They have the ideal that we must gather together, become friends, and all that blah, and it never takes place. Because the principle is wrong – my country and your country, my God and your God. The Russians have their ideal and the others have theirs. So if one really realizes, feels the depth of this: all time, the whole of it, is now, it is like lightning that changes.

RE: When you say, all time is now, is 'now' always happy?

K: Why should it be happy?

RE: Quite, that's my point.

K: Why should it be anything? You know, there is something here that we should go into. What is it to be nothing? Because we want to be something. The wanting is a sense of lacking. I haven't got a good house, I want a better house. I don't know all the knowledge in books, I must read. So there is this tremendous craving. And what is the craving for? We want peace, we crave peace, and we live violently.

RE: We always look for the sources of the violence outside ourselves.

K: That's it, and therefore we say, non-violence. A human being is violent, living violently, fighting, quarrelling, in conflict, and at the same time he is working for peace!

RE: I'll tell you where my 'happy' came in – I wasn't using 'happy' in the sense that I think would cause a problem. It was just that I remember a big exhibition at Olympia: Mind, Spirit and something or other; and there were many little booths of various religious persuasions, and all the people in them were smiling. They were selling this sort of smiling, 'blissed out' quality. And I ached to have one booth where everybody had a splitting headache!

K: Quite! So, sir, the word 'change' implies, I am this, I must be that. We are conditioned from childhood to that.

RE: To expect.

K: So heavily conditioned. I see a small car, I must have a bigger car. I see you on television, and why am I not there! You know there is this tremendous craving, not just for publicity, but the inner craving for God, for illumination, for living a right life, that we must all be together. Why do we have such craving?

RE: I don't know. There is a great unlovedness about it, the feeling that you are not actually loved, and that possibly the larger car will put its arms round you in a way that the smaller car doesn't, will make up for it! It is a displaced feeling of lack of affection, I would have thought.

K: Partly. Is it the sense of insufficiency in oneself? I am not loved.

RE: That feels to me very real.

K: I am not loved. I am not loved by that woman or man and I must be loved by that woman or man. But that leads to another very complex question: what is love?

RE: I would tend to say, usually, possessiveness.

K: Of course it is. Possessiveness, attachment, jealousy, sexual pleasure, desire for more.

RE: It is also self-love.

K: We call all that area 'love'. Someone said to me, how can there be love without jealousy? Which means without hate! And one needs to ask too: what is the relationship between love and death? So there are these two questions: what is love, and what is that state of love with death? In the ordinary sense of the word 'love' is there any relationship at all? And if there is a relationship, how does that show, manifest itself?

RE: I see love in the ordinary sense we are talking about as a series of faulty insurance schemes against death, where the insurance house is bound to collapse. But you still take out the insurance.

K: First of all, we never ask that question.

RE: The connection between death and love, no. As we are plunging into love we certainly don't.

K: Now, if I put that question to you, if I may, what is your response to it, what is the relationship? Is there any relationship? If there is, what is its nature?

RE: Well, love in the sense of possession feels like an attempt to ward off death, to have it not happen. Possession, in the terms we are talking about, it is an attempt to have a permanence where there can be no permanence. So it is an attempt to contradict the fact that things die.

K: That's it. Death is impermanence.

RE: Death is impermanence, a permanent word to describe an impermanent happening.

K: Death is impermanence and possessiveness is hoping for permanence.

RE: Absolutely, an attempt to make it go on for ever. It is curious how cheap love poetry has always got everything going on for ever, while good love poetry is usually about things collapsing.

K: What is the relationship then? What is the relationship between darkness and light? That is, darkness, when there is no moonlight, no stars, nothing, the darkness in a forest. I have been in that, dark, absolutely impenetrable darkness. And the sun comes up and everything is light. What is the relationship between the two?

RE: You tell me.

K: I don't think there is any. Light is light. Let me put it another way. What is the relationship between good and bad, is there any relationship at all?

RE: Before talking of good and bad, let's take dark and light. If I am asked to describe something, I do need the presence of one before I can do the other. For instance, if I am describing this forest in which I can't see a tree, that is darkness, then of course when the light comes up the trees become visible.

K: So you are judging light and darkness according to your perception.

RE: Yes, that's right.

K: That's obvious. But move a little further, deeper. What is the relationship between that which is good and that which is so-called evil or bad? Is the good born out of the bad? Because I know what is bad, or experience that which is painful, and all the rest of it, I am moving from, or trying to get away from, the bad to the good.

RE: I would use good or bad to describe very temporary effects.

K: No, is good temporary? That which is good, that which is beautiful, is not temporary.

RE: Why not?

K: Let's look at the first question for a minute. If the good, or any other word you like to use, is the outcome of the bad, has its roots in the bad, then it is not good, it is part of the bad. So every opposite has its roots in its own opposite.

RE: Yes, I get that.

K: So is there a good which is not born out of the bad?

RE: Not something that I could give that word to, because we have already used it in a certain way.

K: Give it another word, it doesn't matter. These are good old-fashioned words, the good, the beautiful, the true. Now, I question altogether whether there is an opposite at all.

RE: To good, or to any opposite?

K: To any opposite. Of course there is man, woman, tall, short, I am not talking about that.

RE: These are conveniences.

K: Yes, apart from the convenience, is there something so absolute and not related to the relative?

RE: I would always be conditional myself about handling that. I couldn't do it in any way. I would be very frightened of people who do because they become murderers.

K: No, on the contrary!

RE: What do you mean?

K: I mean the freedom of goodness, not the misuse of freedom. The misuse of freedom is what is happening in the world. But freedom is good, it has the quality of goodness in it. I don't like to use the word moral virtue, that has no meaning, but that sense of depth in it.

RE: We are somehow alongside fear again, an absence of fear.

K: Of course. That's why we said, is it possible to be totally free of fear? Not just what might happen, of which I might be afraid, or that which has happened of which I am afraid, but these two elements, the past and the future, are the 'now'. So can the 'now', which is fear, be completely wiped away?

RE: The presence of 'now', as you handle it, is almost dependent on one's having these fictions of past and future with one.

K: That's right.

RE: So even to talk about 'now' is risky.

K: But one has to use that word. You are sitting there, I am sitting here, that's now.

RE: But you have to dig the scalpel further.

K: Of course. I mean, you have to have a little bit of subtlety in this!

RE: Yes, that's right. But the fear remains until the knife has gone much deeper.

K: Of course. So what is fear? Not theoretically, but actually in one's heart, in one's brain, what is fear, how does it come about? What is the source, the root, the beginning of it?

RE: Roughly, off the top of my head, it is a feeling of not being in the right place, of not feeling you are where you should be. An 'ought' is involved in fear, the ought to be.

K: We have said that. The ought to be, I ought to be. But what is the root of it? We said fear is like a vast tree. There is a marvellous tree here, an oak, it covers the ground, an acre. Now our fear is like that. But the root of that oak is there, in the centre, though the branches are enormous.

RE: What is the root, how would you describe the root? Or are you asking me to describe it?

K: Not to describe it. The *fact* of it is time and thought. Time and thought are the root of fear. We are trying to understand whether it is possible to be completely free, psychologically, of fear. And the root of that, the beginning from which the oak tree grows, and becomes enormous, the root of it is time and thought – time being, I will be, if I am not, I am frightened. Thought says, 'I have been, and my God, I hope I will be'.

RE: Is there a sort of fear that is not connected with thought? Or is all fear connected with thought?

K: It is all connected with thought.

RE: If suddenly something happens to you that terrifies the organism...

K: At that second there is no fear, but then thought comes in.

RE: Yes, thought intervenes rapidly, faster than light, and then there is reactive fear.

K: Then the question arises: can thought be active in certain areas, writing a letter, talking, being fully active there, and in other areas, in the psychological world, not active at all?

RE: Discursive thought I have never understood at all. I have never had any feeling even for putting sentences together. I have always felt that the things that make sense to me have always come like sudden flashes.

K: Our thought is linear.

RE: Well, we are trained in a linear way, but I have never felt comfortable with it. That's the schooling, isn't it, that's where you pass or fail your exams.

K: Thinking is always a series of connections, associations.

RE: So are you running a school here in Brockwood based on thought to stop thinking?

K: No, thought is absolutely necessary in certain areas, which also require a great deal of attention, knowledge, capacity, skill, ingenuity, and invention. But is it that this same activity has spilled over, extended into, the other area?

RE: Very good, that's excellent. To know *where* it is useful, to have it as a useful tool.

K: Of course. If I understand, really see the depth, the seriousness of that, then I will question why it is that thought is always moving, active, in the psychological world. The psychological world is the 'me', my consciousness, my failure, my success, my reputation, my 'I must be', my 'I must not be', my faith, my belief, my dogma, my religious attitude, politics, fear, pain, pleasure, suffering, all that is 'me'. All that is memory, the 'me' is memory.

RE: And the 'me', if you are brought up like a lot of us in this country...

K: ... all over the world.

RE: ... all over the world maybe, in a sort of Bunyan tradition of hold your own, you are responsible for yourself, I mean, again there is an element in that which makes sense. There is also an element in it that is quite destructive.

K: So thought and time are the root of fear. Then one asks the question: why does thought come into this area, the realm of the psyche?

RE: I wonder. It appears to stop danger. When you have a thought it is like asbestos to hold something hot, you have the illusion that the thought enables you to control something which in an uncontrolled state might be overwhelming.

K: So there is the thinker who holds something hot and thought that says, 'don't hold it'.

RE: Yes, beware.

K: So there are two separate entities. The thinker and the object of which you think. Now, what is the thinker?

RE: A thought.

K: Right, but thought says, 'I am the thinker *separate from.*'

RE: Yes.

K: To realize that the observer, the thinker, the experiencer and the observed, the thought, the experience are one, are not separate,

187

sir, that means a tremendous, inward, psychological revolution. It means there is no division, there is no conflict. And when you then give attention to the fact, the fact is burnt away. But thought will be kept to plant a tree, to bring that flower into being.

RE: That makes sense, yes.

K: So if you give attention to that, it will never create problems.

RE: Yes, I understand. Everything we are saying is bringing something to a T-junction. Because we can't conceive of it, it is uncomfortable for us to think that we have to shed various ways of handling the world.

K: The other day somebody said, 'you have to burn your icons'.

RE: Burn your icons, indeed. Yes, and that's uncomfortable, and there is no way past it.

K: So when you burn your icons, death is – you understand?

RE: Yes.

K: And also, I don't know if you have gone into this, not theoretically but actually, what then is creation? Not invention, I am not talking about that. Invention is born out of knowledge, the scientist can invent more atom bombs, or something new, but it is always born out of knowledge.

RE: Creation, then, in what sense?

K: Creation which is not born out of knowledge. Because knowledge is limited.

RE: Certainly in whatever I have done, in my humdrum way, there have been odd moments, writing something where certainly it was not any form of pre-knowledge that created it. My boundaries seemed to be almost illusory, I was not confined for some reason, and then something else is fed in, and you write or do something that has a muscle which is not yours.

K: No, let's be clear. Must creation always be expressed, be put into writing, expressed in a sculpture, in painting?

RE: No, I don't see why it should have to be expressed.

K: So if both of us see the fact that creation cannot be born out of knowledge...

RE: Yes, for sure.

K: There can be vast invention of various kinds, at various levels and so on, born out of knowledge. But is there a state of the brain or mind where knowledge is not?

RE: And where creation is? Well, I think there must be, I am sure that there is.

K: First of all, I who have been writing, or inventing, call that 'creation'. Or Leonardo paints something and I say, 'what a marvellous creation'. We have used that word to cover invention and also...

RE: ... to refer to a product. Thus when you get a sketch by a master, for example, an incomplete thing, part of a process, it somehow makes you tingle in a way that maybe the finished thing doesn't.

K: Of course.

RE: The patron, the man who has paid for the picture, somehow comes into it, frequently at the stage when it has to be completed. Whereas the energy, whatever was going on in the making of it, didn't have to push it to that conclusion, and is present at an early stage.

K: You see, this has been one of the most ancient questions: is there a state of mind, brain, where knowledge ends? Knowledge is useful in other directions, but don't let's confuse things. Only with the complete ending of knowledge is there something new. And *that* is creation.

RE: The end of knowledge is creation itself, yes.

K: That requires not a discipline of conformity but tremendous alertness, a sense of deep watchfulness so that the other doesn't slip in.

RE: You have to shed everything then, you wouldn't be who you are. It is a scary thought.

K: We had better stop now.

What Is Your Secret?

Bernard Levin, author, journalist, and broadcaster.

Bernard Levin: Krishnaji, what is the secret? What do you know that the rest of us don't know?

Krishnamurti: Oh, I don't know about that!

BL: But you must know something. Look at you – serene, realized, content, with no conflict – how have you managed it? What is it?

K: I have never had conflict in my life.

BL: No conflict? You must be almost unique among human beings if that's so.

K: It's not because of circumstances, because I was protected, because of any outside influence that kept me safe. I think it was a realization that conflict destroys not only the mind but the whole sensitivity of awareness. So I've never had conflict; which seemed quite natural to me, it wasn't an effort not to be in conflict.

BL: Well, for most of us it is an effort, so how can we conquer it?

K: I think it comes really when you have a direct perception that conflict destroys human dignity, a human sense of depth. If you have a deep insight into that, it stops immediately – for me.

BL: Ah, what about for *us*?

K: Oh yes, for everybody.

BL: For everybody? Then how do we obtain that? It's almost like finding Nirvana, finding the ultimate goal, isn't it?

K: No, the ultimate goal, if you can put it that way, is to find that which is completely sacred, totally uncontaminated by thought.

BL: Is thought the contaminant then?

K: Yes.

BL: You see, that is a very strange concept for most people.

K: It's not a concept, it's an actuality. Why do you reduce it to a concept?

BL: Well, because that is our way of thinking, we learn to think that thought itself is the most important, the strongest and most powerful means we have.

 K: Of course.

BL: And is that not so?

 K: But thought is very limited.

BL: Go on, why?

 K: Because it's born out of knowledge, out of memory, experience, so knowledge is never complete about anything.

BL: But what is *more* complete than that? You say born out of experience, memory, knowledge; of course it is, but how can we go beyond those?

 K: I think that comes really when you give thought its right place. You need thought to come here, you need thought to have all these lights and cameras and so on. You also need thought to build the atom bomb and the cruise missile. But thought is limited, it is conditioned by knowledge, which is never complete under any circumstances. So when one realizes that, then thought has its right place, then psychologically you don't build an image about yourself or about anything. You see facts as they are.

BL: We all like to think we do that all the time.

 K: Yes, but take for example all the religions, it doesn't matter if it's Christianity, Hinduism, Buddhism or Islam, they are based on thought. Thought, whatever it has created, is not sacred, all the rituals, all the things that go on in the name of God are not sacred.

BL: You're talking about the rituals, and about the structure, the hierarchies of the churches, but what about the original teaching? You wouldn't say that about the teaching, for example, of Christ or Buddha, would you?

 K: I would say that. Because they have been put into print and translated by Man to accommodate himself, they're called revelations in Christianity, and in Buddhism there is something definite handed down from the Buddha through his disciples, but that is still not a direct perception, direct understanding, a direct and vital insight into that which is eternal.

BL: But how else can such teaching be transmitted – after all you write books and appear on television?

 K: Yes, unfortunately.

BL: I mean, that is the way these things *are* transmitted – how else can they be transmitted?

K: If you could see, for example, that the word is not the thing, the book, whatever is printed, is not the real thing, they're only a means of communication by people who have seen something and then want to communicate it to others.

BL: Surely.

K: And during the communication it gets twisted and the person becomes all important, not what he said.

BL: Well, that I think is what I meant a moment ago about the churches. The churches institutionalize the great teacher, the great leader, the great seer and distort it, as you say, but that doesn't affect the teaching. After all, let us take something we're all familiar with – the Sermon on the Mount – Christ spoke those words, they have been written down and now we can read them for ourselves. They are still Christ's words, are they not?

K: Could we put the whole thing differently? One has to be a light to oneself.

BL: Hm, go on.

K: And you cannot possibly depend on anyone. You cannot have light from another, whoever it is – God or saviours or Buddhas – it cannot be handed down to another, one has to be totally, completely, a light to oneself. That doesn't mean selfishly, doesn't mean egocentric activity, on the contrary to be a light to oneself means to understand oneself so completely that in that understanding there is no distortion of what one is.

BL: Do you mean then that none of us needs any of this teaching handed down to us, that we can all discover these things for ourselves?

K: Every man is the story of mankind – obviously. And if one knows how to read oneself, the story of oneself, which is very complex, which needs a great deal of attention, one has a mind that doesn't distort facts, what is actually seen; with such an attentive, sensitive awareness, which is not a matter of effort, one can read about oneself without any illusion.

BL: But there's a fine line, I think, separating what you say about that attention from what we do most of the time, which is to concentrate on ourselves.

K: That is merely egocentric activity.

BL: Well, indeed, of course it is but then we *are* egocentric.

K: So as we are egocentric, and that's creating havoc in the world, why don't we realize the mischief that we are bringing about?

BL: Well, that's a question I should ask you – why don't we realize it?

K: Either we are totally indifferent to the world and what is happening or we are so consumed by our own desires and pleasures that it doesn't matter what happens as long as we fulfil.

BL: But must we not even seek happiness?

K: Happiness is a side-effect, not an end in itself.

BL: No, but I mean let's take happiness that does not depend upon anyone else's suffering, let us say that no one else is harmed, is it wrong then to seek the condition of happiness for ourselves or indeed for others – for our loved ones?

K: What do you mean by that word 'happiness'?

BL: Well, what the world means by it is innocent pleasure, if you like.

K: That's all. As long as one has pleasure you call that happiness. Is pleasure love, is love desire?

BL: Well, it is part of it clearly.

K: No, no.

BL: I mean that is how we use the word, as we live it at the moment.

K: Yes, we accept that, that's our human condition, and we never seem to break through it. So what will make human beings throughout the world break through it, finish with all this?

BL: But why should we, after all love is one of the most – I mean I want to know what you think about this, I'm not telling you – but is not love one of the most beneficial aspects of mankind?

K: It is, but it is not to be identified with desire, with pleasure, sex, fulfilment, a sense of having fun in life, all that which is *called* love. I think that is not love.

BL: What is?

K: I think one can come to realize what love and compassion, which are also intelligence, really are, when we discover what love is not – it is certainly not ambition.

BL: I can see that is true of selfish ambition, ambition to exert power over people. But what about the ambition to do good, to help people?

K: You *do* good, you're not *ambitious* to do good, then it becomes selfish, a self-centred activity, you *do* good, finish.

BL: But we live in a world which depends on these things, don't we?

K: We live in a world that thought has created, we live in a world where we have given tremendous importance to thought, and thought has created all these problems, the atom bomb, wars and the instruments of war, national divisions, religious divisions.

BL: It has indeed created those things but has it not also created good things in the world?

K: I was going to say that – surgery, medicine.

BL: And art.

K: Art, all the other things, of course. But the most destructive part of thought is that under which we are living, with eternal wars. And nobody seems able to stop it, nobody wants to stop it, because of commercialism and all the rest of it.

BL: Well then how can we stop it? And we'd better start I suppose with ourselves.

K: Yes, that's all.

BL: How do we do that?

K: After all, human consciousness is the consciousness of mankind. It's not my consciousness or your consciousness, it's the consciousness of humanity, and the content of that consciousness is put there by thought, greed, envy, ambition, all the conflicts, misery, suffering, an extraordinary sense of isolation, loneliness, despair, anxiety, all that is there in our consciousness. Belief – I believe in God, I believe in faith, and belief brings about atrophy of the brain.

BL: But do you reject belief itself?

K: Yes.

BL: You do?

K: Completely.

BL: You don't leave much standing do you, Krishnaji!

K: Of course not, that's why I said one has to be free of all the illusions that thought has created to see something really sacred which comes about through right meditation.

BL: And what is *right* meditation? You are suggesting that there is also a wrong meditation.

K: Oh, all the meditations and all the rest of it being put forward now by the gurus (laughing) are nonsense.

BL: Why?

K: Because first you must put the house in order.

BL: But isn't this the way to put it in order?

K: Ah, you see, that's wrong. They think that by meditating you put the house in order.

BL: And that is not so?

K: No, on the contrary you must put the house in order first, otherwise if you don't it becomes an escape.

BL: But we need surely to escape from the ego, from the self, from these desires, these demands in ourselves, and surely the silence of meditation is a valid path to that, isn't it?

K: You see, this question is very complex. Putting the house in order means no fear, the understanding of pleasure, the ending of sorrow. From that arise compassion, intelligence, and the process of that – we'll call it process for the moment – is part of meditation and then to find out whether thought can ever stop, which means time has to have a stop. And then out of that comes the great silence, and it is in that silence that one can find that which is sacred.

BL: Well, as far as I'm concerned, and I'm sure this is true of most people, to stop thought, to switch off the mind is the most difficult thing in life.

K: You see it is again rather complex. Who is it that switches off the mind?

BL: I suppose what I have to say is, it is the mind itself.

K: Itself.

BL: Which I suppose is impossible.

K: No, when one realizes that the observer is the observed, the controller is the controlled, the experiencer is the experience, when one realizes it not intellectually, verbally, but actually, profoundly, then that very perception stops it. It's like seeing danger. If you see danger you move away from it. For example, a human being who is perpetually in conflict may 'meditate', he may do all kinds of things but the conflict still goes on; but when he sees the psychological danger, the poison of conflict, then he'll stop it, there's an end of it.

BL: But from what you say, it seems to me that there is no path to this.

K: Oh, no.

BL: Well, how do we get there? I mean to get somewhere where there is no path seems to be a very difficult idea indeed.

K: Look, these paths have been laid down by thought, there's the whole Hindu idea of progression, the Buddhist, the Christian way, but truth is not a fixed point. So you can't have a path to it.

BL: But there must be a path, or I hope there's a path, to the ending of conflict.

K: There is no path, but there is an ending of conflict, sorrow and all that when one realizes – no, let's put it this way, when there's actual sensitive awareness of what one is without any distortion, awareness of it without any choice, out of that there's the ending of all this mess.

BL: Well, when you say that there is only this awareness of what one is, full awareness without choice, without illusion, it sounds as though we all have to sit around waiting for instant revelation.

K: Oh, then you can sit around for a million years!

BL: Exactly.

K: As we have done.

BL: Indeed we have.

K: You see, then we have to find out what action is. Is there an action that doesn't create conflict, in which there is no regret, which under all circumstances, whether we live in a poor or an affluent society, is and must always be correct? To find that out one has to go into the question of what our action is now. It is either idealistic action concerned with the future or it is action based on past memories, which is knowledge. Now, is there an action independent of the future, of time? That's the whole point, isn't it?

BL: We can't stop time in its tracks, it rolls on.

K: Time by the watch, by the day, goes on, but is there psychological, inward time? There isn't, we have created that set-up.

BL: So it seems then that whatever the thing is, it is complete and instantaneous, it is not something you build up layer by layer.

K: Absolutely not. There is not a gradual process; then it is not enlightenment, because you allow time into it to gradually become something.

BL: You know, in this context I would like to ask you something. You have a school here, what do you teach the children? If you cannot build this up for them, for any of us, old or young I presume – what do you teach?

K: The academic subjects.

BL: Yes, but in these areas...

K: Of course, and also point out all this. How to live correctly, what it means.

BL: Philosophers throughout the ages have discussed that very point, how to live correctly – right living, as Socrates called it.

K: Yes, right living.

BL: Can you teach that?

K: You can point out. You can say don't be a slave to society, don't be this or that, but you have to show it, to point out, then it's up to them.

BL: But can we live in the real world that we do live in where we have to catch trains and go to offices and buy bread in the shop...?

K: Yes, I've done all those.

BL: How can we combine all the pressures of the mundane around us?

K: I wouldn't do anything under pressure.

BL: You wouldn't – I wish *I* didn't!

K: No, I refuse to be under pressure, either intellectually or psychologically. I don't mind starving, I don't mind having no job, but I refuse to be put in that position.

BL: You see this is what I really meant when I asked what is the secret, because you say you will never be put under pressure, and indeed I can see and understand that, one has only to look at you or read or listen to you to know that, but what about the rest of us? How do we get out from under the burden?

K: If we all say we won't be under pressure...

BL: We all are under pressure all the time.

K: No, we won't be.

BL: How can we refuse it? How can we live in the real world, the job is waiting for us, we're going to be late, we've got an appointment.

K: Just a minute, that brings up the issue whether society can be changed. The communists and the socialists have tried it, various systems are trying to change society. Now, what is society? It's an abstraction from our personal relationship. If our personal relationship changes radically, society changes. But we're not willing to change, we admit wars, we accept all this terrible state of existence.

BL: Yes, we do. How do we stop it?

K: Revolt against it. Not revolt by becoming a communist or that kind of stuff but revolt psychologically against it.

BL: But that presumably must be done by each individual. This is not something that can be done collectively.

K: Again, what do you mean by 'individual'?

BL: Well, we're all independent, separate personalities.

K: Are we?

BL: Well, aren't we?

K: I doubt it. We're not individuals, we are the result of a million years of collective experiences, memories, all that. We think we are individuals, we think we are free, we are not. To us freedom means choice. Choice means confusion, you don't choose if you are clear.

BL: You said once, one of your most striking phrases as I remember, that your purpose was to set Man free.

K: Yes, it sounds... (laughs)

BL: It's the most important thing in the world after all, but how do you go about that? How do we set ourselves free, because presumably *we* have to set ourselves free is what you meant. How do we set ourselves free?

K: To be aware of our conditioning. What is our conditioning?

BL: Well, that surely varies from individual to individual.

K: I doubt it. We are conditioned by fear, conditioned by pleasure, which are common to all mankind. We are conditioned by our anxieties, our loneliness, our desperate uncertainty, all these are the factors that condition the mind.

BL: And can we simply put them aside?

K: No, you put a wrong question there; if one sees the consequences, the pain, everything this conditioning entails, it stops naturally. That is intelligence, there is no entity which says I must stop it.

BL: And then we are free?

K: What do you mean by 'free'?

BL: Well, what I mean by it is to be rid of these fears, anxieties, these impossible desires, vain yearnings.

K: Yes, that is freedom.

BL: It certainly seems so to me.

K: Unless there is that freedom you cannot be a light to yourself, unless there is that freedom, meditation is meaningless.

BL: You see, everybody thinks it is the other way round. You have reversed this, haven't you?

K: That is a fact.

BL: We think of the systems, the beliefs, the faith, the work as a means to getting to this state of freedom, but you start with a state of freedom.

K: Belief atrophies the brain. If you keep on repeating, repeating, as they do, your brain atrophies.

BL: Then can we just do it by one great leap into freedom?

K: Yes, that is by insight into all this.

BL: Instantaneously? And any of us can do it?

K: Yes, anybody who is attentive, inquiring, exploring, who is trying to understand this terrible confusion of life.

BL: At any age?

K: No, of course not, a baby, a child, can't do it!

BL: But we don't have to spend a lifetime in practising it?

K: Of course not. Death is waiting for you.

BL: It is waiting for all of us.

K: For all of us.

BL: Thank you very much, Krishnamurti.

Can One Have Lucidity in this Confused World?

Huston Smith, *professor of philosophy at the Massachusetts Institute of Technology.*

Huston Smith: Krishnamurti, maybe I have only one question which in one way or another I will be coming back to in various ways. Living as we are in this confused and confusing world, torn by conflicting voices without and conflicting tensions within, with hearts that seem star-crossed and tensions that never go, is it possible in such a life, such a world, to live with total lucidity? And if so, how?

Krishnamurti: I wonder, sir, what you mean by that word 'lucidity'. I wonder whether you mean clarity.

HS: That's what comes to mind first, yes.

K: Is this clarity a matter of intellectual perception or is it a perception not merely with a fragment of your being, but with the totality of one's being?

HS: It certainly has the ring of the latter.

K: It is not fragmentary, and therefore it is not intellectual, emotional or sentimental. So is it possible in this confused world, with so many contradictions, not only outwardly with such misery and starvation, while there are many rich societies, but also inwardly, where there is such insufficiency psychologically, can a human being living in this world find within himself a clarity that is constant, that is true in the sense of not contradictory, is it possible for a human being to find this?

HS: That's my question.

K: I don't see why it shouldn't be found by anybody who is really quite serious. Most of us are not serious at all, we want to be entertained, to be told what to do, we want someone else to tell us how to live, what this clarity is, what truth is, what God is, what righteous behaviour is, and so on. Now if one could discard completely all the authority of psychological specialists and also of the specialists in religion, if one could really deeply negate all authority of that kind, then one would be relying totally on oneself.

HS: Well, I may be right off-centre, and contradicting what you are suggesting, because now you have said it seems to you possible, my immediate impulse is to ask you – how?

K: Wait, sir.

HS: But you would say I am looking to authority.

K: What is necessary is freedom from authority, not the 'how'. The 'how' implies a method, a system, a way trodden by others, and someone to tell you: do this and you will find it.

HS: Now, are you saying that to ask you how this lucidity is to be achieved is an inappropriate question?

K: No, not at all. But the 'how' implies a method, a system. The moment you have a system and method you become mechanical, you just do what you are told. That's not clarity. It is like a child being told by its mother what it should be from morning 'til night and therefore it becomes dependent on the mother or father. So to have clarity, the first essential is freedom, freedom from authority.

HS: I feel in a kind of bind here, because this freedom is attractive and I want to go towards that, but I also want to pick your mind and ask you how to proceed? Am I moving away from my freedom if I ask that?

K: No, but I am pointing out the difficulty, the implication of the word 'how'. It implies intrinsically a mind that says: please tell me what to do.

HS: Yes, but I ask again, is that a mistaken, a wrong question?

K: I think that it is. If you ask, what are the things, the obstructions that prevent clarity, then we can go into it. But if you say right from the beginning, what is the method – well, there have been a dozen methods and they have all failed, they have not produced clarity, enlightenment, or a state of peace in Man. On the contrary these methods have divided Man; you have your method, and somebody else has his method, and these methods are everlastingly quarrelling with each other.

HS: Are you saying that once you abstract certain principles and formulate them into a method, this becomes too crude to meet the intricacies?

K: That's right, the intricacies, the complexities and the living quality of clarity.

HS: So that the 'how' must always be immediate, from where one stands, the particular individual.

K: I would never put the 'how' at all, the 'how' should never enter into the mind.

HS: Well, this is a hard teaching. It may be true and I am reaching for it, and yet I don't know that it's possible – I don't feel it is possible to relinquish completely the question of 'how'.

K: Sir, I think we shall be able to understand each other if we could go a little slowly, not into the 'how', but into the things that prevent clarity. Come to clarity through negation, not through the positive method of following a system.

HS: Fine, all right. The negative approach, that is good.

K: I think that is the only way. The positive way of the 'how' has led Man to divide himself, his loyalties, his pursuits; you have *your* 'how', there is the 'how' of somebody else, the method of this and that, and then we are all lost. So if we could set aside the question of 'how' for the time being, probably you will never put it afterwards. I hope you won't.

HS: Well, we'll see.

K: So what is important is to find out what the obstructions, the hindrances, the blocks are that prevent clear perception of human anxiety, fear, sorrow, the ache of loneliness, the utter lack of love and all that.

HS: Let's explore the virtues of the negative. What are these?

K: First of all I feel, there must be freedom, freedom from authority.

HS: Could we stay a moment on this matter of authority. When you say we should renounce all authority, it seems to me that the goal of total freedom and self-reliance is a valid one, and yet along the way it seems to me that we rely, and should rely, on all kinds of authorities in certain spheres. When I go to a new territory and I stop to ask the filling station attendant which way to go, I accept his authority because he knows more about that than I do.

K: Obviously the specialist knows a little more than the layman. The expert, whether in surgery or technology, clearly knows much more than anyone not familiar with that particular technique. But we are considering not authority in a speciality like that but the whole problem of authority.

HS: We need to understand the areas in which there is specialized authority, which we should accept, and where...

K: ... authority is detrimental, is destructive. So there are two problems involved in this question of authority: there is the authority of the expert – let's call him that for the moment – which is necessary, but also the authority of the man who says, 'psychologically I know, you don't'.

HS: Yes, I see.

K: This is true, this is false, you must do this, you must not do that.

HS: So one should never turn over one's life to...

K: ... to anybody. Because the different religions throughout the world have said, give your life to us, we will direct, shape it, we will tell you what to do. Do this, follow the saviour, follow the church and you will have peace. But, on the contrary, churches and religions of every kind have produced terrible wars and brought about the fragmentation of the mind. So the question is not freedom from a particular authority, but the whole conceptual acceptance of authority.

HS: Yes, I can see that one should never abdicate one's own conscience.

K: No, I am not talking here about conscience.

HS: Well, I am thinking of conscience in the sense of how I should live my life, how I should live.

K: But we started out by asking: why is it that Man who has lived for two million years and more, why is Man not capable of clear perception and action? That was the question.

HS: Right, and your first point is that it is because he doesn't accept full responsibility...

K: I haven't come to that yet. I am saying that we must approach this problem negatively, which means I must find out what are the blockages.

HS: The obstacles.

K: The obstacles that prevent perception. Now one of the major blocks, or hindrances, is this total acceptance of authority.

HS: So be ye lamps unto yourself.

K: That's right, you must be a light to yourself. To be a light to yourself you must deny every other light, however great that light be, whether the light of the Buddha or of X, Y or Z.

HS: Perhaps accept it here or there but nevertheless you retain the say-so as to where you find it might be valid.

K: No, because that is my own authority. What authority have I? My authority is the authority of society. I am conditioned to accept authority, and when I reject the authority of the outer I accept the authority of the inner. And my authority of the inner is the result of the conditioning in which I have been brought up.

HS: All right. The only point that I am not quite sure about is that it seems to me while assuming, accepting, affirming and maintaining one's own freedom...

K: Ah, you can't. Sir, how can a prisoner, except ideologically or theoretically, *accept* that he is free? He is in prison, and that is the fact from which we must move.

HS: I see.

K: Not accept, obey a fanciful ideological freedom that doesn't exist. What exists is that Man has bowed to this total authority.

HS: All right, and that is the first thing we must see and remove.

K: Absolutely. That must go completely for someone who is serious, who wants to find out the truth, to see things very clearly. That is one of the major points. And this means freedom not only from authority but from the fear which makes him accept authority.

HS: Right, that seems true also. Behind the craving for authority is fear which we look to authority to be free from.

K: That's right. And fear makes Man violent; he engages not only in territorial violence, but also in sexual and various other forms of violence. So freedom from authority implies freedom from fear, which in turn implies the cessation of every form of violence.

HS: If we stop violence then our fear recedes?

K: Let's put it the other way round. Man is psychologically, linguistically violent; in daily life he is violent, which ultimately leads to war. Man has accepted war as his way of life, whether in the office, at home, or on the playing field. Everywhere he has accepted war as a way of life, which is the very essence of violence, aggression, and everything it involves. So as long as Man accepts violence, lives a way of life which is violent, he perpetuates fear, and therefore more violence, and in so doing also accepts authority.

HS: Yes, so these three are a kind of vicious circle, each playing into the other.

K: And the churches say, live peacefully, be kind, love your neighbour, which is all sheer nonsense. This is merely a verbal assertion that has no meaning at all. It is just an idea because the morality of society, which is the morality of the church, is immoral.

HS: So in trying to see the things that stand between us and lucidity and freedom, we find authority and fear and violence working together to obstruct us. Where do we go from there?

K: It's not going somewhere, but understanding this fact that most of us live a life in this ambience, in this cage of authority, fear and violence. One can't go beyond the cage, unless one is free from it, not intellectually or theoretically, but actually free from every form of authority, not the authority of the expert, but the feeling of dependence on authority. Now, is it possible for a human being to be completely free of fear? Not only at the superficial level of one's consciousness, but also at the deeper level, what is called the unconscious.

HS: Is it possible?

K: That is the question, otherwise you are bound to accept the authority of somebody, any Tom, Dick or Harry with a little bit of knowledge, a little bit of cunning explanation or some intellectual formula, you are bound to fall for it. So the question is whether a human being, heavily conditioned as he is by the propaganda of the church, of society, morality and all the rest of it, whether such a human being can really be free from fear. That is the basic question.

HS: That's what I wait to hear.

K: I say it is possible, not in abstraction, but actually possible.

HS: And my impulse again is to say – how?

K: And again, you see, when you say 'how', you stop learning, you cease to learn. Because we are learning; learning about the nature and structure of human fear. At the deepest level and also at the most superficial level, we are learning about it. When you are learning, you can't ask suddenly, how am I to learn. There is no 'how' if you are interested, if the problem is vital, intense, if it has to be solved to live peacefully, then there is no 'how', you say, let's learn about it. So the moment you bring in the 'how' you move away from the central fact of learning.

HS: Let's continue then on the path of learning about this.

K: So, what does it mean to learn?

HS: It means to perceive how one should proceed in a given domain.

K: No, sir, surely. Here is a problem of fear. I want to learn about it. First of all I mustn't condemn it, I mustn't say, it is terrible, and run away from it.

HS: It sounds as though you have been condemning it in one way or another.

K: No, I want to learn. When I want to learn about something, I look, there is no condemnation at all.

HS: Well, we were going at this through a negative route.

K: Which is what I am doing.

HS: And fear is an obstacle.

K: About which I am going to learn. Therefore I cannot condemn it.

HS: Well, it's not good, you are not advocating it.

K: I am neither advocating nor not advocating it. Here is a fact of fear. I want to learn about it. The moment I learn about something I am free of it. So learning matters. What is implied in learning? First of all to learn about something there must be complete cessation of condemnation or justification.

HS: Yes, I can see that. If we are going to understand something we need to keep our emotions out of it.

K: If I want to learn about that camera, I begin to look at it, undo it, go into it. So to learn about fear there must be no condemnation, no justification of it, and therefore no verbal escape from the fact of fear. But the tendency is to deny it.

HS: To deny the reality.

K: The reality of fear, the fact that fear is causing all these things. To deny by saying: I must develop courage. We are going into this problem of fear because it really is a very important question: whether the human mind can ever be free of fear.

HS: It certainly is.

K: Which means, whether the mind is capable of looking at fear, not as an abstraction, but actually at fear as it occurs.

HS: Facing fear. Yes, we should do this, and I agree with you that we can't deny it.

 K: To face it, being aware of fear. To learn about fear there must be no condemnation or justification. That's a fact. So can the mind look at fear? What is fear? There is every kind of fear: fear of the dark, fear of one's wife, fear of one's husband, fear of war, fear of a storm, so many psychological fears. And you cannot possibly have the time to analyze all of them, that would take a lifetime, and even then you will not have understood them.

HS: So it is the phenomenon of fear itself rather than any...

 K: ... any particular fear.

HS: Right, now what should we learn?

 K: Wait, go slowly. Now to learn about something you must be in complete contact with it. I want to learn about fear. Therefore I must look at fear, I must face it. Now to face it implies a mind that does not want to solve the problem of fear.

HS: To look at fear...

 K: ... is not to solve the problem of fear. This is very important to understand because if I want to solve fear I am concerned more with the *solution* of fear than with *facing* fear. If I say, I must solve it, I am beyond it already, I am not looking.

HS: You are saying that if we are trying to solve the problem of fear we are not truly facing it?

 K: Quite right, sir. You see, to face fear the mind must give complete attention to it, and if you give partial attention to fear, which is to say, I want to solve it and go beyond it, you are not giving it complete attention. There are several problems involved in this. We generally consider fear as something outside us. So there is the question of the observer and the observed. The observer says, I am afraid, and he puts fear as something away from him.

HS: I am not sure. When I feel afraid, I am afraid, I feel it very much in here.

 K: In here, but when you observe it, it is different.

HS: When I observe fear...

 K: ... then I put it outside.

HS: No, again that doesn't seem quite right.

K: All right, at the moment of fear there is neither the observer nor the observed.

HS: That is very true.

K: That is all I am saying. At the crisis, at the moment of actual fear there is no observer.

HS: It fills the horizon.

K: Now, the moment you begin to look at it, face it, there is this division.

HS: Between the fearful self and the...

K: ... the non-fearful self. So in trying to learn about fear, there is this division between the observer and the observed. Now is it possible to look at fear without the observer? This is really quite an intricate and complex question, so one has to go into it very deeply. As long as there is an observer who is going to learn about fear there is a division.

HS: That's true, we are not in full contact with it.

K: Therefore in that division is the conflict of trying to get rid of fear or to justify fear. So is it possible to look at fear without the observer? So that you are completely in contact with it all the time.

HS: Well, then you are experiencing fear.

K: I wouldn't like to use the word 'experience', because experience implies going through something.

HS: All right. But it seems better than 'looking at', because that does seem to imply a division between an observer and the observed.

K: We can use the word 'observing' or being aware of fear without choice, since choice implies the observer, choosing whether I like or don't like this or that. So when the observer is absent, there is choiceless awareness of fear. Then what takes place? That's the question. The observer creates the linguistic difference between himself and the thing observed. Language comes in there, and the word prevents complete being in contact with fear.

HS: Yes, words can be a screen.

K: That is all we are saying. So the word mustn't interfere.

HS: We have to go beyond that.

K: But is that possible, to be beyond the word? Theoretically we say, yes, but we are slaves to words.

HS: Yes, far too much so.

K: The mind has to become aware of its own slavery to words, realizing that the word is never the thing. So that the mind is free of the word 'to look'. All that this implies. Sir, I mean, the relationship between two people, husband and wife, is the relationship of images.

HS: Obviously.

K: You have your image of her, and she has her image of you. The relationship is between these two images. Now, the real human relationship is when the images don't exist. In the same way the relationship between the observer and the observed ceases when the word is not. So one is directly in contact with fear.

HS: We pass through the screen.

K: Yes, now there is fear at the conscious level, which one can understand fairly quickly. But there are the deeper layers of fear, in the so-called hidden parts of the mind. Now is it possible to be aware of that without analysis? Analysis takes time.

HS: Surely it is possible.

K: You say that it is possible. Is it? There is the whole reservoir of fear, the whole content of the unconscious – its content is the unconscious. Now, to be aware of all that, not through dreams, again that takes too long.

HS: Are you asking whether we can be explicitly aware of the full reach of mind?

K: Yes, the full content, full reach of the mind; both the conscious as well as the deeper layers, the totality of consciousness.

HS: Can we be explicitly aware of all that? I am not sure.

K: I say it is possible. It is only possible when you are aware during the day of what you say, the words you use, the gestures, the way you talk, the way you walk, what your thoughts are, to be completely and totally aware of all that.

HS: Do you think all of that can be before you in total awareness?

K: Yes, sir, absolutely. When there is no condemnation and no justification, when you are directly in contact with it.

HS: It seems to me that the mind is rather like an iceberg with a whole region of it...

K: It is possible to see the whole of it if, during the day, you are aware of your thoughts, your feelings, your motives, which demands a mind that is highly sensitive.

HS: We can certainly be aware of much, much more than we usually are. When you say we can be aware...

K: Totally, yes sir.

HS: . . .of all the psychological factors...

K: I am showing you, I am showing you. If you deny it, if you say, it is not possible, then it is not possible.

HS: No, I'd like to believe that.

K: It's not a question of belief. I don't have to believe in what I see. It's only when I don't see that I have belief in God, or in this or that.

HS: For me it is a matter of belief, maybe not for you because you...

K: Belief is the most destructive part of life. Why should I believe that the sun rises? I see that the sun rises. When I do not know what love is then I believe in love.

HS: Like so many times when I listen to you speak it seems to me like a half-truth which is stated as a full truth, and I wonder whether that is for the sake of emphasis, or whether you really mean to carry it all the way.

K: No, sir, to me it really is.

HS: We have been speaking of the elements that block us, the things that block us from a life of lucidity and freedom, authority, violence, fear. I wouldn't like to spend all the time on these obstacles. Is there anything affirmative we can say about this condition?

K: Sir, anything affirmative indicates authority. It's only the authoritarian mind that says, 'let's affirm'. Which is in opposition to negation. But the negation we are talking about has no opposite.

HS: Well, when I ask you for an affirmative statement it doesn't seem to me that I am deciding to invoke authority. I just want to hear if you have something interesting to say which I will then stand judgement on.

K: With regard to what?

HS: As to whether it speaks to my condition, and to the state of life that it seems to me we are groping for in our words to describe.

K: Are you implying, sir, that life is only in the present? Is life to be divided into the past, present and future, which becomes fragmentary, or is there a total perception of living?

HS: Well, again, as so often, it seems to me that the answer is both. In one sense it is a unity and it is present and the present is all we have, but Man is a time-binding animal, as they say, who looks before and aft.

K: So Man is the result of time, not only evolutionary but chronological as well as psychological. He is the result of time: the past, the present and the future. Now, he lives mostly in the past.

HS: Yes, mostly.

K: He *is* the past. He is the past because he lives in memory.

HS: Not totally.

K: Wait, sir. Follow it step by step. He lives in the past and therefore he thinks and examines and looks from the background of the past.

HS: Which is both good and bad.

K: No, it is not a matter of a good or bad past. He lives in the past, examines everything from the past, and projects the future from the past. So he lives in the past, he is the past. And when he thinks of the future or the present, he thinks in terms of the past.

HS: It seems to me that most of the time that is true, but there are new perceptions, new experiences that break through the whole momentum of the past.

K: New experiences break through only when there is an absence of the past.

HS: Well, it seems to me it is like a merging of things that we perforce bring with us from the past, but bring to play upon the novelty, the newness, of the present. It is a fusion of the two.

K: But if I want to understand something new I must look at it with clear eyes. I can't bring the past with all the recognition process, with all the memories, and then translate what I see as new. Surely, the man who invented the jet engine, must have forgotten, or be completely familiar with the propeller, and then there was an absence of that knowledge in which he discovered the new. That is the only way to operate in life. That is, I must be completely aware – there must be complete awareness of the past, but an absence of the past to see the new or to come upon the new.

HS: I am conceding reluctantly here because I think I see what you are saying, I think I agree with the point that you are making, but it is also true that one operates in terms of the symbols that one has. It is not as though we begin de novo.

K: But we *have* to begin de novo because life demands it, because we have lived in this way, accepting war, hatred, brutality, competition, anxiety, guilt, all that we have accepted, we live that way. I am saying that to bring about a different quality, a different way of living, the past must disappear.

HS: We must be open to the new.

K: Yes, therefore the past must have no meaning.

HS: That I can't go along with.

K: That is what the whole world is objecting to. The established order says: I cannot let go for the new to be. And the young people throughout the world say: let's revolt against the old. But they don't understand the whole complication of it. So they say, what have you given us, except examinations, jobs, and repetition of the old pattern – wars, favourite wars.

HS: Well, you are pointing out, it seems to me, the importance of not being slaves to the past. And that is very true.

K: The past being tradition, the past being the pattern of morality, which is the social morality, which is not moral.

HS: But at the same time there is only one generation, namely ourselves, that separates the future generation from the caveman.

K: I agree with all that.

HS: If the caveman were to be totally rescinded we would start right now.

K: Oh, no, to break through the past demands a great deal of intelligence, a great deal of sensitivity to the past. You can't just break away from it.

HS: OK, I am convinced.

K: So the problem really is can we live in a different way? A different way in which there are no wars, no hatred, in which the human being loves the human being without competition, without division, saying you are a Christian, you are a Catholic, you are a Protestant, you are this. That is all so immature. It has no meaning. It is an intellectual, sophisticated division. And that is not a religious mind at all, that is not religion. A religious mind is a mind that has no hatred, that lives completely without fear, without anxiety, in which there is not a particle of antagonism. Therefore a mind that loves – that is a different dimension of living altogether. And nobody wants that.

HS: And in another sense everybody wants that.

K: But they won't go after it. They are distracted by so many other things, they are so heavily conditioned by their past that they hold on to it.

HS: But I think there are some who will go after it.

K: Wait sir, very few.

HS: The numbers don't matter.

K: The minority is always the most important thing.

HS: Krishnamurti, as I listen to you and try to listen through the word to what you are saying, it seems to me that what I hear is that, first, I should work out and each of us should work out his own salvation, not leaning on authority outside; second, not to allow words to form a film between us and actual experience, not to mistake the menu for the meal; and third, not to let the past swallow up the present, take possession of it, by responding to a conditioning of the past, but rather to be always open to the new, the novel, the fresh. And finally, it seems to me you are saying something like the key to doing this is a radical reversal in our point of view. It is as though we were prisoners straining at the bars for the light, and looking for the glimpse of light that we see out there and wondering how we can get out towards it, while actually the door of the cell is open behind us if only we would turn around, we could walk out into freedom. This is what is seems to me you are saying. Is this it?

K: A little bit, sir.

HS: All right, what else?

K: Surely, sir, the fact is Man is involved in everlasting struggle, conflict, caught in his own conditioning, and straining, struggling, beating his head to be free. And we have accepted from religions and all the rest of it that effort is necessary, that it is part of life. To me that is the highest form of blindness, of limiting Man – to say that you must live everlastingly in effort. But to live without effort requires the greatest sensitivity and the highest form of intelligence; which doesn't mean, well, I won't struggle, I'll become like a cow. One has to understand how conflict arises, the duality in us, the conflict between the fact of 'what is' and 'what should be'. If there is no 'what should be', which is ideological, which is non-real, which is fiction, and you see 'what is' and face it, live with it without the 'what should be', then there

213

is no conflict at all. It is only when you compare, evaluate with 'what should be', and then look with 'what should be' at the 'what is', that conflict arises.

HS: There should be no tension between the ideal and the actual.

K: No ideal at all. Why should we have an ideal? The ideal is the most idiotic form of conceptual thing, why should I have an ideal? The fact is burning there, why should I have an ideal about anything?

HS: Well, now once more when you speak like that it seems to me that you break it into an either/or. Not the ideal but the actual, whereas it seems to me the truth is somehow both of these.

K: Truth is not a mixture of the ideal and the 'what is', then you produce some messy mélange. There is only 'what is'. To take a very simple example: we human beings are violent. Why should I have an ideal of non-violence? Why can't I deal with the fact? – of violence without non-violence. The ideal is an abstraction, a distraction. The fact is I am violent, Man is violent. Let us tackle that, let us come to grips with that, and see if we can't live without violence. There is no dualistic process in that. There is only the fact that I am violent, Man is violent, and is it possible to be free of that. Why should I introduce the idealistic nonsense?

HS: No dualism, you say, no separation, and in your view is it the case that there is no separation?

K: Absolutely.

HS: Is there any separation between you and me?

K: Physically there is. You have got a black suit, are a fairer person than me, and so on.

HS: But you don't feel dualistic.

K: If I felt dualistic, I wouldn't sit down to discuss with you, then we are just playing intellectual games.

Why Is Your Teaching So Difficult To Live?

Renée Weber, professor of philosophy at Rutgers University.

Renée Weber: My general question has to do with what one might call a sense of all or nothing in what you say. Take, for example, teaching and education. One of the things you seem to say is that a teacher who isn't completely free from fear, sorrow and all the human problems, cannot really be a genuine teacher. That leaves the impression that one is either perfect or useless.

Krishnamurti: I think there must be a misunderstanding here.

RW: Hopefully.

K: Because if one says that until one is perfect, or whatever word one likes to use, and is free from certain states of mind, one cannot teach, that would be an impossible situation, wouldn't it?

RW: Yes.

K: The student, or whoever is learning from you, will be lost. So is it possible for the educator to say, I am not free, you are not free, we are both conditioned, we have various forms of conditioning, let's talk about it, let's see if we can get free of it. That way you can break it up.

RW: Don't you think the educator has at least to understand this process better than the student?

K: Perhaps he has read more about it, has studied a little more.

RW: But he may not necessarily know how to do it better.

K: So in communicating with the student, or in communicating with himself, the educator realizes that he is both the teacher and the student. Not that he has learnt, and then transmits, but rather the teacher is both educating and being educated. He is doing both.

RW: You are saying he is not an oracle who delivers. If he is open he is learning and teaching at the same time.

K: That's a really good educator, not one who just says, 'I know and I'll tell you all about it'.

RW: Which means that such a person has to be, I suppose, free from faults such as pride.

K: Those are obvious things. Suppose I am an educator and am full of arrogance, vanity, ambition and all the rest of it, the usual nonsense that goes on in human beings. In talking with the student or with somebody I am learning, learning that I am arrogant and that the student is also arrogant in his way, so we begin to talk about it. And a discussion like that, if one is honest and really self-critical, self-aware, has tremendous possibilities.

RW: But you are saying that this process can take place between teacher and student even though neither of them is perfect?

K: I wouldn't use that word, I don't know what perfection is – then we go off into something else. But if we could establish a relationship with the student or with each other in which an open dialogue takes place, a free, self-critical, self-aware dialogue of questioning, doubting, inquiring, then we are both learning, are both communing with each other's point of view, with each other's difficulties. So in that way, if one really wants to go very deeply into the matter, you help each other.

RW: It's not necessarily my view but suppose somebody says: that raises a problem because it may make the student feel that the teacher doesn't know any more than he does, it may undercut his trust.

K: I would tell him, look, I have studied a bit more than you have. I have gone into, for instance, various Indian, Buddhist philosophies, I have studied, I know a little bit more about it.

RW: Exactly.

K: It doesn't mean I am something extraordinary.

RW: So you feel if the teacher just very honestly...

K: That's his function.

RW: ... speaks of the strengths and the weaknesses: 'I know more, but I don't know everything'.

K: Say I am discussing Buddhism, for example, or Aristotle or Plato – take Plato. You have studied more than I have. I haven't studied Plato at all, but you have. So you say, look, I know a little more, naturally, otherwise I wouldn't be your professor.

RW: Exactly, otherwise I shouldn't be, it would be dishonest.

K: But as I haven't read Plato or Aristotle or any of these people, I would say, look, I haven't read them but I am willing to go into this very thoroughly, not from any particular point of view, not from Aristotle's, Plato's or the Buddhist point of view, but as a human being dealing with another human being, let's discuss these things: what life is about, what existence is for, whether there is justice at all in the world, which there isn't, and so on.

RW: I think that makes it far clearer because at least under those circumstances, caring and self-critical adults would feel that they can teach others. Whereas if they have to be perfection itself, then who could do it?

K: But there are very few people who are self-critical, honest with themselves, aware of what they think, whether they put their thoughts into words properly and so on. I mean one has to be tremendously honest in all this.

RW: What do you think makes one person capable of that and not another? You say there are so few people who are totally honest. Why is that so?

K: That's a fact, some people are serious, some are not.

RW: What quality does it take for a person to be very honest with himself?

K: Not to be afraid of discovering what you are, not to be ashamed, not to be frightened to discover. Being able to say simply, this is what I am: I am a lot of words, a lot of other people's ideas, I am incapable of thinking anything for myself, I am always quoting, I am depending on the environment and pressure and this and that. Unless one is self-aware and self-critical you end up like a...

RW: So it takes at least the awareness and courage to say it.

K: I don't like to use the word 'courage'.

RW: What word would you use?

K: A man who is really serious, who wants to investigate all this, is naturally fearless, he will say, all right, if I lose my job, I lose my job.

RW: But let's say even without the outside judgement, like a job, don't you think many people feel or fear that if I look all this straight in the face, even for myself, it will make the problem worse, not better? That's what they fear.

217

K: It would bring about much more uncertainty.

RW: That's it, and therefore...

K: Face that uncertainty. Rather than saying, well, it will bring me greater uncertainty, greater problems, so I won't do anything – which is really a senseless existence.

RW: Well, you would probably say it is running away and hiding.

K: Yes, partly hiding.

RW: They might also reason – I have heard people say this – that the other thing will disintegrate me, I won't be able to function as a sane person.

K: What you call sanity may be insanity. What is going on in the world is quite insane. If you want to fit into that insanity, all right, be one of the insane. But suppose you don't want to be insane, then you say, sorry, I'm against the current or not going along with it.

RW: This brings up a second question that comes up many, many times; it's related to this one but it's broader. Both here and in India, what puzzles and confuses most people, including me, is that we feel you talk about a certain state of integration, of sanity, or whatever, you even use the word 'light', and several of us have said, yes, I have tasted that from time to time, I know a little bit of that.

K: Most people say that.

RW: Exactly. Then we say, it seems to disappear or somehow leak away, it gets thinner.

K: It slips away.

RW: Your answer has been, if it ever slips away then you have never experienced it in the first place, because it is not the kind of thing that can come and go. Could you clarify that? It has confused people and made them very unhappy.

K: What is the problem? The problem is, I have experienced something, clarity or a sense of wholeness, a holistic way of living, I have had a glimpse of it, and it has gone. It may have lasted a day, or it may have lasted a week but it has gone. And I remember it, it has left a mark, it has left a remembrance, and I would like to have it back again. I would like it to continue, or to live with it all the time, have it as part of my life, or find a way of remaining with it. So the question is: that state, that thing that happens so rarely in a human life, was that invited, asked for, or did it come naturally, unexpectedly, without any preparation, without any drill? It came naturally, it came when *you* were not, when you had no problems, etc, etc, it came then. And now it has gone and you are back in your old state of mind and you want it back. You want to see if you can't somehow remain with it all the time.

RW: Yes, but it isn't that you want it back because...

K: You want to live with it.

RW: It seems the best way to cope, you feel that everything comes out intelligently.

K: Yes, you have had an experience or a state of mind that has happened spontaneously, it came uninvited, it happened when you were not thinking about yourself.

RW: Yes, you suddenly feel together.

K: You are not concerned with yourself all the time and when you are absent from yourself then that happened. Then you say, I could see in that state everything very clearly.

RW: Exactly.

K: There were no problems I couldn't tackle, there was nothing, no resistance, no hindrance, nothing.

RW: That's right.

K: So what am I to do?

RW: Exactly.

K: The question really is this: that state of mind, or whatever you like to call it took place when the self was not, when the ego, the personality, the problems, the mess one has, the ambitions, the greed and so on, were temporarily in abeyance. That was when it happened.

RW: That's my first question. The self is not. Now you said 'temporarily in abeyance'. That means it just moved into the background, it left the centre of the stage.

K: Perhaps, I am saying.

RW: Or did it just dissolve?

K: No, of course not. If it dissolved the other thing would never survive.

RW: Exactly, so somehow it was pushed...

K: No, it happened. You are walking down a lane full of trees and beauty, you are looking at all the beauty of it and you suddenly say, 'by Jove, look at that'. At that moment the self, with all its hideous problems, is not.

RW: All right.

K: With its pleasures and joys and all the rest of it. And when it goes, you are back to your old self. The question then is, is it possible to be free of the self? Not how to get that state of mind back or how to live with it, or to capture it by some drill or system of meditation. All those ways are encouragement of the self.

RW: All right. So can we go back to that state for a minute. In that state, because let's say I was totally with that...

K: Not *you* were.

RW: How would you put it?

K: I would say, that state brought about a feeling that you saw everything very clearly.

RW: Yes.

K: Your problems, everything very clearly.

RW: Yes. Something didn't always get in the way and make an obstacle. Nothing got in there, it was unobstructed. Now what brings it on and what makes it go again?

K: What brings it on? That's very simple. When there is no self.

RW: But what triggers that? Why is there suddenly no self?

K: Because you are not concerned with your problems, you are looking at those orange trees, at the beauty of those flowers. For a single second *you* are not.

RW: And the next second *you* are back.

K: Then you say, now I am back, for God's sake I wish I had that. One doesn't realize that the very demand for it...

RW: ... blocks it.

K: Not only blocks it, emphasizes the self.

RW: Because it is *I* who want it.

K: Of course. Back again to the old resistance. That's why I said one requires a great deal of simple humility and honesty in this, not all the arrogance of knowledge and that kind of thing. That denies the other.

RW: But do you think – I will tell you why this question is important to people – if one has had a glimpse of this, is it helpful or not?

K: We must be a little careful. What do you mean by *this*? It is not something mysterious, occult, something brought about through phony meditation and all that kind of stuff.

RW: I didn't mean that; by *this*, I mean...

K: I would say: that state.

RW: A glimpse of that state, yes.

K: I am saying that state is not something mysterious, not something that you have to go through a lot of process to have.

RW: I understand that, but you have agreed it is rare.

K: Because human beings are so terribly selfish, they are mostly concerned with themselves in different ways.

RW: Yes, subtly or obviously.

K: Yes, the subtle becomes a little more difficult to see, but it is still the same thing.

RW: All right, let's say that if you have had a glimpse of that state of being...

K: Not of being.

RW: ... of functioning. What would you call it?

K: A state in which the self was absent. The self means time, the self means evolution, the self means this accumulation of memories, problems and all the terrible things by which the self makes itself manifest.

RW: All right.

K: Power, position, dependence on people. When for a single second that is not, the other is. The other is nothing extraordinary.

RW: It is not exotic, romantic.

K: Obviously.

RW: Yes, but then the question that keeps coming up, and it came up, remember, in India, in Madras. All your friends there asked the question: if that state has been, why does it come and go? Why is that state a way of life for some people and for others it is a very sporadic, occasional glimpse?

K: It is very simple. The one with whom it remains is unselfish. You seem not to give importance to the state of mind when there is no self.

RW: What does that mean?

K: Not to be selfish with all its complexities.

RW: By that you don't necessarily mean to be altruistic? You don't mean that at all.

K: That is social work.

RW: OK, so not to be selfish...

K: Nor becoming a monk or a hermit or trying to become something.

RW: Right. So what does it mean not to be selfish? I am me – that's what the ordinary person would say, I'm me, I have to make my decisions, I have to...

K: What does selfish mean? To be concerned with the self in different, gross or subtle or most refined ways, hiding under every kind of cover in the name of helping people, in the name of a guru. It's all there, you can see it blatantly.

RW: I understand. Now, to take your description...

K: Not my description, the actuality.

RW: OK, if somebody said, well, what about people who are not intellectuals, not meditators, not the ones who run to gurus, just simple people who don't think much about themselves – that's not what you mean either.

K: Of course not. First of all: thinking is common to all mankind. It is shared by everyone. By top scientists as well as the poorest, uneducated, unsophisticated human being – he thinks too – so it is shared by all human beings.

RW: Yes.

K: It is shared by all human beings, so it is not my thinking, not individual thinking. Thinking is shared by you, by me, by her, by that person. But we have said, *my* thinking.

RW: You feel it is shared as a collective process?

K: Not collective, it is simply shared. I don't have to live with it as collective or non-collective, it is so. Sunlight is shared by all human beings, it is not *my* sunlight.

RW: Is it analogous?

K: Of course.

RW: Somebody could say: but only I know my thoughts, and I don't know your thoughts, I don't know his thoughts.

K: No, we are saying 'thinking', why should I know your thoughts?

RW: Thinking is different from the product.

K: Of course. The expression of thinking may vary, the scientist would put it in the most complicated scientific way and the poor villager, the poor uneducated man says, 'I want this'. But thinking is shared by all human beings.

RW: As a function, yes.

K: And you may express it differently because you have read Plato and I haven't. So I may put it in simpler language.

RW: But, you know, we were pursuing how the selfishness of most human beings...

K: I am showing it to you. So when I say it is my thinking not your thinking, I know expressions of that vary – right? You are a Platonist, I am not, you are a Buddhist, I am not, and if you are a Christian you express your thinking in a certain...

RW: ... symbol system.

K: ... symbols, jargon and all the rest of it. To you the saviour is important, to me it is not, I don't believe in all that. So your expression and my expression vary, and we think that these varying expressions give individuality.

RW: I understand.

K: But this is not so. Thinking is shared by all of us, it is not yours or mine.

RW: You are saying that the activity of thinking itself, which is shared, is the central thing, not the outcome or content.

K: That's right.

RW: Whereas we fasten on the outcome and content.

K: I paint, I am an artist. Being an artist I feel myself superior to, better than others, and so on. So I never see that my thinking is the same as yours, because my expression of it on a canvas is different. That gives me a feeling that I am different. You can't paint but I can. But see the beauty of the idea that we all share the sun, the sunlight. You may build a marvellous house to protect yourself from the sun and I may live in a hut, in a small cottage, but we share that thing. But the moment I *identify* myself with my expression as a painter, with a big house, then the difference arises. So identification is one of the factors of selfishness. And attachment to that identification, and holding on to your opinions. I say I have tremendous faith in Jesus and suppose you haven't – then I am definitely a believer, I am separate from you.

RW: Right.

K: But you also believe in something else.

RW: Let's say – for example, not me now – that the other person believes that people who believe in something are gullible and stupid and my superiority is there, I believe in nothing.

K: The moment you identify with your superiority, there *you* are.

RW: Right, I am modern, I believe in nothing.

K: The moment you identify with that it is the same thing. And selfishness is so extraordinarily clever in its own way, it can hide behind all the most brutal things and the most subtle forms of expression, producing constant refinement of the self, making itself more and more selfish.

RW: The 'selfless' *self* being the most dangerous. Because it really fools itself!

K: Right. That's why I said that a great sense of humility and honesty is needed, not double talk about anything. When one wants this way of life, one lives very honestly, scrupulously, and if you are honest you are naturally very clear in your humility. Then this doesn't require evolution.

RW: How does that relate to confidence or lack of confidence, this absolute honesty with oneself?

K: Why should we have confidence?

RW: Let's say trust in your own awareness.

K: Why should you have?

RW: Can I give you one obvious answer? I think people who don't have it are the most self-centred, they are always insecure, worrying all the time.

K: Most people are neurotic.

RW: All right, that's very common. But I mean you don't feel that this unprotectedness that you speak of, this open selflessness...

K: We must understand very clearly what we mean by selflessness or openness. You can't use these words lightly. I mean we have more or less said what the nature of the self is. It creates gods and worships gods. That is another form of selfishness.

RW: But would you say that of anything it creates: is art a form of it?

K: The moment I identify myself with the expression that I have created and which I worship, or of which I say, how marvellous, or which brings me profit and all the rest of it, that's a movement of the self. So to live without identification – whether with your experience, your knowledge, or the expression of your creation by hand or mind. That is why the other thing becomes so rare.

RW: Do you think anybody does it at all?

K: I hope so.

RW: I mean, it certainly is a very difficult thing to understand for most people.

K: Because they don't apply it.

RW: They want to. Now why don't they do it?

K: They don't want it, they do what they want. If they want it, they will do it.

RW: That is a difficult step to follow. Let's say, many of the people who are seriously interested in these ideas ...

K: But they don't want it.

RW: ... but for years they try.

K: No, you can't *try* this. It's like a man trying not to be violent.

RW: I understand. But you are saying they don't really want to. And the proof is if they really wanted to they would do it.

K: Of course, they wanted to go to the Moon, and they did it.

RW: But that's easier.

K: Ah, no.

RW: It *is* easier.

K: No, that also requires a great deal of energy.

RW: But it's something outside myself.

K: Even there you have to have energy.

RW: That's true.

K: Even there you must have coordination, cooperation, efficiency and all that. Now if you apply all that to yourself and say, look, I really want this thing, to live a life without any conflict, of course you can do it.

RW: Can I go back to the example of the Moon landing? I can apply energy, passion, effort to something external to me, but here it is my very self I am working on, and it is a kind of dying to the self.

K: No, we said at the beginning of this conversation that there must be a certain quality of honesty, quality of learning, which is humility, not confidence, not all that stuff.

RW: Not trust, not confidence.

K: Of course not. Trust what?

RW: That you are being honest, that you are seeing clearly.

K: No, either you are honest or you are not. You see it.

RW: You mean when you are, you know it directly.

K: Quite. Look, it's simple. When I know I am ambitious, and I pretend not to be ambitious; when I want to be the head of something, and talk about how absurd power is. It's so simple all this; when I want to dominate people and at the same time say I am democratic. It becomes so childish.

RW: But you have said that if one really were serious and wanted to do it, it would happen.

K: Of course.

RW: You see, it sounds so simple and people have heard you say that and they have tried and it doesn't happen!

K: You can't *try* it. You don't *try* not to put your hand in the fire! You know fire burns and you don't go into it.

RW: But is it analogous?

K: It *is*. You realize that this selfish, complex way of living creates problem after problem, that in solving one problem you have ten other problems. That happens in this country politically, and it is happening all over the world. When I realize that way of living is meaningless and that its basis is deep, unexplored selfishness – we have more or less defined the word 'selfishness' – I realize that, and say: do I want to live that way? Most people *do* because that is the easiest way – the easiest way because you run with the pack. And if you don't, you say, sorry, I don't want any of that.

RW: All right, suppose you are at that point, then what is the next step?

K: Then I may be a professor, I may be a cook, anything. I will carry on.

RW: What has changed?

K: What has changed is my whole way of looking at life, not my profession. I may be a carpenter, I have to earn my living that way, but there is no longer a sense of 'I am a carpenter'. It's a function that I carry out. But the function doesn't give me a status.

RW: You are saying that there is not necessarily change from an external point of view, it is how I relate myself to everything, how I view the world.

K: Not how you relate. The moment you say 'how *I* relate', then you are emphasizing the self.

RW: Yes. How would you put it?

K: Why is it that we want identification? The name, the form.

RW: The name, the form, I have to know what house to go to at night, which children to feed.

K: Look at it much more deeply. Why do I want to know who my great-great-grandfather was? Who cares? What matters is what I am *now*. Who cares whether somebody is a prince or a queen? All that is so childish.

RW: That's easier to see. Some people don't care about that but still they would have ...

K: Just a minute. The vast majority want that so that they can dominate the world. Look at it, it is happening right under your nose.

RW: Undeniably, I realize that. I suppose my question is: those few who say they want the other, still they don't do it. Why don't they do it?

K: It's not a lack of will because will has nothing to do with it. Obviously. Will is desire. I desire to be non-violent, but I am still violent.

RW: But earlier you said if people were serious in really *wanting* that, they would do it. You don't mean desire?

K: See what has happened now. I say it is possible because I feel it, I live that way for myself. I say it is possible and you say, show me how. I've shown it to you but your intention may be very, very superficial, you are satisfied with mere description, analysis, definition, and take that with you, make an idea out of it and say: now, how am I to carry out that idea?

RW: Yes, that's the wrong way.

K: You are gone, you are finished.

RW: All right, I come to you, I am serious. I say I would like to live in an intelligent way without the self. I am serious. What do I do next?

K: It's fairly clear, isn't it? Not what you *do* next. It is what you *don't do*, because negation is the most positive thing. So you say, look, what is it I don't need to do?

RW: What is it that we don't need to do?

K: What you don't need to do is to make an effort. Effort means achievement. Say I recognize that there is a possibility of living that way, and I make an effort to achieve it. The maker of the effort is still the same.

RW: That's clear. But there is a paradox because at the same time you have said today and said before, that the person has to be very serious about this, and consider that is the most important thing there is.

K: It is so. When you say it is the most important thing – wait a minute. To kill another human being in the name of your country, your God, in the name of Christ and so on, they have done all this. To realize that to kill a human being is the greatest evil, sin, or whatever you like to call it. That is simple to realize. And you say, by Jove, I won't kill, even if my God, Mr President or the Prime Minister asks me. Did you read what that well-known Argentine author said? I have forgotten his name.

RW: Jorge Luis Borges?

K: Something like that. He said that the Falklands War was like two bald old men fighting over a comb. (Laughter)

RW: That's wonderful! And you think we do that most of the time? You are implying that this is what happens in many guises in the so-called struggles of the world?

K: In the so-called civilized world, and in the primitive world as well. So we are asking: is it possible to live in this world without a single problem, without a single conflict? And problems exist, conflict will exist as long as human beings are selfish. We have come to that point. Selfish in the deepest and in the superficial sense of the word. Now if you say that to me, I say, 'Look, I am a serious human being, I see all the rubbish that is going on in the world and so I put that aside, I am out of it completely. Not physically, I can't get out of it physically, but inwardly, psychologically, I am out of it, which has already made me different. Not that I am aware of my difference, but I am out of that current.'

RW: Out of that current?

K: Yes, out of that current, to which probably ninety-nine per cent belong.

RW: Are you saying I cease to add to that?

K: No, I don't belong to it, I don't think in that way, I don't look at life in that way. So I say, now what is the thing that makes the self so important? What shouldn't I do? What are the things that are unnecessary?

RW: What can I let go, as you said earlier.

K: Attachments. And that implies a tremendous lot, the implications of it. To be unattached means to have an extraordinarily quick, subtle mind, because usually I am attached to so many things.

RW: And they tie up the energy.

K: Yes, I may be attached to that table. It is a very old table, one has bought it at great expense, that chest of drawers over there is also very old, and I get attached to that; or I get attached to some knowledge, or to knowledge altogether.

RW: Are you saying that attachment takes that energy and constricts it?

K: No, that attachment is a form of selfishness.

RW: I put part of me there?

K: Not a part, that *is* me.

RW: That *is* me.

K: If I am attached to that chest of drawers, which is very old, and fetches a lot of money, and I say, 'My God, it's mine, I must look after it', I am attached to it, I become the furniture! I am attached to my wife, my husband, my children, my God, my experience, my knowledge. All those are expressions of 'me'.

RW: You are really saying I am built up by all those things. That's how the 'me' comes into being.

K: Of course. Attachment is 'me'.

RW: Yes, is 'me'. And so in asking the question, what can I let go ...?

K: ... attachment.

RW: ... attachment is the first thing.

K: Of course. If you are unattached there is freedom, there is no fear. But I am attached to that furniture, to my body, to my experience, and I am frightened of dying and therefore invent God who will protect me and I worship that which I have invented. How do you think the Christian world is built up? Or any of the religious cultures? By thought.

RW: You make it sound so clear and logical and even so simple, yet we agree that it is not easy. Why is it so difficult?

K: I wouldn't call it easy, it is complex.

RW: Why is it so difficult to live that way?

K: With respect, you are putting the wrong question. Why is it that people are living *this* way, which is wars, problems, conflict, all the misery that is going on in the world, why do they accept all that? Why do people want all that?

RW: You are turning the question around.

K: Of course.

RW: You are saying that *this* is the difficult way to live.

K: This is the most *impractical* way.

RW: And yet *this* is what we choose. That is what you are saying.

K: Yes, that's the only question. Why do people want to live that way, night after night, entertainment, whether religious, political, sport, and wars? Why do they want to live that way? Partly because it is traditional.

RW: Yes. We are used to it, so it seems easier.

K: We are used to it, and living that way you don't have to think.

RW: Yes, it's less demanding, even if it is more painful.

K: Of course. Less demanding, but painful with all the misery. And they want all this, all the colleges, all the universities, everything goes along with this.

RW: Yes, although I suppose that what you have brought out ...

K: It is not a dichotomy.

RW: No, it is not a dichotomy but – how can I put it – in that other state of being ...

K: You see, you say, 'other state of being'. It is not being.

RW: What is it?

K: You see it cannot be described. Wait a minute. Being implies becoming.

RW: I don't think of it that way. Being is not becoming, being is just dwelling in the moment.

K: All right, wait a moment. Being means what?

RW: It's a state that is not dualistic, I am not striving, I am not ...

K: Which means what? An acorn is an acorn, it doesn't pretend to become an apple. It *is*. Right?

RW: Yes.

K: Who can say, 'it is', and nothing else? You understand?

RW: Not altogether.

K: You see, we are used to this perpetual, contradictory movement, moving forward or backward, it is a constant movement. So nobody in that state of movement can say, 'it is'. Only when that movement stops can you say, 'it is'.

RW: Exactly. But that's living in something that is timeless.

K: Which means not *that*. Don't bring in timeless – it becomes too complicated. But if you say it is not this perpetual, restless movement of thought – which has created all this awful mess...

RW: It just *is*.

K: You can't say it until you...

RW: Until you are in it. And then you don't say it.

K: Of course, it is not just an idea.

RW: I realize that. But I suppose the question is the one we started out with: at times some people have an inkling, a glimpse of that.

K: Yes, we have been through that.

RW: And they are therefore aware to some degree of a difference.

K: No, they are aware only that they want *that* so that they can live better. Look, don't most people, having had great delight in something, once it's gone remember it and say, please ...

RW: They'd like it back.

K: Keep it at that level. Look at everything, the cinema, television, sex – that's the predominating thing here, everybody plays up to it, women dress that way, you know the whole thing. I am not for it or against it, I am saying this is the way they all want it. And I say, all right, have it your way, but that way is going to destroy you. It is going to destroy the Earth, through pollution, and so on, all for your movement. And I say, I am sorry, you are all rather odd, neurotic people; if you don't mind, I don't want to join you.

RW: You bring that example up because the problem is turning something into an object of desire.

K: Of course.

RW: And whether that is a peaceful state of being or an object or a sexual experience...

K: The moment you desire you belong to that which is desired.

RW: Yes. You've made that into an object and I am here and it is there and I want it.

K: Suppose you hate me – I hope you don't! – suppose you hate me and I hate you back, that's the normal state.

RW: Yes, unfortunately.

K: You slap me, I slap you. But if I say, all right, I don't want to be slapped, I don't want to slap you, leave me alone, just carry on, if you want to go that way, carry on. Do you see what takes place? You leave that current. Then they say, by Jove, he is a very strange man. Either he is mentally odd or he is a hero or a saint and we will worship him, which becomes another form of entertainment!

This is what is happening. So the man says, please don't do any of these things. If you want to come the door is open, but *you* must come through the door, I'm not going to push you through the door, you must come, it's up to you. It is not callousness or indifference or lack of compassion. It is so, if you want it, take it. The food is there, but if you are not hungry, all right.

RW: But they are hungry.

K: I know, of course they are hungry, poor chaps, but they fall into all kinds of traps. You have had in this country guru after guru, religious gurus, Catholic gurus, Protestant gurus and Hindu gurus, Buddhist gurus, every type of guru has come here.

RW: Atheist gurus.

K: And atheist gurus. And I say, sorry, you can keep them all. Or, to quote the Bible, not the New but the Old Testament, 'false gods'. I think it is so terribly simple that we miss it. Our minds are so complicated, so clever, so cunning – we are used to that.

RW: But is it so simple?

K: It's not.

RW: But you said it is so simple that we miss it.

K: Of course.

RW: What, just to let go of the self and to stop identifying?

K: Yes, that's the beginning of it.

RW: That takes overcoming years of conditioning!

K: No.

RW: How can that be simple?

K: Conditioning is the movement of thought.

RW: Yes.

K: So to be aware of this whole movement of thought, not to deny it, not to say, how am I to step out of it – to be aware of this. Look what thought has done, technologically, religiously, all the hierarchical structure of the Christian world. You have heard all the evangelists in this country!

RW: Krishnaji, I would like to ask you something. We don't have to use it on tape if you don't want to, it's up to you. It's a question that comes up often and I ask it with real, sincere respect. For all the people – that includes me – who have come many times to hear you, the question that comes up over and over again is: 'Why is it so clear to one person and however hard that person tries, gives of

himself to explain it, to clarify it to others, the others can't do it?'
Are you saying it can be done by everybody?

K: I say if *one* can do it, everybody can do it.

RW: But that's what is being questioned. If that were so, wouldn't everybody do it?

K: Please listen. First of all, we are so heavily conditioned as Christians, as Buddhists and so on, and this conditioning implies, you know, the whole of it. Now, if I am also ambitious to be principal of a school or to become President of this country, do you think I am going to give that up for something that sounds...

RW: ... vague.

K: Not vague, very clear! I understand it intellectually, it is something that may be rather difficult, and it means I may not want to become President.

RW: That's true.

K: So I prefer the President to this!

RW: On the other hand, I think being President will bring me happiness, and if I am convinced this will bring me greater happiness why would I not make the trade...

K: Because there's no guarantee.

RW: OK.

K: You exchange.

RW: Exactly, that's what I wanted to bring out. I have to let go of that and jump into the unknown.

K: Ah, no. *This* is false!

RW: *This* is false?

K: Therefore leave it.

RW: But with no guarantee.

K: Of course.

RW: We agree.

K: I mean it's like someone giving up something in order to get something.

RW: Exactly. That's the wrong model, and people are afraid they'll fall between the cracks and have nothing. I'll give *this* up, but I won't understand or realize the other, so I will have nothing.

K: So I'll give this up if you guarantee me the other.

RW: Exactly.

K: All the religious structures have been based on that.

RW: So you have answered the question really. You have said, if people were completely serious and meant it, they could do it too, they could understand that.

K: It's so simple. It's like a man who says, look, you don't know how to swim. I'll help you to swim but you won't enter the water, you are frightened already, you won't move. But if he says, I'll guarantee you won't sink because you have got this, that and the other, then you'll...

RW: And he can't say that, it's impossible to say it.

K: No, it would be sacrilegious to say that.

RW: I know. That would be impossible, and that's the problem.

K: That's how all the gurus make money! All the churches in the world have made money that way.

RW: You say it's so simple and that we have cluttered up our intellect, but a very simple farmer who doesn't clutter up his intellect cannot do it either.

K: Of course not, because he is dull, the opposite of the other.

RW: Exactly.

K: It requires a good mind, it requires clear perception of things as they are.

RW: An unclutteredness.

K: Absolutely, to see things as they are.

RW: A good mind but one not cluttered with content.

K: With concepts. Concepts is good enough, not cluttered with ideals, concepts. After all, there is no justice in the world. Right? That's so obvious.

RW: There is very little.

K: There is none. Because you are clever, I am not. You are tall, I am short. You were born rich, I was born in a hovel. You have every opportunity, I haven't. You ride in the best cars and I walk. You have got a good brain and I haven't. You are free, I am not. It's so clear, there isn't justice. We want justice but there isn't any.

RW: What follows from that? Therefore what? Nature has distributed things unequally?

K: First accept that, see that there is no justice, right?

RW: There is no equality, I would put it that way.

K: There is no equality. No, no justice.

RW: All right, in that sense. What follows?

K: What follows is what happens to me when I see that there is no justice. I am a poor man, there is no justice in the world. Either I become bitter, angry, violent.

RW: Or depressed.

K: Of course, depressed. So if I don't do any of those things I am not talking about equality, I am not even looking for equality. Then I am a free man.

RW: That step is not clear.

K: As long as I am comparing I am caught in the trap.

RW: It will rankle.

K: I am caught in the trap. So I don't compare. Personally, I've never compared. It may sound odd, it may sound crazy, but it's a fact.

RW: Do you think though if you were a farmer with six children to feed, and you saw the landlord riding around, that you wouldn't compare?

K: Of course, I would feel angry.

RW: It would be natural.

K: It would be rancour because I want to beat him, I want to be like him.

RW: Yes, you want to feed your children and...

K: Yes, and all the rest of it follows. But if there is no feeling of comparison – ah, that is a different way of living!

RW: That's very interesting. Thank you very much.

What Is Meditation?

Chögyam Trungpa Rinpoche, Tibetan Buddhist meditation master, and founder of the Naropa Institute, Colorado.

Krishnamurti: You know, sir, in all the organized religions, with their dogmas, beliefs, traditions and so on, the person and personal experience have played a great part. The person has become extraordinarily important, not the teachings, their reality, but the person. Human beings throughout the world have emphasized the person of the teacher. The person represents to them tradition, authority, a way of life, through him they hope to attain or reach enlightenment or heaven or whatever. And most people seek personal experience and that in itself has very little validity, because it may be merely a projection of one's own intentions, fears and hopes. So personal experience has very little validity in religious matters. It has really no value at all where truth is concerned.

Now, to negate personal experience is to negate the 'me', because the 'me' is the very essence of all experience, which is the past; and when religious people go on missions or come over to the West from India or elsewhere, they are really doing propaganda and that has no value with regard to truth, because then it becomes a lie.

So if one puts aside *completely* all the experiences of human beings and their systems, their practices, their rituals, their dogmas, their concepts – that is, if one can actually do it, not theoretically but actually wipe it all out – then what is the quality of the mind that is no longer held in the matrix of experience? Because truth is not something you experience, truth is not something towards which you gradually progress; you don't come to it through infinite days of practice, sacrifice, control, discipline. What you have then is 'personal experience', and when there is 'personal experience' there is the division between the 'me', the person, and the thing that you experience, and though you may try to identify yourself with that experience, with that thing, there is still division.

Seeing all this, how organized religions have really destroyed truth, giving human beings some absurd myth to make them behave, if one can put all that aside, what place has meditation in all this? What place has a guide, a guru, a saviour, a priest? Recently I saw somebody from India preaching transcendental meditation; you attend his class and practise every day and the idea is you will have greater energy and ultimately reach some kind of transcendental experience. It is really – I can't put it too strongly – it is really a great calamity when such things happen to people. When they come from India, from China or Japan to teach people meditation, they are doing propaganda. And is meditation a thing that you practise daily, which means conforming to a pattern, imitating, suppressing? You know what is implied in conformity. Can such conformity to any pattern, it doesn't matter what it is, ever lead to truth? Obviously not.

Then, if you actually see, not just theoretically, but actually see the falseness of practising a system, however absurd, however noble, that it has no meaning, what is meditation? What, first of all, is traditional meditation? – whether it be Christian, Hindu, Buddhist, Tibetan or Zen, you know all the varieties of meditation and their schools. For me, all that is not meditation at all. Then what is meditation? Perhaps we could discuss that?

Chögyam Trungpa: Yes, I think so.

K: Why should one make meditation into a problem? We human beings have enough problems, both physically and psychologically, why add yet another one with meditation? And is meditation a way of *escaping* from one's problems, an avoiding of what actually is, and therefore no meditation at all? Or is meditation the *understanding* of the problem of living? Not avoiding but understanding daily living with all its problems. If that is not understood, if that is not put in order, I can go and sit in a corner and follow somebody who teaches me transcendental or some nonsensical meditation and it will have no meaning at all. So what is it to you to meditate, what does it mean? I hope I have not made it too difficult for you to answer because I deny all that kind of meditation, the practice of constantly repeating a word, as they do in India, in Tibet, as they do all over the world, Ave Maria or some other words, repeat, repeat, repeat, it means – nothing. You make the mind more absurd and grotesque than it is.

So if we may, together, inquire into this question. Is it because there is a long established tradition that you must meditate, and therefore we meditate? When I was a small boy I vaguely remember that being a Brahmin we went through a certain ceremony, we were told to sit quietly, close our eyes, meditate, think about something or other – the whole thing was set going. So if we could together examine and share what is meditation, what the implications of it are, why one should meditate at all. Because if you make meditation into another problem, then for God's sake avoid it! So could we together go into this? Seeing the traditional approaches, and seeing their absurdity. Because unless the human being becomes a light to himself, nothing matters: if you depend on somebody else then you are in a state of perpetual anxiety. So could we examine this traditionally first. Why should one meditate?

CT: Don't you think that meditation happens as part of the living situation of a man?

  K: Sir, a human being has innumerable problems. He must solve those first, mustn't he? He must bring order in the house in which he lives, the house that is the 'me' – my thoughts, my feelings, my anxieties, my guilt, my sorrow – I must bring order there. Without that order how can I proceed further?

CT: The problem is that if, while trying to solve the problem, you are looking for order, then doesn't it seem to be looking for further chaos?

  K: So I do not look for order. I inquire into disorder and I want to know why there is disorder, I do not want to find order, then I have all the gurus and all the gang coming in! I don't want order, I only want to find out why in one's life there is such chaos and disorder. A human being must find out, not ask someone else to tell him if there is disorder.

CT: Well, you can't find out intellectually.

  K: Intellect is part of the whole structure, you can't deny the intellect.

CT: But you can't use intellect to solve intellectual problems.

  K: No, you can't solve these problems at any level except totally.

CT: Quite, yes.

  K: That is, sir, to solve the human problem of disorder, does that need meditation – in the ordinary accepted sense of the word?

CT: I wouldn't say in the ordinary, conventional sense of meditation, but meditation in the extraordinary sense.

K: What do you mean by that, if I may ask?

CT: The extraordinary sense of meditation is to see the disorder as part of the direction.

K: To see disorder.

CT: To see disorder as order, if you like.

K: Ah, no. To see disorder.

CT: Well, if you see disorder then it becomes order.

K: First I must see it.

CT: See it clearly.

K: So that depends, then, on how you observe disorder.

CT: Not trying to solve it.

K: Of course not. Because if you try to solve it, you solve it according to a set pattern...

CT: A set pattern.

K: ... which is the outcome of your disorder, the opposite of your disorder. If you try to solve the disorder it is always according to a preconceived idea of order. That is, the Christian order, Hindu order, whatever order, socialist order, communist order. Whereas if you observe entirely, what is disorder? Then, there is no duality in that.

CT: Yes, I see.

K: How is one to observe this total disorder, in which human beings live? The disorder when you see television, the commercials, the hectic violence, the absurdities. Human existence is a total disorder – killing, violence and at the same time talking about peace. So we come to the question: what is observation of disorder? Do you see it from the 'me' as separate from the thing that is disorder?

CT: That is already disorder.

K: Isn't it! So do I look at disorder with the eyes of my prejudices, my opinions, my conclusions, my concepts, the propaganda of a thousand years – which is the 'me'. Or do I look at disorder without the 'me'? Is that possible? That is meditation. You follow, sir? Not all the rubbish they talk about. To observe without division, to observe without the 'me', who is the very essence of the past, the 'me' that says, 'I should, should not, I must, I must not'. The 'me' that says, 'I must achieve, I must gain God', or

whatever it is. So can there be an observation without the 'me'?
You see, if that question is put to an orthodox meditator he will
say, 'there can't, because the 'me' is there. So I must get rid of the
'me'. To get rid of the 'me' I must practise.' Which means I am
emphasizing the 'me'! Through practice I hope to deny practice,
through practice I hope to eradicate the result of that practice,
which is still the 'me', so I am caught in a vicious circle.

So the traditional approach, as one has observed it in the world,
emphasizes the 'me' in a very subtle but strengthening way – the
'me' that is going to sit next to God – which is an absurdity! The
'me' that is going to experience Nirvana or Moksha or heaven,
enlightenment – it means nothing. So we see the orthodox
approach is really holding the human being in the prison of the
past, giving him importance through his personal experience.
Reality isn't a 'personal' experience. You can't personally experience
the vastness of the sea, it is there for you to look, it isn't *your* sea.

If you put that aside then the question arises: is it ever
possible to see without the 'me', to observe this total disorder of
human beings, their lives, the way they live, is it possible to
observe it without division? Because division implies conflict,
like India and Pakistan, like China and America and Russia, all
that. Division politically breeds chaos, division psychologically
breeds endless conflict, both inwardly and outwardly. Now to
end this conflict is to observe without the 'me'.

CT: I wouldn't even say observe.

K: To observe 'what is'.

CT: Well, when you observe then you are judging.

K: No, that is not what I mean. You can observe through criticism,
through evaluation. That's partial. To observe totally, in that
there is no evaluation at all.

CT: A total observation. Then there is no observer.

K: Therefore what is meditation then?

CT: That *is* meditation.

K: That *is* meditation. So in observing disorder, which is
essentially meditation, in that observation there is order, not
the order which the intellect creates. So meditation is not a
personal search for personal experience. Meditation is not the
search for some transcendental experience that will give you
great energy to become more mischievous.

Meditation is not personal achievement, sitting next to God. Meditation is then a state of mind in which the 'me' is absent, and therefore that very absence brings order. And that order must exist to go any further. Without that order things become silly. It's like these people who go around dancing, chanting and repeating 'Krishna' and all that silly stuff, that is not order. They are creating colossal disorder! As the Christians are creating great disorder, as the Hindus, the Buddhists are. As long as you are held within a pattern you must create disorder in the world. The moment you say, 'America must be the superpower', you are going to create disorder.

So the next question is: can the mind observe without time and without memory, which are the material of the mind? Memory and time are the material of the mind. Can it observe without those two elements? Because if it observes with memory, the memory is the centre, the 'me'. Right? And time is the 'me' also, time is the evolution of the brain cells as becoming. So can the mind observe without memory and time? Which is only possible when the mind is completely still. And the traditional people recognize this, so they say, 'we must practise in order to be silent!' So control your mind – you know the tricks they play.

CT: I don't see any particular importance in laying emphasis on the stillness of the mind because if one is able to see the non-dualistic way of looking at situations then you have further energy that will flow out.

K: You can only have further energy to flow, greater energy, when the mind is quiet.

CT: But to put the emphasis on stillness ...

K: No, we said, observe disorder, without the 'me', its memories, its structure of time, then in that quality there is a quietness of the mind which is observing. That stillness is not an acquired, practised thing, it comes naturally when you have order.

You see, sir, all one can do is to point out and help the person to go to the door, it is for him to open the door, you can't do any more than that. This whole idea of wanting to help people means, you know, you become a do-gooder. And a do-gooder is not a religious man at all. Shall we go on with this?

CT: I think so. There is a further thing that can be clarified, when you put emphasis on absolute peace.

K: Ah! I said, sir, complete order is complete quietness of the

241

mind. Quietness of the mind is the most active mind.

CT: That's what I want you to say.

K: It's the most dynamic thing, it isn't just a dead thing.

CT: People could misunderstand.

K: Because they are used only to practice which will help them to *become* – that is death. But a mind that has gone, inquired into all this in this way, becomes extraordinarily active and therefore quiet.

CT: That's what I mean, yes.

K: It's like a great dynamo.

CT: Yes.

K: The greater the speed the more the vitality. Of course, Man is seeking more energy, he wants more energy, to go to the moon, to go and live under the sea. He is striving for more and more and more. And I think the search for more does lead to disorder. The consumer society is a disorderly society. The other day I saw some paper tissue, Kleenex, which was beautifully decorated!

So our question is: does the observation of disorder bring order? That is really a very important point because for most of us effort is demanded to bring about order. Human beings are used to effort, to struggling, fighting, suppressing, forcing themselves. Now all that has led to disorder, socially, outwardly and inwardly.

The difficulty with human beings is that they have never observed a tree, a bird, without division. Since they have never observed a tree or a bird totally they can't observe themselves totally. One can't see the total disorder in which one lives, there is always an idea that somewhere there is a part of me that is order which is looking at disorder. So they invent the higher self, which will bring about order in disorder – God is in you and pray to that God, he will bring about this order. Always there is this effort. What we are saying is that where there is the 'me' there must be disorder. And if I look at the world through the 'me', the world outside or the world inside, there is not only division, but that brings about conflict, that division creates chaos and disorder in the world. Now to observe all that totally, in which there is no division, such observation is meditation. For that you don't have to practise, all that you have to do is to be aware of what exactly is going on inside and outside, just to be aware.

How Can One Overcome the Despair of Bereavement?

A member of the audience at one of Krishnamurti's public talks in Saanen, Switzerland.

Questioner: Three years ago my son and my husband died. I still find it extremely hard to let go the memory of the utter despair. There must be a way, perhaps you may know it. I have come from a long distance and found help from your talks – could you speak about death and detachment, please?

Krishnamurti: First of all, let us talk over together what it means to be attached and what difference there is between attachment and detachment. What is attachment? Why is one attached to a country, to a person, to some experience, ideology, definite conclusion? Why do people do this throughout the world, depending upon their circumstances, their social and moral environment, and so on? Man has repeated this pattern over and over again. I've had an experience, something that stirs me deeply, brings colour to my life, gives it meaning, and I hold on to the memory of that experience, which has gone, which is *dead*. Why do we do this, my friend asks me – why do human beings, wherever they live, cling in some form or another, to their land, their property, their wealth, their wives, their husbands, and so on? Why? Please, we're talking over together, my friend and I – you, the audience, are listening. Why do we cling, why are we attached? The word attachment comes from the Italian *attaccare*, which means to grip something and hold on to it.

Is it because we are inwardly insufficient in ourselves? Is it because there is loneliness that there is a sense of possession, whether it is of a piece of furniture or a house or a person? To possess something, to say, 'it is mine' gives a great deal of pleasure. Is it that we human beings, you and I, have nothing deeper, more

243

vital, and therefore we hold on to something very superficial, something that may pass away? We know, unconsciously, that it is passing away – but we still hold on. We may hold on to an illusion. The root meaning of that word is to play. And we play with illusions, and seem to find that very satisfactory. Or we invent a subtle form of ourselves at a different level and cling to that.

So we create all these things and hold on to them. Why? Is it that one is afraid to be nothing, to have nothing to hold on to? Is it because possessing, holding, clinging to something, gives us a great sense of security, a sense of well-being, because life is very uncertain, dangerous, incredibly brutal? You see, the world is becoming more and more like a concentration camp.

So why are we attached, each one of us, to something? And when we look at the different forms of attachment, why do we not see the consequences of it, the fear, the anxiety, the pain? To see it, and not allow for time to end it. That is, I'm attached to my wife; and I see, both intellectually and deeply, that this attachment has many painful, desperate consequences. I may see it logically, intellectually, rationally, but I can't let go because I am afraid to be alone, to be lonely. Yet I see all this, because my friend and I are fairly intelligent, we are both looking at it. But then I may say, time will allow me to be free of this attachment, gradually I'll understand, gradually I'll let go. That attitude of gradualness is stupidity, because either I see the whole thing and end it immediately or I am foolish, I like clinging to something, to a memory that is dead, gone.

So intelligence is to see the whole movement of attachment, both the inward and outward, whole process of it, and the very perception of it is to end it. Intelligence is not to postpone, not to allow time to dull the mind, the brain, because if one postpones, neglects, accepts, you are living in a pattern that is already over, in the memory of the dead past. And so the brain is living with something that is finished, with something that is past. And living in the past always dulls the quality, the vitality of the brain.

So we have examined, you and I, sitting on a bench in the forest, attachment. And now let's examine what is detachment. Is detachment the opposite of attachment? If one pursues detachment, and makes that another form of attachment, you are doing exactly the same thing as before. I hope this is clear. That is, if detachment is the opposite of my attachment, then there is conflict. Right? There is conflict between my attachment and 'I should be detached'. And then my whole attention or my energy is spent trying to be detached, while knowing I'm attached.

So we have to find out what the relationship is, if any, between attachment and detachment. Or is there no relationship whatsoever? When there is an ending of attachment, there is no need to use the word 'detachment'. There is the ending of it. But for most of us, our brain is conditioned to this process of opposites.

And one has to question if there is an opposite at all. At the physical level there are the opposites, tall, short, wide, broad, ugly, beautiful and so on. But psychologically, inwardly, is there an opposite at all, or only *what is*? And we invent the opposite in order to get rid of *what is*. I hope you and I, sitting on that bench, are talking about this, and understanding each other. There is no authority between two friends. There is no assertion between two friends who have gone into this matter. So it is a mutual, cooperative understanding. It is not that one is telling the other, they are both travelling together, along the same path with the same intensity, with the same depth.

Now assume that is clear between us two, that there is no relationship between attachment and detachment, that there is only the ending of attachment and nothing else. Now is love attachment? I am attached to spending every evening with my friend, sitting on the bench, talking over my problems. And when we don't meet I miss him. So we are asking each other, is love attachment, is it possessing somebody, holding on to someone or something, whether it is the idea of God, whether it is the idea of liberation, freedom, or to the idea, the concept, that it is in possession that love grows? So we are asking: what is the relationship between attachment and love? My friend is married, has had several marriages, and he's rather wounded by all that. He's rather unhappy. And he thinks that he still loves his present wife. And he says to me, 'I can't lose her, I must hold on, because my life is empty without her.' You know all this, don't you? He says, 'I can't let her go. She wants to do something totally different from me, and it may take her away from me. So I plead with her, I suppress my wanting something else, and I go along with and follow her. But inwardly there is conflict all the time, between her and me.' You know all this, don't you? It's not a new story, is it?

Now I have reduced the whole immensity of love, which is extraordinary, which I don't understand, to something so trivial. That is, I'm attached, possessive, I don't want to lose. If I lose I'm unhappy. And this I call love. So *is* it love? Please, don't agree. Don't say it's not. If it is not, that is the end. But most of us, like my friend, are afraid to look at the complexity of it. My friend wants to change the subject, because if he really sees that attachment is not love, then can he go to his wife and say, 'I love you, but I'm not attached to you.' What would happen? She might throw a brick. Or walk away, because her whole life is to be attached, to the furniture, to ideas, to children, to the husband – you follow?

So then what is my relationship, having seen that love is not attachment, is not jealousy, not ambition, competition. To me that's a reality, not just a verbal structure. And what is my relationship to her who is quite different? Go on, it's your problem, not mine.

She will not accept what to me is truth. See what is involved in this. How painful it all is. It's nothing superficial, it touches the very core of one's being. And what shall I do? Have patience? Patience, being patient, doesn't require time. Patience is not time. Whereas impatience has the quality of time in it. Think it over. When I realize my wife is different from me, finds everything which I think is totally wrong, and I have to live in the same house and so on, do I have patience, and realize that patience is not a process of time? Do I realize that? Not patience therefore in the sense of putting up with it, allowing time to resolve it – I can't do anything but perhaps some other day, another week, another year, we'll settle everything. Then I tolerate the situation. And is this tolerance love? Go on, think it out. To put up with something knowing it is wrong, wrong in quotes, and saying, 'well, time will gradually eliminate it', which means I get really impatient to have a result. So I put up with it. So what shall I do? Go on. Divorce? Run away? Leave her my house, my goods etc? And say goodbye, and disappear altogether?

Or I'm asking, can my love, its intensity, can that bring about a change in her? Please, you're asking these questions. Can I, who have understood this whole phenomenon in all its depth, will that quality of love, compassion, intelligence, bring about a change in her? If she's at all sensitive, if she's at all observant, listening to what I'm saying, wanting us to understand each other, then there is a possibility of her changing. If she puts up a wall, as most people do, then what am I to do? Go on. Don't look at me, look at yourselves. You see, one of our peculiarities is that we want a definite answer, we want something settled, because then I'm free, then I can do what I want. There is no definite answer to this question, it depends on the quality of your attention, your intelligence, your love.

And then another friend says, 'my son and husband are dead. I'm attached to their memory. I'm getting more and more desperate, more and more depressed. I'm living in the past, and the present is always coloured by the past, so what am I to do?'

So we decide to talk over the problem of death. You and the speaker, sitting on a bench, with birds singing all around us, with a thousand shadows and the river running swiftly, making sweet sound, and she raises this question. She says, 'I'm quite young, but any moment an accident can happen, and there may be death, not only of my son and my husband, but also my own death.' She says, 'let's talk about it.'

From time immemorial, historically, culturally, through paintings and statuary, Man has always asked, 'what happens after death?' One has gathered a lot of experience, knowledge, struggled to be moral, ascetic, gone into the depths of oneself. If death is the end, then what is the point of all this, what is the point of all this struggle, pain, experience, knowledge, wealth? And death is always waiting at the end of it. I may belong to a sect, accept certain customs because of that, which is again an isolating process. And death is the common factor for all of us: for the guru, for the Pope, or the innumerable other popes in the world. So that's a fact, we all want to understand the significance, the depth of that extraordinary event – and it is extraordinary. And what is the relationship between death and living? Please, I hope you're following all this – I'm asking my friend. She says, go ahead, I follow verbally anyway, I understand this.

Various civilizations throughout the world have tried to overcome death. They've said that life after death is more important than the now. So they prepared for death. And there are people nowadays who say, we must help our patients, our friends, to die happily. We never ask, what is more important, essential, is it before death, the many years before death, or after death? I'm asking my friend. Naturally she says, 'it's before death, the long years one has lived, maybe ten, fifteen, thirty, fifty, ninety – those long years before the ending. That is the period of living. That is far more significant than the ending of it.'

Why don't we ask this question, not what is after, or how to help me die happily. But what is my life that I have lived for eighty years? It has been one constant battle, with occasional lulls when there has been no pain, no struggle, something like that occasionally, rarely, happens. But the rest of my life has been struggle, struggle. And I've called that 'living'. That's what we are all doing, not only my friend and I, but all human beings are doing that, struggling to find work, wanting more wealth, being oppressed by the tyranny of a totalitarian state, and so on. It has been a vast jungle. That has been my life. And I cling to that, to the struggle, to the pain, to the anxiety, to the loneliness – that's all I have. Right? *That* has become all important.

So I'm asking, we're asking each other, what is it that dies? Now this becomes a rather complex question. My friend and I have time, it's Sunday morning and we've no work, so we can sit down and go into it. Is it the individual that dies? Please, inquire as a friend, who is it that dies? Apart from the biological ending of an organism, which has been ill-treated, has had several illnesses, that inevitably comes to an end. You may find a new drug that may help Man to live 150 years, but at the end of those 150 years, that extraordinary thing is there waiting. Is my consciousness, the whole of it, with all its content, is it mine? That is, my consciousness is its content, the content is my belief, my dogmas, my superstitions, my attachment to my country, patriotism, fear, pain, pleasure, sorrow and so on, all that is the content of my consciousness, and yours. So both of us, sitting on that bench, recognize this fact, that the content makes up consciousness. Without its content consciousness as we know it doesn't exist. So my friend and I see the logic of it, the rationality of it, and so on. We agree to that.

Then, is this consciousness which I have clung to as mine, and my friend's consciousness which she clings to as hers, calling ourselves individuals, is that consciousness unlike other consciousnesses? Right? Please be clear on this point. That is, if you're lucky enough to travel, observe, talk over with other people, you'll find that they are similar to you. They suffer, they are lonely, they have a thousand gods and you may have one God, they believe, they don't believe, and so on. On the periphery, there may be variations. You may be tall, or you may be short, you may be very clever, may be scholarly, have read a great deal, you're capable, you've a certain technique, efficiency, it's all on the periphery, on the outside. But inwardly, we are similar. This is a fact. Therefore our conditioning, which says we are individual, separate souls, is not a fact. This is where my friend begins to squirm, because she doesn't like the idea that she is not an individual. She can't face the fact, because all her conditioning has been that. So I say to my friend, look at it, don't run away from it, don't resist it, look at it. Use your brains, not your sentiment, not your desire – just look at it, is that a fact or not? And she accepts it, vaguely.

So if our consciousness is similar to all mankind, then I am mankind. You understand? Please understand this, the depth and beauty of this. If I am mankind, the entire mankind, then what is it that dies? You understand? Either I can contribute to, or I move away from, that entire consciousness which is 'me', I cleanse the whole of my being from that. So that I am not individual, so that I am the whole of humanity.

Then is there emptying of the consciousness, which is my beliefs, my anxiety, my pain, my blah blah, all that? Is there an ending to all that? If I end it, what importance is it? What importance or value to humanity is it? I am humanity, I am asking this question. What value, what significance has this when, after a great deal of intelligence, love, I observe this and in that observation there is the total ending of those contents? Has it any value? Value in the sense of moving humanity from its present condition. You understand? Surely it has, hasn't it? One drop of clarity in a bucket of confusion, that one drop begins to act.

And my friend, the questioner, says, 'I'm beginning to understand the nature of death. I see that if I'm attached to, if I hold onto things, death has a grip on me. If I let them go, each day as they arise, I am living with death. Death is ending, so I'm ending, while living, everything that I will lose when I die.' So the question my friend asks is, 'can I let go every day what I have accumulated, end it, so that I am living with death, and therefore there is a freshness, not living in the past, in memories?'

From this arises a very complex question. What is immortality? All this is arising from one question – sorry! What is immortality? That which is beyond mortality, beyond death. As we have said before, where there is a cause, there is an end. There is an end to the effect and the cause remains and creates another effect. It's a constant change. And we are asking: is there a life without any causation? Please, do you understand what I'm saying? We live with causes – you know, I don't have to go into that. All our life is based on many, many causes. I love you because you give me something. I love you because you comfort me. I love you because I'm sexually fulfilled, and so on. That is a cause, and the effect is the word I use, which is 'love', which it is not. Any motive I have is a causation. So I'm asking my friend, is it possible to live without any cause, not belong to any cause, in the sense of an organized cause, or to have any cause in myself? Knowing that if there is a causation there is an ending, which is time.

Now we're going to find out together if, in our daily relations, in our daily activity – not some theoretical but actual activity – one can live without a cause. Look into it, my friend, don't look to me, but look at it, look at the question first. Knowing that when I say, 'I love you', because you give me something in return, there is always in that relationship of causation the ending of that relationship. So we're asking each other, is there a life without cause? See the beauty of it, first, see the depth, see the vitality of that question, not the mere words. We have said that love has no cause – obviously. If I love you because you give me something, it's merchandise, a thing of the market. So can I love you, can there be love, without wanting anything physically, anything psychologically, inwardly, nothing in any form? So that is love, which has no cause, therefore it is infinite. You understand? Like intelligence, it has no cause, it is endless, timeless; so too is compassion.

Now if there is that quality in our life, the whole of our activity changes completely. That's enough for that question. I hope my friend who put it has understood.

Who Are You?

A member of the audience at one of Krishnamurti's public talks in Saanen, Switzerland.

Questioner: Who are you?

Krishnamurti: Is that an important question? Or should the questioner ask who he is, not who I am, but who he is? If I tell you who I am, what does it matter? It is only out of curiosity, isn't it? It is like reading a menu in the window, you have to go into the restaurant to eat the food. Standing outside and reading the menu won't satisfy your hunger. So to tell you who I am is really quite meaningless.

First of all, I am nobody. That's all, it is as simple as that – I am nobody. But what is important is: who and what are you? The question as put implies that there is somebody 'great', therefore I am going to imitate you, the way you walk, the way you talk, the way you brush your teeth, or whatever. I am going to imitate you, which is part of our pattern. There is the hero or man who is enlightened, or the guru, and you say, 'I am going to copy everything you do' – it becomes so absurdly silly. It is childish to imitate somebody. And are we not the result of many imitations? The religions have said – they don't use the word 'imitate' – surrender yourself, follow me, I am this, I am that, worship. All this is what you are. In school you imitate. Acquiring knowledge is a form of imitation and of course there is the fashion – short dress, long dress, long hair, short hair, beard, no beard – imitate, imitate. And also we imitate inwardly, psychologically, we all know that.

But to find out who you are, who *you* are, not who the speaker is, is far more important, and to find out who you are you have to inquire. You are the story of mankind. If you really see that it gives you tremendous vitality, energy, beauty, love, because you are no longer a small entity struggling in a corner of the Earth. You are part of this whole humanity. That has a tremendous responsibility, vitality, beauty, love. But most of us won't see this, most of us are concerned with ourselves, with our particular little problem, particular little sorrow and so on. And to step out of that narrow circle seems almost impossible because we are so conditioned, so programmed, like computers, that we cannot learn something that is new. Now the computer can but we can't!

See the tragedy of it. The machine that we have created, the computer, can learn much faster, infinitely more than the brain can, and the brain that has invented it is sluggish, slow, dull because we have conformed, obeyed, followed, there is the guru, there is the priest, there are the rich – you follow? And when you do revolt, as revolutionaries and terrorists do, it is still very superficial – changing the pattern of politics, of so-called society, society being merely the relationship between people, and we are talking of a revolution that is not physical but psychological in which there is no conformity – no inward feeling of conformity. Conformity exists when there is comparison. And to have a mind which is totally free from comparison is to observe the whole history of humanity that is embedded in you.

Sources

Since Krishnamurti's death, schools that seek to apply his approach to education have continued in India, the United States and England.

The *School* in England is residential, international and co-educational, and provides secondary and higher education for 14 to 24-year-olds.

The *Krishnamurti Centre* accommodates adult guests who wish to study Krishnamurti's teachings in quiet surroundings, whether by the day, on weekends, or for a week or so.

The *Krishnamurti Foundation* maintains the Krishnamurti archives and distributes books and audio and video recordings.

The address for all three is:

Brockwood Park, Bramdean, Hampshire, SO24 0LQ, England.

Brockwood Park School: 01962 771 744
  fax: 01962 771 875

The Krishnamurti Centre: 01962 771 748

Krishnamurti Foundation: 01962 771 525
  fax: 01962 771 159

Soul: An Archaeology
Readings from Socrates to Alice Walker

Edited by Phil Cousineau

What does soul mean? Is it, as in Aristotle's classic definition, the 'life-giving principle'? Is it the shiver up your spine when Aretha Franklin sings the blues? Or is it the simple, breathtaking beauty of a Pablo Neruda poem?

Soul offers a range of stories, essays, poems, myths and songs that illustrate the ways in which soul has been expressed through the ages and explores its myriad dimensions – philosophical, spiritual, theological and even alchemical. Selections include writing from such literary and historical luminaries as Carl Jung, James Joyce, Thomas Aquinas, St Teresa of Avila, D. H. Lawrence, Jack Kerouac, John Keats, Milan Kundera, T. S. Eliot, Wassily Kandinsky and many, many more.

'Place this enriching book near your bed or some other intimate place and read it slowly over many years. Here you'll find both pleasure and enlightenment, for Phil Cousineau has a remarkable talent for giving the glow of beauty to matters of the utmost importance and depth.'
THOMAS MOORE, AUTHOR OF *CARE OF THE SOUL*

'This wonderful volume is a treasure house of wisdom and hope.'
JOAN HALIFAX, AUTHOR OF *THE FRUITFUL DARKNESS*

'Phil Cousineau writes with brilliance but always from the heart. Indeed, he pays honor to that "inner universe that is as vast as the outer one."'
ROBERT JOHNSON, AUTHOR OF *HE, SHE AND WE*

'Cousineau fires our night sky with flaming soul-bursts from every age and quarter . . . If there is a world soul – an anima mundi – it would address our times in something like Cousineau's voice.'
HUSTON SMITH, AUTHOR OF *FORGOTTEN TRUTH AND THE WORLD'S RELIGIONS*

Pure Heart, Enlightened Mind
The Zen Journal and Letters of An Irish woman in Japan

Maura 'Soshin' O'Halloran

A statue stands in the grounds of Kannonji monastery in Northern Japan of a 27-year-old Irish woman who became a Zen monk and is now venerated as a Buddhist saint.

Maura 'Soshin' O'Halloran went at the age of 24 to Japan, where she began to study in an old temple tucked away in the back streets of Tokyo. From there she moved to a remote temple in Northern Japan and started her formal Zen training. One thousand days later she received the dharma transmission of her Roshi. Six months later, while returning to Ireland, she met her tragic death in a road accident.

Pure Heart, Enlightened Mind is a collection of Maura's journals and letters home during the three year period of her training. They serve as a powerful record of one woman's journey to her destiny. Through her lively, humorous and sharp observation, Maura eloquently describes the rigours, hardships and ultimate joys of Zen training and temple life. Through her writing she reveals an endless sense of compassion that will deeply touch all those who read this book.

'She resembles no one so much as Thérèse of Lisieux the great 19th century Roman Catholic saint who also died in her 20's . . . One senses here a kindred purity and gumption. In the late 20th century this is sanctity enough.'

PHILIP ZALESKI, *NEW YORK TIMES*

Zen Speaks
Shouts of Nothingness

A beautifully illustrated introduction to the philosophy and wisdom of Zen Buddhism.

Tsai Chih Chung
Translated by Brian Bruya

Zen has been described as the greatest 'non-religion' in the world. A wholly Chinese invention, Zen has evolved into a traditional way of life for those free spirits who come to understand that life is everything and nothing.

Zen Speaks is an illustrated adaptation of the early Zen Buddhist classics of the thirteenth century. Collected and popularised by the bestselling Chinese illustrator Tsai Chih Chung, the book includes over 100 Zen tales for today's reader bringing to life the spirit and philosophy of Zen, its ineffable insights, its rich unfolding of spiritual beauty and peace, and its unveiling of the intangible charm of uncertainty and nothingness.

Each story is told in a series of richly illustrated cartoons, with a text that is at once irreverently humorous and yet replete with wisdom and understanding. Complete with the original Chinese text, in beautiful decorative panels along the sides of each page, Zen Speaks vividly and entertainingly brings the essence of Zen philosophy to life.

SOUL: AN ARCHAEOLOGY	1 85538 493 0	£9.99	☐
PURE HEART, ENLIGHTENED MIND	1 85538 452 3	£7.99	☐
ZEN SPEAKS	1 85538 442 6	£4.99	☐

All these books are available from your local bookseller or can be ordered direct from the publishers.

To order direct just tick the titles you want and fill in the form below:

Name: _____

Address: _____

_____

_____ Postcode: _____

Send to: Thorsons Mail Order, Dept 3, HarperCollins*Publishers*, Westerhill Road, Bishopbriggs, Glasgow G64 2QT.
Please enclose a cheque or postal order or your authority to debit your Visa/Access account —

Credit card no: _____

Expiry date: _____

Signature: _____

— to the value of the cover price plus:
UK & BFPO: Add £1.00 for the first book and 25p for each additional book ordered.
Overseas orders including Eire: Please add £2.95 service charge. Books will be sent by surface mail but quotes for airmail despatches will be given on request.

24 HOUR TELEPHONE ORDERING SERVICE FOR ACCESS/VISA CARDHOLDERS **– TEL: 0141 772 2281.**